# NATIONAL GEOGRAPHIC
## *Student Atlas*
### *of the*
# World

NATIONAL GEOGRAPHIC SOC:
WASHINGTON, D.C.

# About the Earth

# The Continents

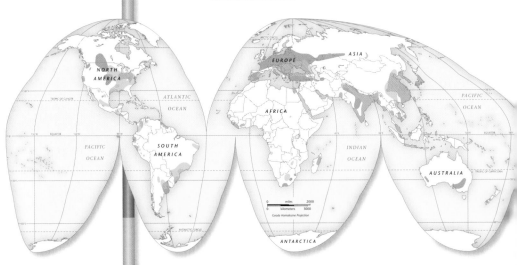

## Resources

*Inside covers:*
**Measurement Conversion Charts &
World Facts**

MERCURY

VENUS

EARTH

MARS

SUN

JUPITER

SATURN

URANUS

NEPTUNE

• PLUTO

# The Earth in Space

**A**t the center of our solar system is the sun, a huge mass of hot gas that is the source of both light and warmth for Earth. Third in a group of nine planets that revolve around the sun, Earth is a terrestrial, or mostly rocky, planet. So are Mercury, Venus, and Mars. Earth is about 93 million miles (150 million kilometers) from the sun, and its journey, or revolution, around the sun takes 365¼ days. Farther away from the sun, five more planets—Jupiter, Saturn, Uranus, and Neptune (all made up primarily of gases) plus tiny, mostly icy Pluto—complete the major heavenly bodies that make up our solar system. The solar system, in turn, is part of the Milky Way galaxy.

▲ *Nine planets* orbit the sun, held in place by its gravitational field. Mercury's orbit (below) is the shortest: 88 Earth days; Pluto's is the longest: 248 Earth years.

PLUTO

MERCURY

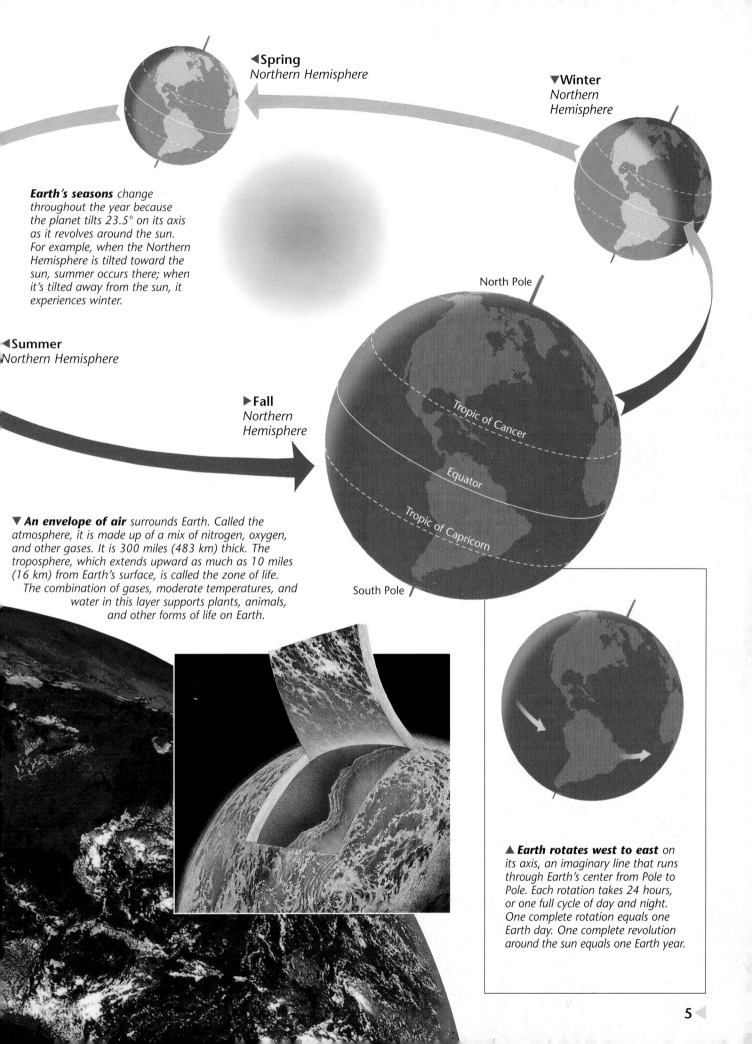

◀**Spring**
*Northern Hemisphere*

▼**Winter**
*Northern
Hemisphere*

**Earth's seasons** *change
throughout the year because
the planet tilts 23.5° on its axis
as it revolves around the sun.
For example, when the Northern
Hemisphere is tilted toward the
sun, summer occurs there; when
it's tilted away from the sun, it
experiences winter.*

◀**Summer**
*Northern Hemisphere*

▶**Fall**
*Northern
Hemisphere*

North Pole

Tropic of Cancer

Equator

Tropic of Capricorn

South Pole

▼ **An envelope of air** *surrounds Earth. Called the
atmosphere, it is made up of a mix of nitrogen, oxygen,
and other gases. It is 300 miles (483 km) thick. The
troposphere, which extends upward as much as 10 miles
(16 km) from Earth's surface, is called the zone of life.
The combination of gases, moderate temperatures, and
water in this layer supports plants, animals,
and other forms of life on Earth.*

▲ **Earth rotates west to east** *on
its axis, an imaginary line that runs
through Earth's center from Pole to
Pole. Each rotation takes 24 hours,
or one full cycle of day and night.
One complete rotation equals one
Earth day. One complete revolution
around the sun equals one Earth year.*

# Learning About Maps

## MAP PROJECTIONS

**M**aps tell a story about physical and human systems, places and regions, patterns and relationships. This atlas is a collection of maps that tell a story about Earth.

Understanding that story requires a knowledge of how maps are made and a familiarity with the special language used by cartographers, the people who create maps.

Globes present a model of Earth as it is—a sphere—but they are bulky and can be difficult to use and store. Flat maps are much more convenient, but certain problems result from transferring Earth's curved surface to a flat piece of paper, a process called projection. There are many different types of projections, all of which involve some form of distortion: area, distance, direction, or shape. *Web Link*

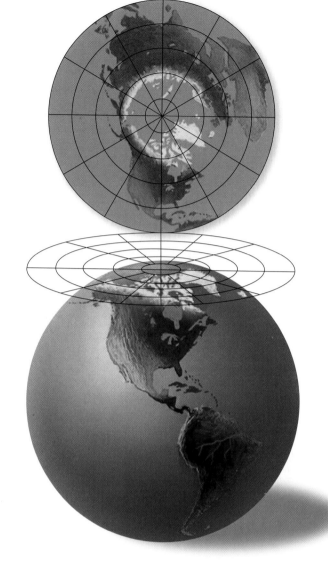

▲ **Azimuthal Projection Map.** *This kind of map is made by projecting a globe onto a flat surface that touches the globe at a single point, such as the North Pole. These maps accurately represent direction along any straight line extending from the point of contact. Away from the point of contact, shape is increasingly distorted.*

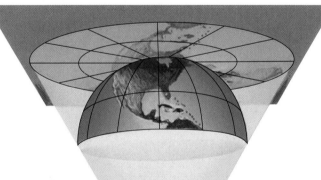

▲ **Making a Projection.**
*Imagine a globe that has been cut in half as this one has. If a light is shined into it, the lines of latitude and longitude and the shapes of the continents will cast shadows that can be "projected" onto a piece of paper, as shown here. Depending on how the paper is positioned, the shadows will be distorted in different ways.*

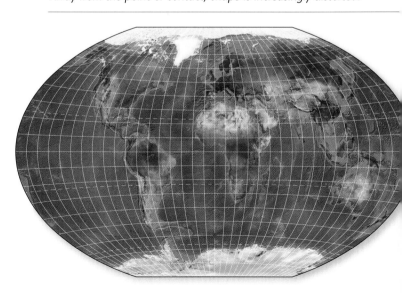

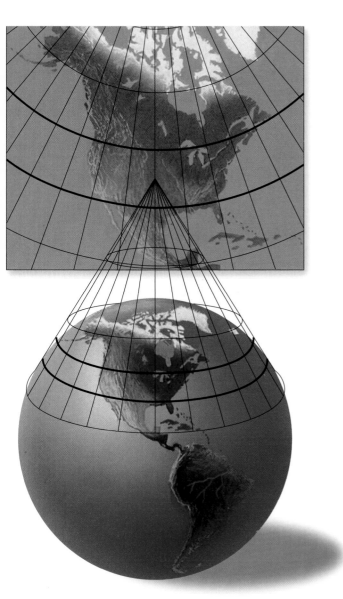

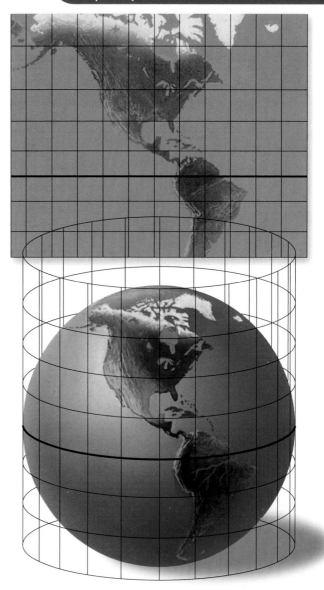

▲ **Conic Projection Map.** *This kind of map is made by projecting a globe onto a cone. The part of Earth being mapped touches the sides of the cone. Lines of longitude appear as straight lines; lines of latitude appear as parallel arcs. Conic projections are often used to map mid-latitude areas with great east-west extent, such as North America.*

▲ **Cylindrical Projection Map.** *A cylindrical projection map is made by projecting a globe onto a cylinder that touches Earth's surface along the Equator. Latitude and longitude lines on this kind of map show true compass directions, which makes it useful for navigation. But there is great distortion in the size of high-latitude landmasses.*

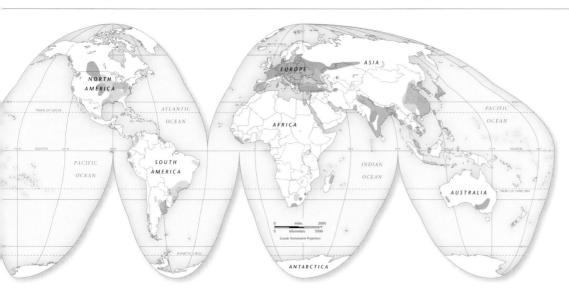

◄ **Other Projections.** *Sometimes cartographers create general purpose world projections, such as the Winkel Tripel (far left), in which distortion of both size and shape is minimized. This creates a reasonably accurate image of Earth. Another general purpose projection is the Goode's Interrupted Homolosine (left), which interrupts ocean areas to preserve the relative size and shape of land areas.*

7

# READING MAPS

People can use maps to find locations, to determine direction or distance, and to understand information about places. Cartographers rely on a special graphic language to communicate through maps.

An imaginary system of lines, called the global grid, helps us locate particular points on Earth's surface. The global grid is made up of lines of latitude and longitude that are measured in degrees, minutes, and seconds. The point where these lines intersect identifies the absolute location of a place. No other place has the exact same address. Web Link

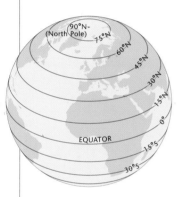

◀ *Latitude. Lines of latitude—also called parallels because they are parallel to the Equator—run east to west around the globe and measure location north or south of the Equator. The Equator is 0° latitude.*

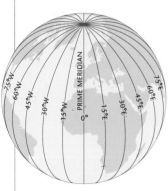

◀ *Longitude. Lines of longitude, also called meridians, run from Pole to Pole and measure location east or west of the prime meridian. The prime meridian is 0° longitude, and it runs through Greenwich, near London, England.*

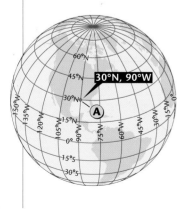

◀ *Latitude and Longitude. When used together, latitude and longitude form a grid that provides a system for determining the exact, or absolute, location of every place on Earth. For example, the absolute location of point A is 30°N, 90°W.*

▲ *Direction. Cartographers put a north arrow or a compass rose, which shows the four cardinal directions—north, south, east, and west—on a map. On this map, point B is northwest (NW) of point A. Northwest is an example of an intermediate direction, which means it is between two cardinal directions. Grid lines can also be used to indicate north.*

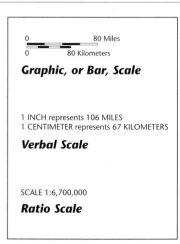

**North arrow**     **Compass rose**

▶ *Scale. A map represents a part of Earth's surface, but that part is greatly reduced. Cartographers include a map scale to show what distance on Earth is represented by a given length on the map. Scale can be graphic (a bar), verbal, or a ratio.*

*To determine how many miles point A is from point B, place a piece of paper on the map above and mark the distance between A and B. Then compare the marks on the paper with the bar scale on the map.*

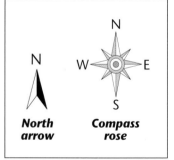

**Graphic, or Bar, Scale**

1 INCH represents 106 MILES
1 CENTIMETER represents 67 KILOMETERS

**Verbal Scale**

SCALE 1:6,700,000

**Ratio Scale**

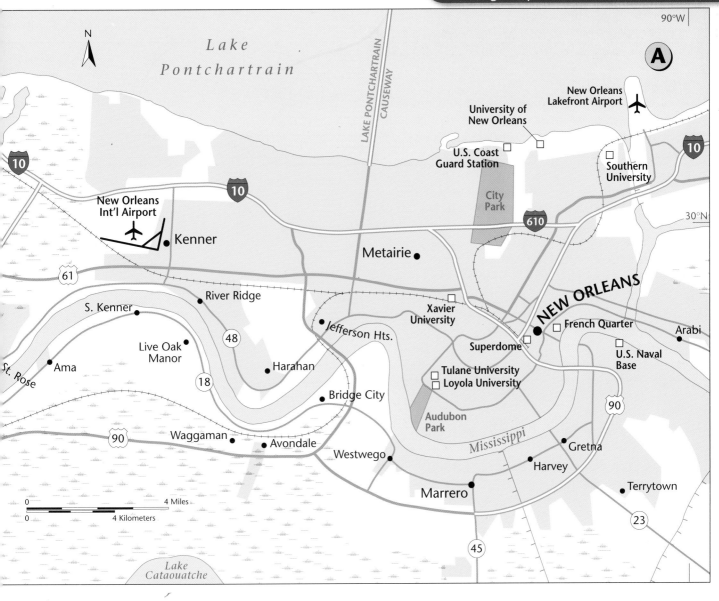

**Symbols.** *Finally, cartographers use a variety of symbols, which are identified in a map key or legend, to tell us more about the places represented on the map. There are three general types of symbols:*

**Point symbols** *show exact location of places (such as cities) or quantity (a large dot can mean a more populous city).*

**Line symbols** *show boundaries or connections (such as roads, canals, and other trade links).*

**Area symbols** *show the form and extent of a feature (such as a lake, park, or swamp).*

*Additional information may be coded in color, size, and shape.*

**Putting It All Together.** *We already know from the map on page 8 which states A and B are located in. But to find out more about city A, we need a larger scale map—one that shows a smaller area in more detail (see above).*

| | | |
|---|---|---|
| Metropolitan area | | Road |
| Lake or river | | Railroad |
| Park | | Runway |
| Swamp | | Airport |
| Canal | | Point of interest |
| Highway | | Town |

# TYPES OF MAPS

This atlas includes many different types of maps so that a wide variety of information about Earth can be presented. Three of the most commonly used types of maps are physical, political, and thematic.

A **physical map** identifies natural features, such as mountains, deserts, oceans, and lakes. Area symbols of various colors and shadings may indicate height above sea level or, as in the example here, ecosystems. Similar symbols could also show water depth.

A **political map** shows how people have divided the world into countries. Political maps can also show states, counties, or cities within a country. Line symbols indicate boundaries, and point symbols show the locations and sometimes sizes of cities.

**Thematic maps** use a variety of symbols to show distributions and patterns on Earth. For example, a choropleth map uses shades of color to represent different values. The example here shows the amount of energy consumed each year by various countries. Thematic maps can show many different things, such as patterns of vegetation, land use, and religions.

A **cartogram** is a special kind of thematic map in which the size of a country is based on some statistic other than land area. In the cartogram at far right, population size determines the size of each country. This is why Nigeria—the most populous country in Africa—appears much larger than Sudan, which has more than double the land area of Nigeria (see the political map). Cartograms allow for a quick visual comparison of countries in terms of a selected statistic.

Web Link

*This globe* is useful for showing Africa's position and size relative to other landmasses, but very little detail is possible at this scale. By using different kinds of maps, mapmakers can show a variety of information in more detail.

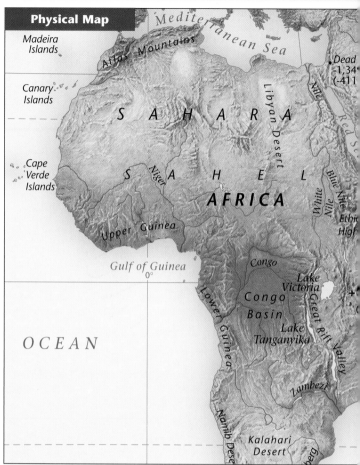

**Physical Map**

Madeira Islands

Canary Islands

Cape Verde Islands

*Mediterranean Sea*

Atlas Mountains

S A H A R A

Libyan Desert

*Nile*

Dead -1,34 (-411

Red Sea

S A H E L

*Niger*

AFRICA

*White Nile*

*Blue Nile*

Ethi High

Upper Guinea

Gulf of Guinea
0°

Congo

Lake Victoria

Congo Basin

Lower Guinea

Lake Tanganyika

Great Rift Valley

O C E A N

*Zambezi*

Namib Dese

Kalahari Desert

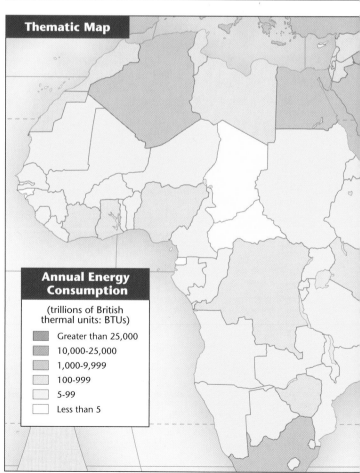

**Thematic Map**

**Annual Energy Consumption**

(trillions of British thermal units: BTUs)

| | |
|---|---|
| | Greater than 25,000 |
| | 10,000–25,000 |
| | 1,000–9,999 |
| | 100–999 |
| | 5–99 |
| | Less than 5 |

## Political Map

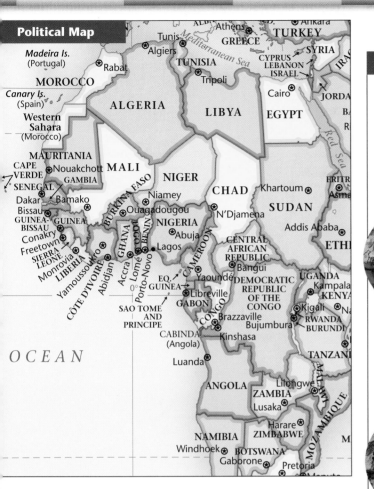

Madeira Is.
(Portugal)

MOROCCO

Canary Is.
(Spain)

Western
Sahara
(Morocco)

ALGERIA

LIBYA

EGYPT

TURKEY

GREECE

TUNISIA

Tunis

Athens

Ankara

CYPRUS
LEBANON
ISRAEL

SYRIA

IRAQ

JORDA

Mediterranean Sea

Algiers

Rabat

Tripoli

Cairo

Red Sea

MAURITANIA

CAPE
VERDE

GAMBIA

SENEGAL

MALI

NIGER

CHAD

SUDAN

ERITR

Asma

Khartoum

Nouakchott

BURKINA FASO

Niamey

Dakar

Bamako

Bissau

GUINEA-
BISSAU

GUINEA

Conakry

Freetown

SIERRA
LEONE

Monrovia

LIBERIA

Yamoussoukro

CÔTE D'IVOIRE

Abidjan

GHANA

Accra

TOGO

Lomé

BENIN

Porto-Novo

Ouagadougou

NIGERIA

Abuja

Lagos

CAMEROON

N'Djamena

CENTRAL
AFRICAN
REPUBLIC

Bangui

Yaoundé

EQ.
GUINEA

Libreville

GABON

SAO TOME
AND
PRINCIPE

CONGO

Brazzaville

CABINDA
(Angola)

Kinshasa

DEMOCRATIC
REPUBLIC
OF THE
CONGO

Addis Ababa

ETH

UGANDA

Kampala

KENYA

N

Kigali

RWANDA

BURUNDI

Bujumbura

TANZANI

0°

OCEAN

Luanda

ANGOLA

ZAMBIA

Lusaka

Lilongwe

MALAWI

Harare

ZIMBABWE

MOZAMBIQUE

M

NAMIBIA

Windhoek

BOTSWANA

Gaborone

Pretoria

Maputo

## Cartogram

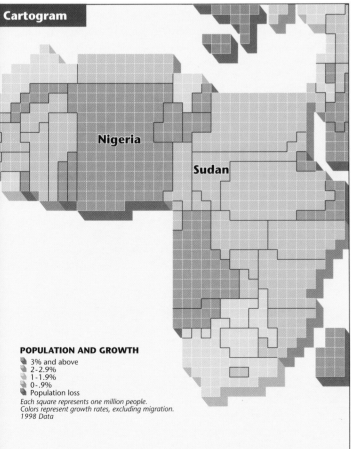

Nigeria

Sudan

**POPULATION AND GROWTH**

- 3% and above
- 2-2.9%
- 1-1.9%
- 0-.9%
- Population loss

*Each square represents one million people.*
*Colors represent growth rates, excluding migration.*
*1998 Data*

## Satellite Image Maps

Satellites orbiting Earth transmit images of the surface to computers on the ground. These computers translate the information into special maps (below) that use colors to show various characteristics. Such maps are valuable tools for identifying patterns or comparing changes over time.

▼ **Cloud Coverage**

▼ **Topography/Bathymetry**

▼ **Sea Level Variability**

▼ **Sea Surface Temperature**

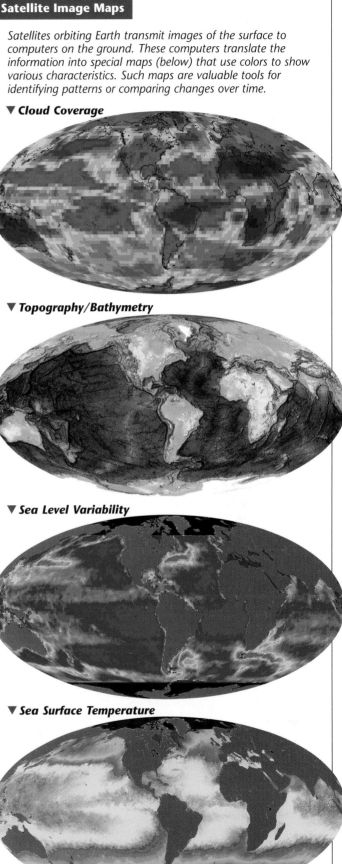

# Physical Systems
## THE PHYSICAL WORLD

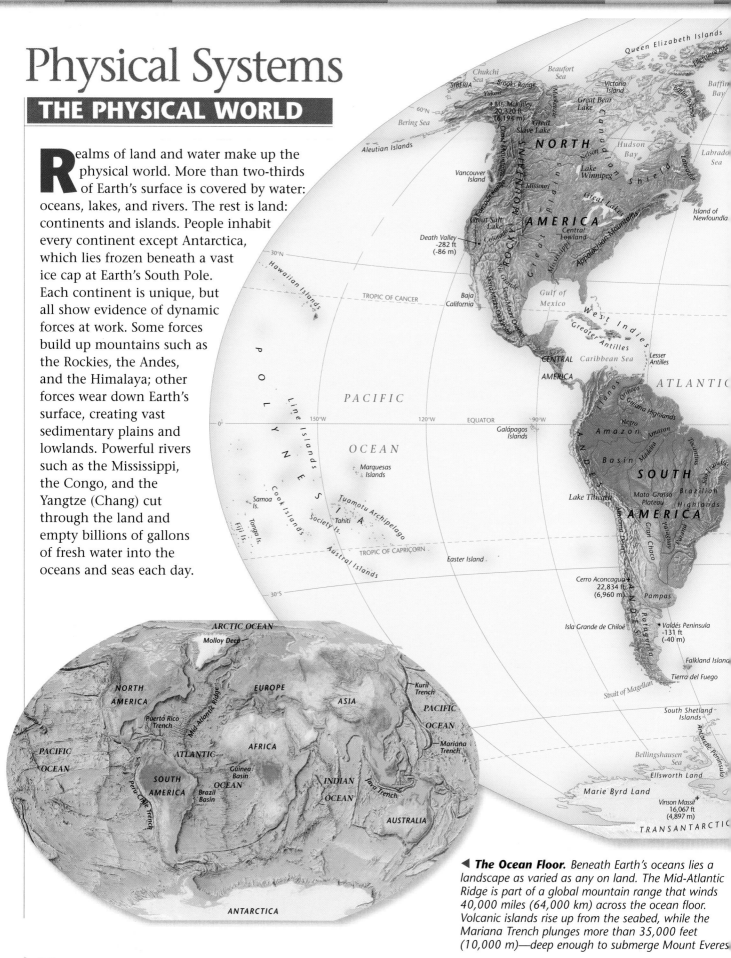

Realms of land and water make up the physical world. More than two-thirds of Earth's surface is covered by water: oceans, lakes, and rivers. The rest is land: continents and islands. People inhabit every continent except Antarctica, which lies frozen beneath a vast ice cap at Earth's South Pole. Each continent is unique, but all show evidence of dynamic forces at work. Some forces build up mountains such as the Rockies, the Andes, and the Himalaya; other forces wear down Earth's surface, creating vast sedimentary plains and lowlands. Powerful rivers such as the Mississippi, the Congo, and the Yangtze (Chang) cut through the land and empty billions of gallons of fresh water into the oceans and seas each day.

◀ **The Ocean Floor.** Beneath Earth's oceans lies a landscape as varied as any on land. The Mid-Atlantic Ridge is part of a global mountain range that winds 40,000 miles (64,000 km) across the ocean floor. Volcanic islands rise up from the seabed, while the Mariana Trench plunges more than 35,000 feet (10,000 m)—deep enough to submerge Mount Everes

ARCTIC OCEAN

GREENLAND

Greenland Sea

Svalbard

Novaya Zemlya

Kara Sea

Laptev Sea

East Siberian Sea

Barents Sea

Iceland

ARCTIC CIRCLE

Norwegian Sea

Scandinavia

Ural Mountains

West Siberian Plain

S I B E R I A

Central Siberian Plateau

Ob

Lena

Angara

60°N

Bering Sea

Kamchatka Peninsula

Aleutian Is.

British Isles

North Sea

Great Britain

Baltic Sea

Northern European Plain

Volga

Irtysh

Ob

Yenisey

Altay Mountains

Lena

Amur

Lake Baikal

Sea of Okhotsk

Kuril Islands

Hokkaido

Ireland

EUROPE

Alps

Danube

El'brus
18,510 ft
(5,642 m)

The Steppes

Aral Sea

Caucasus Mts.

Tian Shan

G O B I

Taklimakan Desert

Kunlun Mountains

A S I A

North China Plain

Yellow (Huang)

JAPAN

Sea of Japan

Korea

Honshu

Azores

Mediterranean Sea

Black Sea

Caspian Sea

Zagros Mountains

Plateau of Tibet

Brahmaputra

Yellow Sea

Yangtze (Chang)

East China Sea

Nampo Shoto

30°N

Madeira Islands

Atlas Mountains

Libyan Desert

Nile

Persian Gulf

Dead Sea
-1,349 ft
(-411 m)

ARABIAN PENINSULA

Red Sea

H I M A L A Y A

Mt. Everest
29,035 ft
(8,850 m)

Ganges

Salween

Ryukyu Islands

Taiwan

PACIFIC

Canary Islands

SAHARA

S A H E L

AFRICA

White Nile

Blue Nile

Gulf of Aden

Ethiopian Highlands

Somali Peninsula

Arabian Sea

INDIA

Deccan Plateau

Bay of Bengal

Andaman Islands

Andaman Sea

Indochina Peninsula

Mekong

South China Sea

Hainan

Luzon

Philippine Sea

Mariana Islands

OCEAN

M I C R O N E S I A

Marshall Islands

Niger

Upper Guinea

Gulf of Guinea

Congo

Lake Victoria

Great Rift Valley

Kilimanjaro
19,340 ft
(5,895 m)

Maldive Islands

60°E

90°E

Sri Lanka

Nicobar Is.

Malay Peninsula

Sumatra

Borneo

Celebes

INDONESIA

Greater Sunda Islands

Moluccas

New Guinea

150°E

EQUATOR

M E L A N E S I A

Bismarck Archipelago

Solomon Islands

Gilbert Islands

0°

Cape Verde Islands

Lower Guinea

Congo Basin

Lake Tanganyika

Zambezi

Seychelles

INDIAN

Java

Arafura Sea

Vanuatu

New Caledonia

Fiji Islands

OCEAN

Namib Desert

Drakensberg

Kalahari Desert

Madagascar

Mascarene Islands

OCEAN

Coral Sea

Great Sandy Desert

Central Lowlands

Great Dividing Range

AUSTRALIA

Lake Eyre
-52 ft, (-16 m)

Great Victoria Desert

Darling

Murray

Mt. Kosciuszko
7,310 ft
(2,228 m)

Tasman Sea

North Island

NEW ZEALAND

30°S

South Sandwich Islands

0        miles        2000

0      kilometers     3000

*Winkel Tripel Projection*

Kerguélen Islands

Tasmania

Auckland Islands

South Island

ANTARCTIC CIRCLE

60°S

MOUNTAINS

Queen Maud Land

Transantarctic Mountains

Victoria Land

ANTARCTICA

◄ **The Physical World.** *Great land-masses called continents break Earth's global ocean into four smaller ones. Each continent is unique in terms of the landforms and rivers that etch its surface and in the ecosystems that lend colors ranging from the deep greens of the tropical forests of northern South America and southeastern Asia to the browns and yellows of the arid lands of Africa and Australia. Most of Antarctica's features are hidden beneath its ice cap.*

# EARTH'S GEOLOGIC HISTORY

**E**arth is truly a living planet. Its outer shell, or crust, is broken into huge pieces called plates. These plates ride on the slowly moving molten rock, or magma, that lies beneath the crust. Their movement constantly changes Earth's surface. For instance, along one convergent boundary—a place where two plates meet—the plate carrying India is colliding with the Eurasian Plate, heaving up the still growing mountains of the Himalaya. Along another convergent boundary, the Nazca Plate dives beneath the South American Plate in a process called subduction. Volcanoes may occur along subduction zones. Along transform zones, such as California's San Andreas Fault, plates grind past each other, triggering earthquakes. The Mid-Atlantic Ridge is a divergent boundary where plates are pulling apart and molten rock is rising to form new ocean floor. At places called hot spots magma breaks through the crust, forming new land, as in the Hawaiian Islands. (Web Link)

▼ *Our Changing Planet. The Latin phrase terra firma implies planet Earth is solid and unchanging. However, Earth's surface has been anything but unchanging. Geologic evidence suggests that moving plates have collided and moved apart more than once over the course of the planet's long history. As the main map shows, the forces of change show no signs of stopping.*

▶ **Pangaea.**
*About 240 million years ago, all of Earth's continents had collided to form a vast land-mass (now called Pangaea) that stretched from Pole to Pole.*

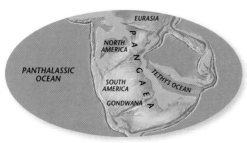

▶ **Drifting Apart.**
*By 94 million years ago, Pangaea had been pulled apart into smaller landmasses. In the warm global climate, dinosaurs evolved into Earth's dominant animal group.*

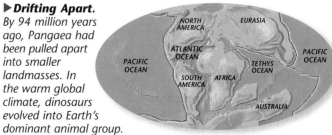

ARCTIC OCEAN

Plate Boundary (uncertain)

E U R A S I A N

P L A T E

ALPS

PLATEAU OF TIBET

H I M A L A Y A

Plateau of Tibet

PACIFIC
OCEAN

ARABIAN

PLATE

I N D I A N

PLATE

PHILIPPINE
PLATE

A F R I C A N

Great Rift Valley

SOMALI

PLATE

PACIFIC

P L A T E

P L A T E

EQUATOR

OCEAN

INDIAN
OCEAN

MID-ATLANTIC RIDGE

A U S T R A L I A N

P L A T E

A N T A R C T I C

P L A T E

| 0 | miles | 2000 |
| 0 | kilometers | 3000 |

Winkel Tripel Projection

### Plate Tectonics

- Divergent boundary
- Convergent boundary
- Transform zone
- ○ Notable earthquake of the 20th century
- ∘ 20th-century quake greater than 6.5 magnitude
- ▲ Notable volcanic eruption of the 20th century
- ▲ Known volcanic eruption during the past 10,000 years
- ○ Hot spot

◀ **Tectonic boundaries**
mark areas of geologic change in ocean floors, along continental margins, and even through continents, as in East Africa's Great Rift Valley. Clusters of volcanoes and frequent earthquakes signal areas of instability.

▶ **Eve of Destruction.**
By 65 million years ago, continents were moving toward their current positions. The impact (✱) of an asteroid in the Gulf of Mexico probably extinguished the dinosaurs and many other species.

NORTH AMERICA    EUROPE    ASIA
ATLANTIC OCEAN    PACIFIC OCEAN
PACIFIC OCEAN    AFRICA
SOUTH AMERICA
AUSTRALIA

▶ **Deep Freeze.**
By 18,000 years ago, the continents resembled their current shapes. A great ice age had the far northern and southern regions locked under huge ice sheets.

EUROPE    ASIA
NORTH AMERICA    PACIFIC OCEAN
ATLANTIC    AFRICA
PACIFIC OCEAN    OCEAN
SOUTH AMERICA    AUSTRALIA
ANTARCTICA

# EARTH'S LAND & WATER FEATURES

The largest land and water features on Earth are the continents and the oceans, but many other features—large and small—make each place unique. Mountains, plateaus, and plains give texture to the land. The Rockies and the Andes rise high above the lowlands of North and South America. In Asia, the Himalaya and the Plateau of Tibet form the rugged core of Earth's largest continent. These features are the result of powerful forces within Earth pushing up the land. Others, such as canyons and valleys, are created when weathering and erosion wear down parts of Earth's surface.

Dramatic features are not limited to the land. Submarine mountains, appearing like pale blue threads against the deep blue on the satellite map, rise from the seafloor and trace zones of underwater geologic activity. Deep trenches form where plates collide, causing one to dive beneath the other.

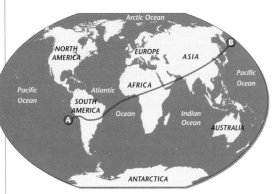

**▼ A Slice of Earth.**
This cross section of Earth's surface extends from Lake Titicaca near South America's Pacific coast to the Kuril Islands in the North Pacific Ocean. It shows towering mountains, eroded highlands, broad coastal plains, and deep ocean basins.

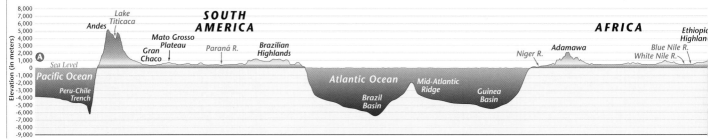

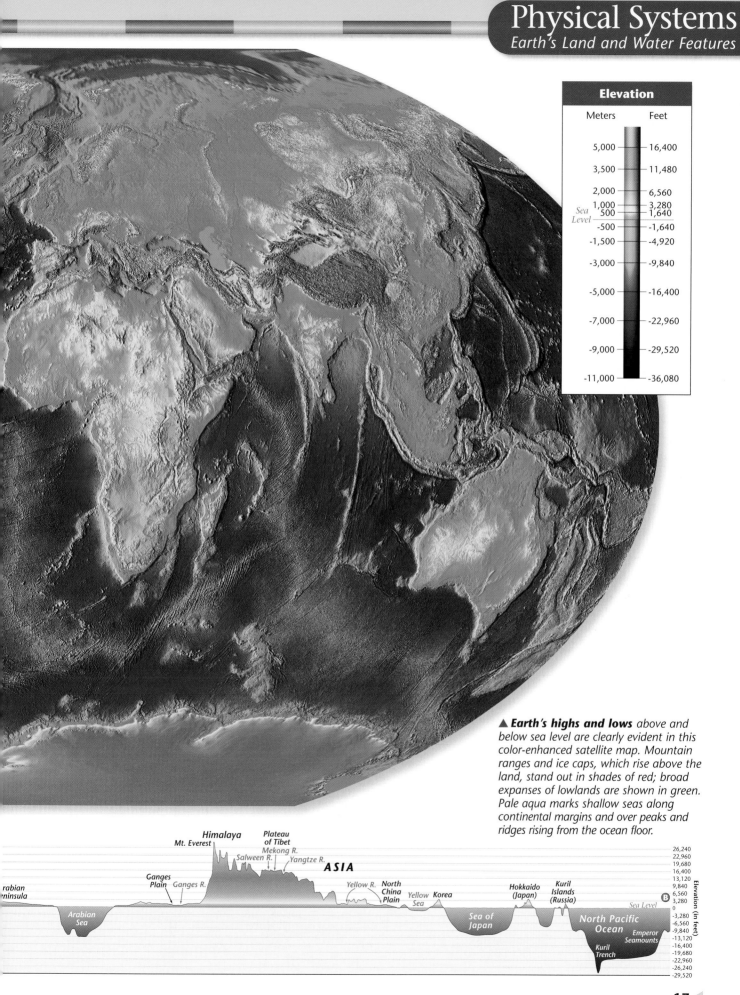

**Elevation**

| Meters | Feet |
|---|---|
| 5,000 | 16,400 |
| 3,500 | 11,480 |
| 2,000 | 6,560 |
| 1,000 | 3,280 |
| 500 | 1,640 |
| -500 | -1,640 |
| -1,500 | -4,920 |
| -3,000 | -9,840 |
| -5,000 | -16,400 |
| -7,000 | -22,960 |
| -9,000 | -29,520 |
| -11,000 | -36,080 |

*Sea Level*

▲ **Earth's highs and lows** *above and below sea level are clearly evident in this color-enhanced satellite map. Mountain ranges and ice caps, which rise above the land, stand out in shades of red; broad expanses of lowlands are shown in green. Pale aqua marks shallow seas along continental margins and over peaks and ridges rising from the ocean floor.*

Himalaya
Mt. Everest
Plateau of Tibet
Mekong R.
Salween R.
Yangtze R.
**ASIA**
Ganges Plain
Ganges R.
Yellow R.
North China Plain
Yellow Sea
Korea
Hokkaido (Japan)
Kuril Islands (Russia)
rabian ninsula
Arabian Sea
Sea of Japan
North Pacific Ocean
Emperor Seamounts
Kuril Trench
Sea Level
Ⓑ

Elevation (in feet)

26,240
22,960
19,680
16,400
13,120
9,840
6,560
3,280
0
-3,280
-6,560
-9,840
-13,120
-16,400
-19,680
-22,960
-26,240
-29,520

# EARTH'S CLIMATES

Climate is not the same as weather. Climate is the long-term average of conditions in the atmosphere at a particular location on Earth's surface. Weather refers to the momentary conditions of the atmosphere. Climate is important because it influences vegetation and soil development. It also influences people's choices about how and where to live.

There are many different systems for classifying climates. One commonly used system was developed by Russian-born climatologist Wladimir Köppen and later modified by American climatologist Glenn Trewartha. Köppen's system identifies five major climate zones based on average precipitation and temperature, and a sixth zone for highland, or high elevation, areas. Except for continental climate, all climate zones occur in mirror image north and south of the Equator. (Web Link)

▼ **Climate Graphs.** *A climate graph is a combination bar and line graph that shows monthly averages of precipitation and temperature for a particular place. The bar graph shows precipitation in inches and centimeters; the line graph shows temperature in degrees Fahrenheit and Celsius. The graphs below are typical for places in the climate zone represented by their background color. The seeming inversion of the temperature lines for Alice Springs and McMurdo reflects the reversal of seasons south of the Equator, where January is midsummer.*

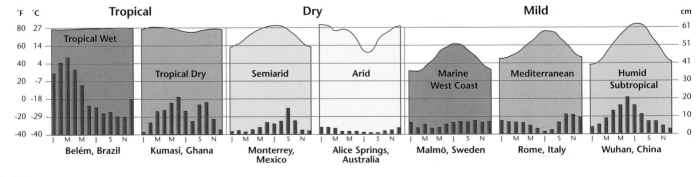

ARCTIC OCEAN

North Atlantic Drift

ARCTIC CIRCLE

EUROPE

Malmö
Minsk

Rome

ASIA

60°N

Lhasa
Wuhan

Kuroshio

North Equatorial
Current

PACIFIC

AFRICA

Kumasi

Kampala

OCEAN

Equatorial
Countercurrent

EQUATOR

150°E

OCEAN

Benguela Current

60°E

90°E

South Equatorial
Current

INDIAN

OCEAN

Agulhas Current

West Australia Current

AUSTRALIA

Alice
Springs

30°S

West Wind Drift

60°S

ANTARCTIC CIRCLE

ANTARCTICA

McMurdo

### Climatic Zones

(based on Köppen System)

**Tropical**
- Tropical wet
- Tropical dry

**Dry**
- Semiarid
- Arid

**Mild**
- Marine west coast
- Mediterranean
- Humid subtropical

**Continental**
- Warm summer
- Cool Summer
- Subarctic

**Polar**
- Tundra
- Ice cap

**High Elevations**
- Highlands
- Uplands

- → Warm ocean current
- → Cool ocean current
- → Prevailing wind

▲**Climate patterns** become apparent when viewed at the global level. A band of tropical wet climate hugs the Equator, and continental climates are present only in the Northern Hemisphere. Tundra and ice caps are found in the high latitudes near both Poles.

| °F | °C | Continental | | | Polar | | High Elevations | | cm | in |
|---|---|---|---|---|---|---|---|---|---|---|
| 80 | 27 | | | | | | | | 61 | 24 |
| 60 | 14 | | | | | | | | 51 | 20 |
| 40 | 4 | | | | | | | | 41 | 16 |
| 20 | -7 | | | | | | | | 30 | 12 |
| 0 | -18 | Warm Summer | Cool Summer | Subarctic | Tundra | Ice Cap | Highlands | Uplands | 20 | 8 |
| -20 | -29 | | | | | | | | 10 | 4 |
| -40 | -40 | | | | | | | | 0 | 0 |

J M M J S N  J M M J S N  J M M J S N  J M M J S N  J M M J S N  J M M J S N  J M M J S N

Des Moines, Iowa, U.S.A. | Minsk, Belarus | Fairbanks, Alaska, U.S.A. | Resolute, Nunavut, Canada | McMurdo, Antarctica | Lhasa, China | Kampala, Uganda

**19** ◀

# CLIMATE CONTROLS

The patterns of climate vary widely. Some climates, such as those near the Equator and the Poles, are nearly constant year-round. Others experience great seasonal variations, such as the wet and dry patterns of the tropical dry zone and the monthly average temperature extremes of the subarctic.

Climate patterns are not random. They are the result of complex interactions of basic climate controls: **latitude**, **elevation**, **prevailing winds**, **ocean currents**, **landforms**, and **location.**

These controls combine in various ways to create the bands of climate that can be seen on the world climate map on pages 18–19 and on the climate maps in the individual continent sections of this atlas. At the local level, however, special conditions may create microclimates that differ from those that are more typical of the region.

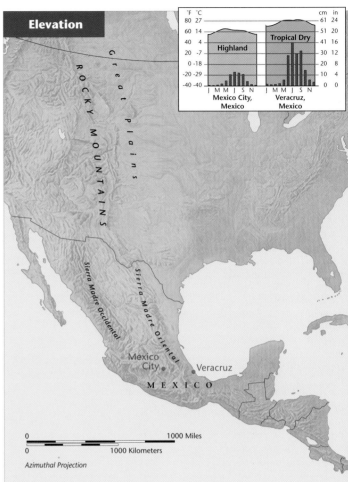

### Elevation

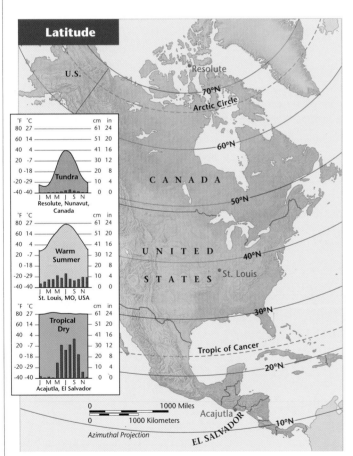

### Latitude

▲ **Latitude.** Energy from the sun strikes the Equator at a right angle. As latitude (distance north or south of the Equator) increases, the angle becomes increasingly oblique, or slanted. Less energy is received from the sun, and annual average temperatures fall. Therefore, the annual average temperature decreases as latitude increases from Acajutla, El Salvador, to St. Louis, Missouri, to Resolute, Canada.

▲ **Elevation.** Not all locations at the same latitude experience similar climates. Air at higher elevations is cooler and holds less moisture than air at lower elevations. This explains why the climate at Veracruz, Mexico, which is near sea level, is warm and wet, and the climate at Mexico City, which is more than 7,000 feet (11,000 m) above sea level, is cooler and drier.

▶ **Landforms.** Air carried by prevailing winds blowing off the ocean is full of moisture. If that air encounters a mountain when it reaches land, it is forced to rise. It becomes cooler, causing precipitation on the windward side of the mountain (see Portland graph). When air descends on the side away from the wind—the leeward side— the air warms and absorbs available moisture. This creates a dry condition known as rain shadow (see Wallowa graph).

### Landforms

## Prevailing Winds and Ocean Currents

▶ **Prevailing Winds and Ocean Currents.** *Earth's rotation combined with heat energy from the sun creates patterns of movement in Earth's atmosphere called prevailing winds. In the oceans similar movements of water are called currents. Prevailing winds and ocean currents bring warm and cold temperatures to land areas. They also bring moisture or take it away. The Gulf Stream and the North Atlantic Drift, for example, are warm-water currents that influence average temperatures in eastern North America and northern Europe. Prevailing winds—trade winds, polar easterlies, and westerlies—also affect temperature and precipitation averages.*

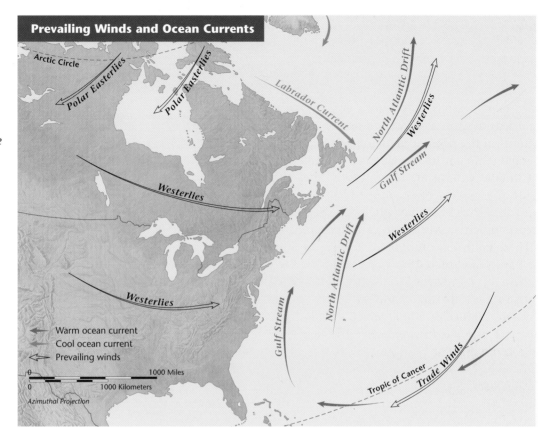

## Location

▼ **Location.** *Marine locations—places near large bodies of water—have mild climates with little temperature variation because water gains and loses heat slowly (see San Francisco graph). Interior locations—places far from large water bodies—have much more extreme climates. There are great temperature variations because land gains and loses heat rapidly (see Wichita graph). Richmond, which is relatively near the Atlantic Ocean but which is also influenced by prevailing westerly winds blowing across the land, has moderate characteristics of both conditions.*

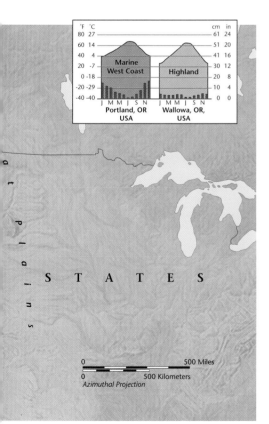

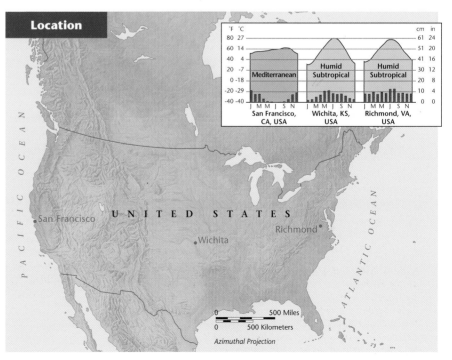

# EARTH'S NATURAL VEGETATION

**N**atural vegetation is the plant life that would be found in an area if it were undisturbed by human activity. Natural vegetation varies widely depending on climate and soil conditions. In the rain forest, trees tower as much as 200 feet (60 m) above the forest floor. In the tundra, dwarf species of shrubs and flowers are adaptations to harsh conditions at high latitudes and high elevations.

Vegetation is important to human life. It provides oxygen, food, fuel, products with economic value, even lifesaving medicines. Human activities, however, have greatly affected natural vegetation. Huge forests have been cut to provide fuel and lumber. Grasslands have yielded to the plow as people extend agricultural lands. As many as one in eight plants may become extinct as a result of human interference. Web Link

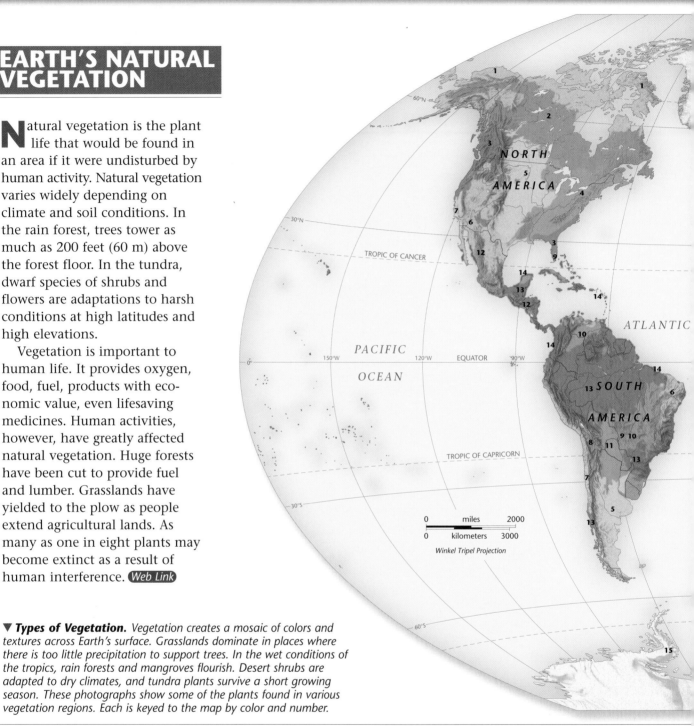

▼ **Types of Vegetation.** *Vegetation creates a mosaic of colors and textures across Earth's surface. Grasslands dominate in places where there is too little precipitation to support trees. In the wet conditions of the tropics, rain forests and mangroves flourish. Desert shrubs are adapted to dry climates, and tundra plants survive a short growing season. These photographs show some of the plants found in various vegetation regions. Each is keyed to the map by color and number.*

▲ **Tundra**

▲ **Northern coniferous forest**

▲ **Temperate broadleaf forest**

▲ **Desert shrub**

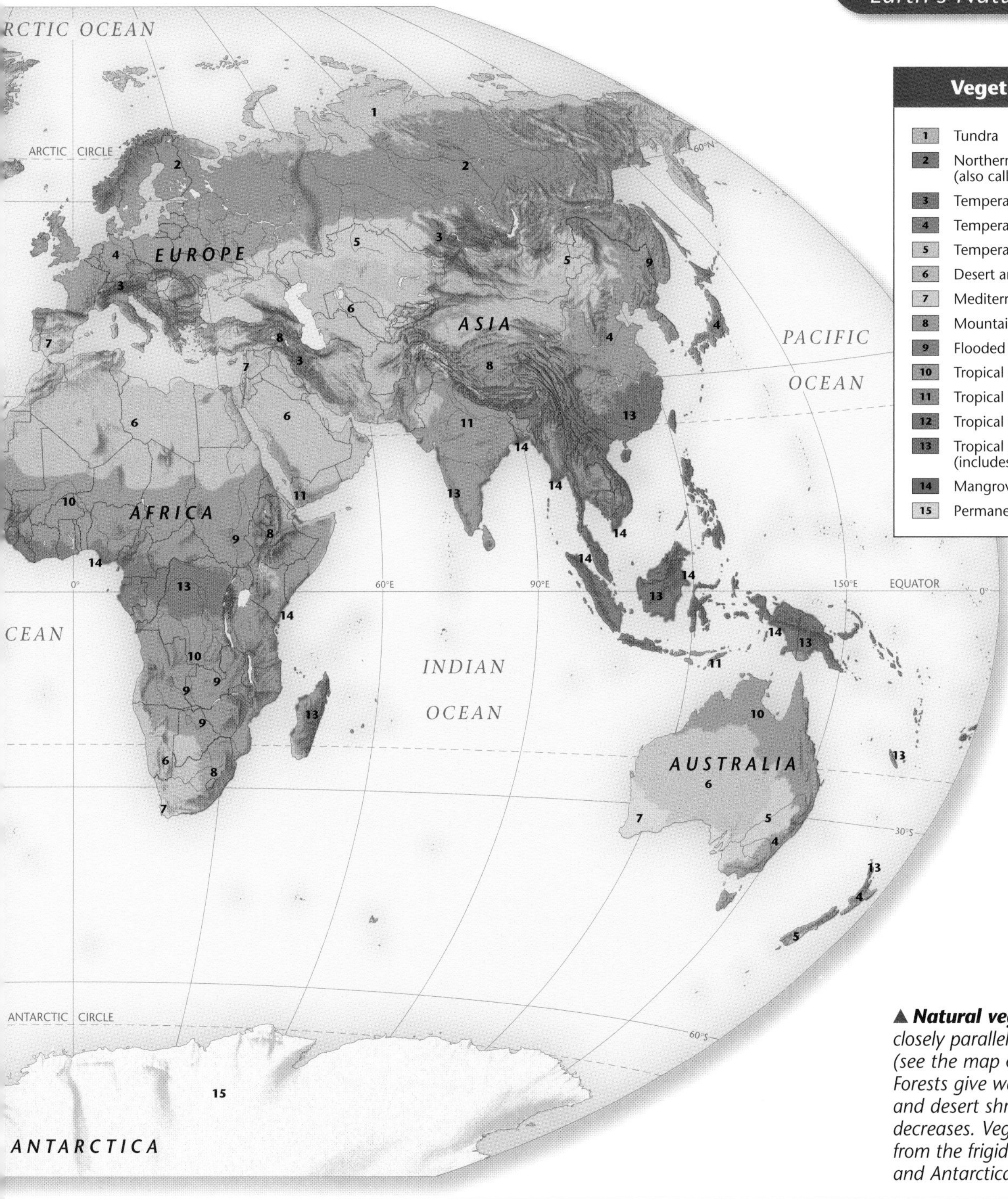

ARCTIC OCEAN

ARCTIC CIRCLE

EUROPE

ASIA

AFRICA

PACIFIC OCEAN

INDIAN OCEAN

AUSTRALIA

ANTARCTIC CIRCLE

ANTARCTICA

60°N

60°E

90°E

150°E

EQUATOR

0°

30°S

60°S

**Vegetation Zones**

| | |
|---|---|
| 1 | Tundra |
| 2 | Northern coniferous forest (also called boreal forest or taiga) |
| 3 | Temperate coniferous forest |
| 4 | Temperate broadleaf forest |
| 5 | Temperate grassland |
| 6 | Desert and dry shrub |
| 7 | Mediterranean shrub |
| 8 | Mountain grassland |
| 9 | Flooded grassland and savanna |
| 10 | Tropical grassland and savanna |
| 11 | Tropical dry forest |
| 12 | Tropical coniferous forest |
| 13 | Tropical moist broadleaf (includes rain forest) |
| 14 | Mangrove |
| 15 | Permanent ice cover |

▲ **Natural vegetation** patterns closely parallel patterns of climate (see the map on pages 18–19). Forests give way to grasslands and desert shrubs as precipitation decreases. Vegetation is absent from the frigid ice caps of Greenland and Antarctica.

▲ **Temperate grassland**

▲ **Tropical grassland**

▲ **Tropical moist broadleaf**

▲ **Mangrove**

23

# Human Systems

## THE POLITICAL WORLD

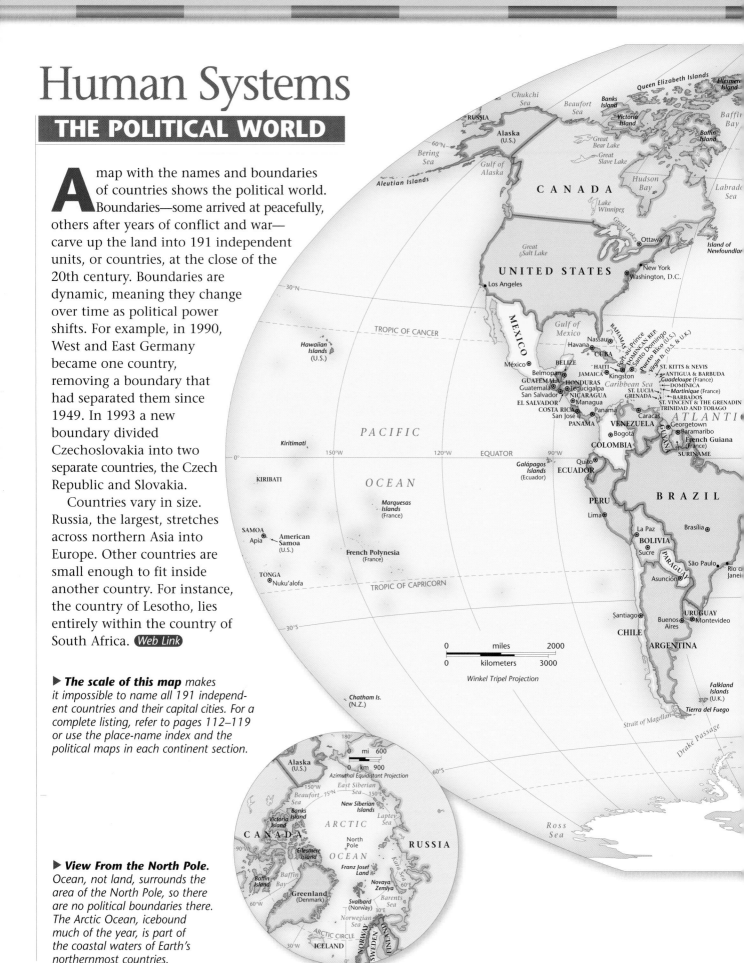

**A** map with the names and boundaries of countries shows the political world. Boundaries—some arrived at peacefully, others after years of conflict and war—carve up the land into 191 independent units, or countries, at the close of the 20th century. Boundaries are dynamic, meaning they change over time as political power shifts. For example, in 1990, West and East Germany became one country, removing a boundary that had separated them since 1949. In 1993 a new boundary divided Czechoslovakia into two separate countries, the Czech Republic and Slovakia.

Countries vary in size. Russia, the largest, stretches across northern Asia into Europe. Other countries are small enough to fit inside another country. For instance, the country of Lesotho, lies entirely within the country of South Africa. **Web Link**

▶ **The scale of this map** makes it impossible to name all 191 independent countries and their capital cities. For a complete listing, refer to pages 112–119 or use the place-name index and the political maps in each continent section.

▶ **View From the North Pole.** Ocean, not land, surrounds the area of the North Pole, so there are no political boundaries there. The Arctic Ocean, icebound much of the year, is part of the coastal waters of Earth's northernmost countries.

▶ **24**

ARCTIC OCEAN

Greenland (Denmark)

Greenland Sea

Svalbard (Norway)

Franz Josef Land

Barents Sea

Novaya Zemlya

Kara Sea

Severnaya Zemlya

New Siberian Islands

Laptev Sea

East Siberian Sea

Norwegian Sea

ARCTIC CIRCLE

ICELAND
Reykjavik

NORWAY

SWEDEN

FINLAND

R U S S I A

60°E

Bering Sea

Sea of Okhotsk

Kamchatka Peninsula

Oslo

Stockholm

Helsinki

EST.

Sakhalin

Hokkaido

UNITED KINGDOM

North Sea

DENMARK

LATV.

LITH.

Minsk

Moscow

Astana

Lake Baikal

Ulaanbaatar

NORTH KOREA

Honshu

JAPAN

IRELAND

BELG.

Copenhagen

Berlin

POLAND

BELARUS

KAZAKHSTAN

MONGOLIA

Pyongyang

Tokyo

Dublin

London

NETH.

GERMANY

Warsaw

UKRAINE

Kiev

Aral Sea

Beijing

SOUTH KOREA

Seoul

Osaka

Paris

SWITZ.

CZECH REP.

SLOVAKIA

MOLD.

Bishkek

KYRGYZSTAN

C H I N A

Kyushu

30°N

FRANCE

AUSTRIA

HUNG.

ROMANIA

Black Sea

GEORGIA

UZBEKISTAN

Tashkent

Dushanbe

TAJIKISTAN

PORTUGAL

ITALY

SLOV.

CRO.

BOS.

YUGO.

BULGARIA

ARM.

AZERB.

TURKMENISTAN

Ashgabat

Kabul

Shanghai

TAIWAN

The People's Republic of China claims Taiwan as its 23rd province.

Taipei

PACIFIC

Azores (Portugal)

Madrid

Rome

ALBANIA

MACED.

Ankara

TURKEY

SYRIA

Tehran

Islamabad

Northern Mariana Islands (U.S.)

Lisbon

SPAIN

Madeira Is. (Portugal)

Canary Is. (Spain)

Rabat

MOROCCO

Western Sahara (Morocco)

ALGERIA

Tunis

Algiers

TUNISIA

Tripoli

GREECE

Athens

Mediterranean Sea

CYPRUS

LEBANON

ISRAEL

Cairo

JORDAN

IRAQ

Baghdad

IRAN

AFGHANISTAN

PAKISTAN

New Delhi

Kathmandu

NEPAL

Thimphu

BHUTAN

BANGLADESH

Dhaka

Calcutta

MYANMAR (BURMA)

Hanoi

Hainan

Philippine Sea

Luzon

Manila

PHILIPPINES

OCEAN

MARSHALL ISLANDS

KUWAIT

QATAR

BAHRAIN

U.A.E.

Riyadh

Muscat

India

Mumbai (Bombay)

Arabian Sea

South China Sea

FEDERATED STATES OF MICRONESIA

LIBYA

EGYPT

SAUDI ARABIA

OMAN

Red Sea

Khartoum

ERITREA

Asmara

YEMEN

Sanaa

Socotra (Yemen)

Yangon

THAILAND

Bangkok

LAOS

Vientiane

VIETNAM

CAMBODIA

Phnom Penh

Mindanao

PALAU

Bay of Bengal

SRI LANKA

Colombo

Sri Jayewardenepura Kotte

KIRIBATI

EQUATOR

NAURU

MAURITANIA

CAPE VERDE

Nouakchott

MALI

NIGER

CHAD

SUDAN

Addis Ababa

DJIBOUTI

ETHIOPIA

SOMALIA

MALDIVES

Male

BRUNEI

Bandar Seri Begawan

150°E

SENEGAL

Dakar

GAMBIA

Bamako

BURKINA FASO

Niamey

N'Djamena

CENTRAL AFRICAN REPUBLIC

Kuala Lumpur

SINGAPORE

MALAYSIA

Borneo

GUINEA-BISSAU

Bissau

GUINEA

Conakry

SIERRA LEONE

Freetown

Monrovia

LIBERIA

CÔTE D'IVOIRE

GHANA

Accra

TOGO

BENIN

Ouagadougou

Yamoussoukro

Abidjan

Lomé

Porto-Novo

NIGERIA

Abuja

Lagos

CAMEROON

Yaoundé

EQ. GUINEA

Bangui

DEMOCRATIC REPUBLIC OF THE CONGO

UGANDA

Kampala

RWANDA

Kigali

BURUNDI

Bujumbura

Nairobi

KENYA

Dar es Salaam

SEYCHELLES

Jakarta

Java

Celebes

I N D O N E S I A

Sumatra

East Timor

New Guinea

PAPUA NEW GUINEA

Port Moresby

SOLOMON ISLANDS

Honiara

TUVALU

SAO TOME AND PRINCIPE

Libreville

GABON

CONGO

Brazzaville

Kinshasa

CABINDA (Angola)

TANZANIA

COMOROS

Moroni

INDIAN

OCEAN

VANUATU

Port-Vila

FIJI

Suva

OCEAN

Luanda

ANGOLA

ZAMBIA

Lusaka

MALAWI

Lilongwe

MOZAMBIQUE

Antananarivo

MAURITIUS

Port Louis

Réunion (France)

Coral Sea

New Caledonia (France)

NAMIBIA

Windhoek

BOTSWANA

Gaborone

ZIMBABWE

Harare

MADAGASCAR

Great Australian Bight

A U S T R A L I A

30°S

SOUTH AFRICA

Pretoria

Maputo

SWAZILAND

LESOTHO

Bloemfontein

Cape Town

Tasman Sea

North Island

Kerguélen Islands (France)

Canberra

Tasmania

NEW ZEALAND

Wellington

South Island

ANTARCTIC CIRCLE

60°S

A N T A R C T I C A

Ross Sea

ATLANTIC OCEAN

ANTARCTIC CIRCLE

30°W

30°E

60°S

Weddell Sea

Antarctic Peninsula

Ronne Ice Shelf

75°S

INDIAN OCEAN

60°E

A N T A R C T I C A

90°W

West Antarctica

South Pole

East Antarctica

90°E

Ross Ice Shelf

60°W

PACIFIC OCEAN

Ross Sea

120°E

0  mi  600

0  km  900

Azimuthal Equidistant Projection

150°E

180°

▶ **View From the South Pole.** *Covered by ice, the continent of Antarctica has been set aside by treaty for scientific research. It has no permanent population and no political boundaries, although 7 countries claim territory there and 23 operate year-round research stations (see map page 111).*

# WORLD POPULATION

Late in 1999 the United Nations announced that Earth's population had surpassed six billion. Although more than 80 million people are added each year, the rate, or annual percent, at which the population is growing is gradually decreasing. Earth's population has very uneven distribution, with huge clusters in Asia and in Europe. Population density, the number of people living in each square mile (or square kilometer) on average, is high in these regions. For example, there are more than 2,000 people per square mile (800 people per sq km)) in Bangladesh. Other areas, such as deserts and Arctic tundra, have less than 2 people per square mile (1 person per sq km). Web Link

▼ **Crowded streets,** like this one in Shanghai, may become commonplace as Earth's population continues to increase and as more people move to urban areas.

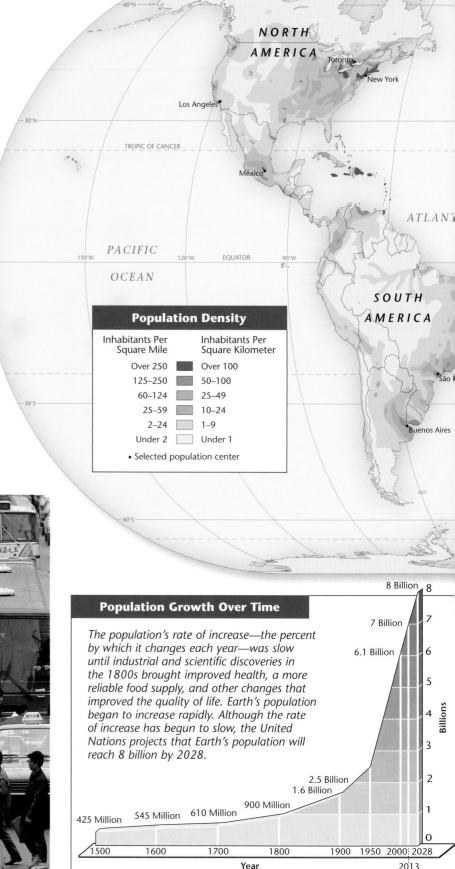

## Population Density

| Inhabitants Per Square Mile | | Inhabitants Per Square Kilometer |
|---|---|---|
| Over 250 | | Over 100 |
| 125–250 | | 50–100 |
| 60–124 | | 25–49 |
| 25–59 | | 10–24 |
| 2–24 | | 1–9 |
| Under 2 | | Under 1 |

• Selected population center

## Population Growth Over Time

The population's rate of increase—the percent by which it changes each year—was slow until industrial and scientific discoveries in the 1800s brought improved health, a more reliable food supply, and other changes that improved the quality of life. Earth's population began to increase rapidly. Although the rate of increase has begun to slow, the United Nations projects that Earth's population will reach 8 billion by 2028.

425 Million · 545 Million · 610 Million · 900 Million · 1.6 Billion · 2.5 Billion · 6.1 Billion · 7 Billion · 8 Billion

Billions

1500 · 1600 · 1700 · 1800 · 1900 · 1950 · 2000 · 2028

2013

**Year**

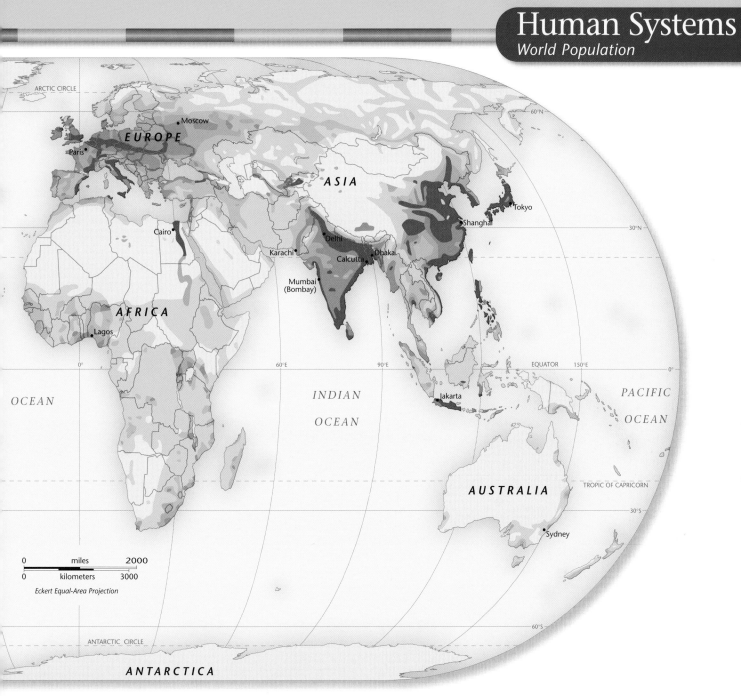

ARCTIC CIRCLE

60°N

EUROPE
Moscow
Paris

ASIA

Tokyo
Shanghai
Cairo
30°N
Delhi
Karachi
Calcutta Dhaka
Mumbai
(Bombay)

AFRICA

Lagos

0°
60°E
90°E
EQUATOR
150°E
0°

OCEAN

INDIAN

OCEAN

Jakarta

PACIFIC

OCEAN

0       miles      2000
0    kilometers    3000
*Eckert Equal-Area Projection*

AUSTRALIA

TROPIC OF CAPRICORN

30°S

Sydney

60°S

ANTARCTIC CIRCLE

ANTARCTICA

## Three Population Pyramids

A population pyramid is a special type of bar graph that shows the distribution of a country's population by sex and age. Italy has a very narrow pyramid, which shows that most people are in middle age. Its population is said to be aging, meaning the median age is increasing. The United States also has a narrow pyramid, but one that shows some growth due to a median age of about 35 years and a young immigrant population. By contrast, Côte d'Ivoire's pyramid has a broad base, showing it has a young population. Almost half its people are younger than 15 years.

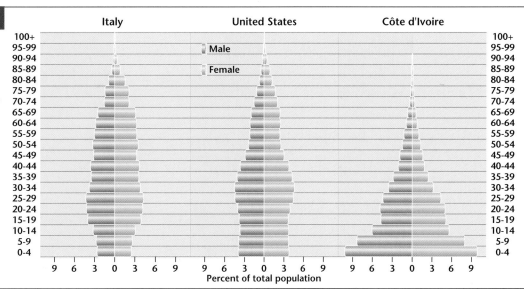

**Italy**          **United States**          **Côte d'Ivoire**

Male

Female

100+
95-99
90-94
85-89
80-84
75-79
70-74
65-69
60-64
55-59
50-54
45-49
40-44
35-39
30-34
25-29
20-24
15-19
10-14
5-9
0-4

9  6  3  0  3  6  9      9  6  3  0  3  6  9      9  6  3  0  3  6  9
**Percent of total population**

# WORLD CITIES

Throughout most of history, people have lived spread across the land, first as hunters and gatherers, later as farmers. But urban geographers—people who study cities—predict that sometime in the next decade more people will be living in urban areas than in rural areas. Urban areas include one or more cities and their surrounding suburbs. People living there are employed primarily in industry or in service-related jobs. Large urban areas are sometimes called metropolitan areas. In some countries, such as Belgium, almost all the population lives in cities. But throughout much of Africa south of the Sahara, less than one-third of the people live in urban areas. Even so, the world's fastest growing urban areas are in Africa and Asia, as shown in the graph below.

Web Link

## Most Populous Urban Areas

*In 1950 New York topped a list of only 8 cities with populations of 5 million or greater. Just 50 years later, New York ranked fifth in a list of 41 cities with populations exceeding 5 million. By 2015, the list is projected to include 59 cities.*

Cities with populations greater than five million for the years:

- 1950
- 2000
- 2015

| North America | South America | Europe | Africa | Asia | Australia/Oceania |
|---|---|---|---|---|---|
| 1 4 6 | 1 6 7 | 4 5 5 | 0 3 6 | 2 23 35 | 0 0 0 |

NORTH AMERICA

Chicago
Toronto
New York
Los Angeles

TROPIC OF CANCER

México
Guatemala City

Bogotá

PACIFIC OCEAN

EQUATOR

ATLANTIC

SOUTH AMERICA

Lima

Belo Horizonte
Rio de Janeiro
São Paulo

Santiago
Buenos Aires

| 0 | miles | 2000 |
| 0 | kilometers | 3000 |

*Winkel Tripel Projection*

## Urban and Rural Populations

*These graphs show the percentages of people living in urban and rural areas in various world regions. Only Asia and Africa are predominantly rural, although both are experiencing rapid urban growth. Asia, which had only 2 cities of five million or more people in 1950, now has 23.*

### United States & Cana

75%    25%

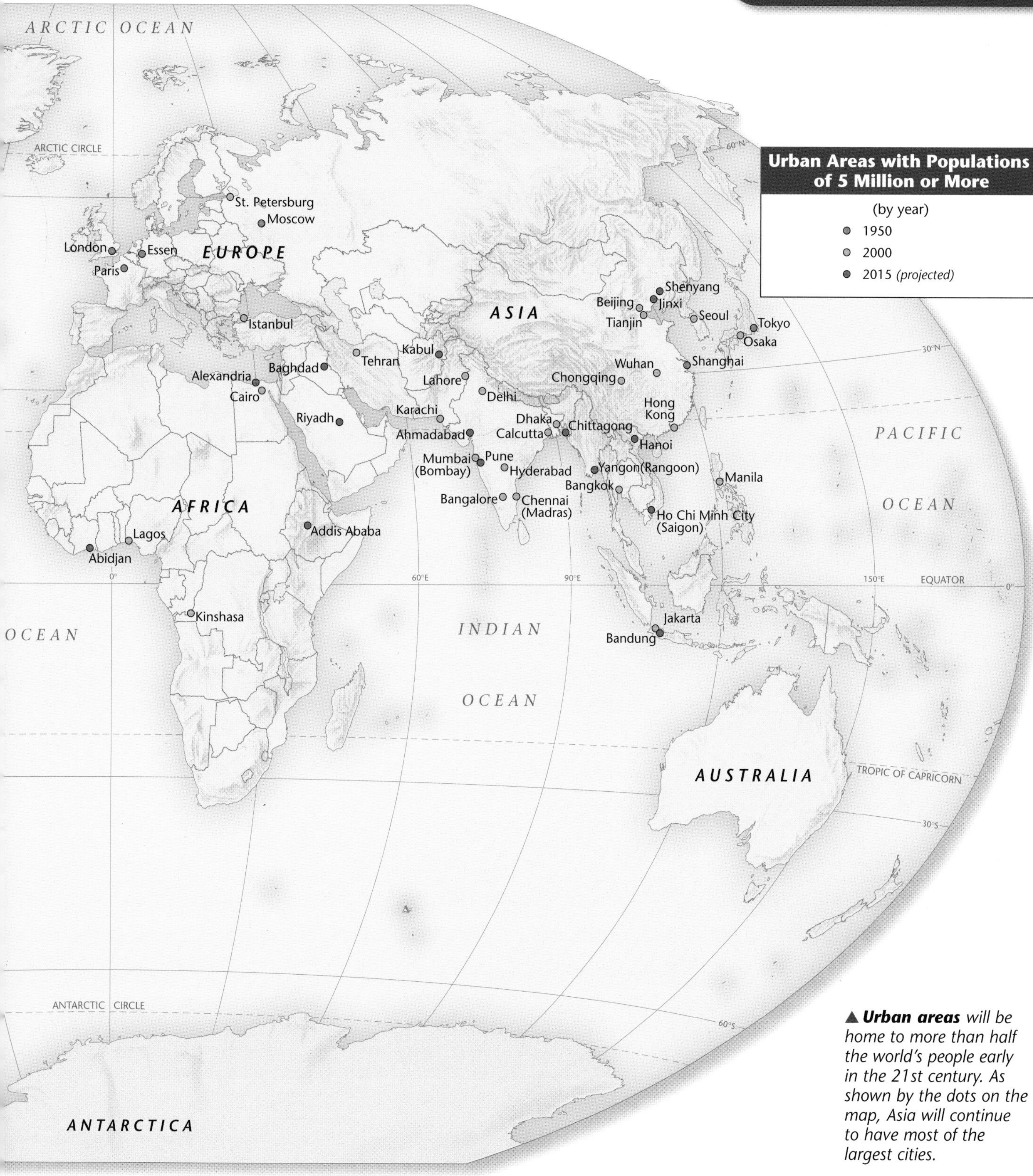

ARCTIC OCEAN

ARCTIC CIRCLE

60°E

EUROPE

ASIA

PACIFIC

OCEAN

AFRICA

INDIAN

OCEAN

AUSTRALIA

ANTARCTICA

**Urban Areas with Populations of 5 Million or More**

(by year)
- 1950
- 2000
- 2015 (projected)

St. Petersburg
Moscow
London
Essen
Paris
Istanbul
Alexandria
Cairo
Baghdad
Tehran
Kabul
Lahore
Delhi
Riyadh
Karachi
Ahmadabad
Mumbai (Bombay)
Pune
Hyderabad
Bangalore
Chennai (Madras)
Dhaka
Calcutta
Chittagong
Chongqing
Wuhan
Shenyang
Beijing
Jinxi
Tianjin
Seoul
Tokyo
Osaka
Shanghai
Hong Kong
Hanoi
Yangon (Rangoon)
Bangkok
Manila
Ho Chi Minh City (Saigon)
Jakarta
Bandung
Lagos
Abidjan
Addis Ababa
Kinshasa

30°N
EQUATOR
150°E
0°
TROPIC OF CAPRICORN
30°S
60°S
ANTARCTIC CIRCLE
0°
60°E
90°E

▲ **Urban areas** will be home to more than half the world's people early in the 21st century. As shown by the dots on the map, Asia will continue to have most of the largest cities.

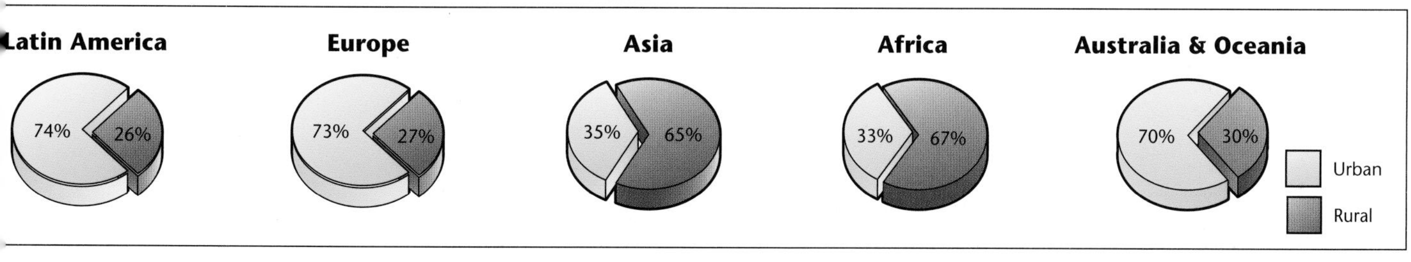

**Latin America**
74% 26%

**Europe**
73% 27%

**Asia**
35% 65%

**Africa**
33% 67%

**Australia & Oceania**
70% 30%

Urban
Rural

# WORLD CULTURES

Culture is all the shared things that define the way a people live—customs and symbols, food and clothing preferences, housing styles, systems of government, music and art forms, language and belief systems. Tracing the diffusion, or movement, of culture traits, or characteristics, is one way that geographers understand how places are connected.

For example, English originated in western Europe, but its widespread use today reflects the far-reaching effects of 19th-century colonial empires. About 6,000 languages are spoken in the world today, many of which will probably become extinct as global trade, communications, and travel blur distinctions among cultures.

Some religions also have spread far from their areas of origin—Islam and Christianity from southwestern Asia and Buddhism from southern Asia.

Web Link

**Major Language Families Today**

- Afro-Asiatic
- Altaic
- Austro-Asiatic
- Austronesian
- Dravidian
- Indo-European
- Japanese/Korean
- Kam-Tai
- Niger-Congo
- Nilo-Saharan
- Sino-Tibetan
- Uralic
- Other

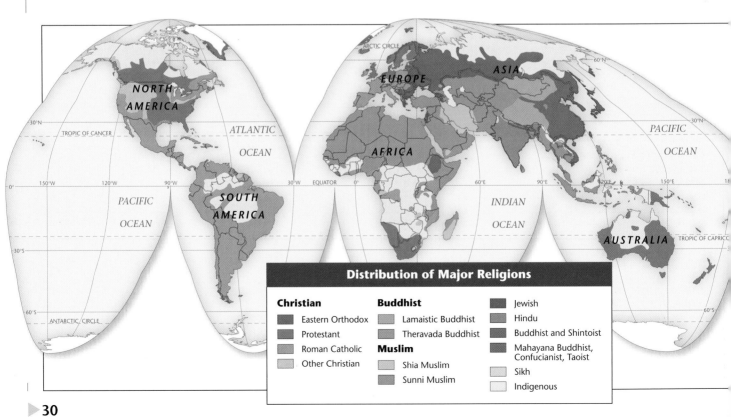

**Distribution of Major Religions**

**Christian**
- Eastern Orthodox
- Protestant
- Roman Catholic
- Other Christian

**Buddhist**
- Lamaistic Buddhist
- Theravada Buddhist

**Muslim**
- Shia Muslim
- Sunni Muslim

- Jewish
- Hindu
- Buddhist and Shintoist
- Mahayana Buddhist, Confucianist, Taoist
- Sikh
- Indigenous

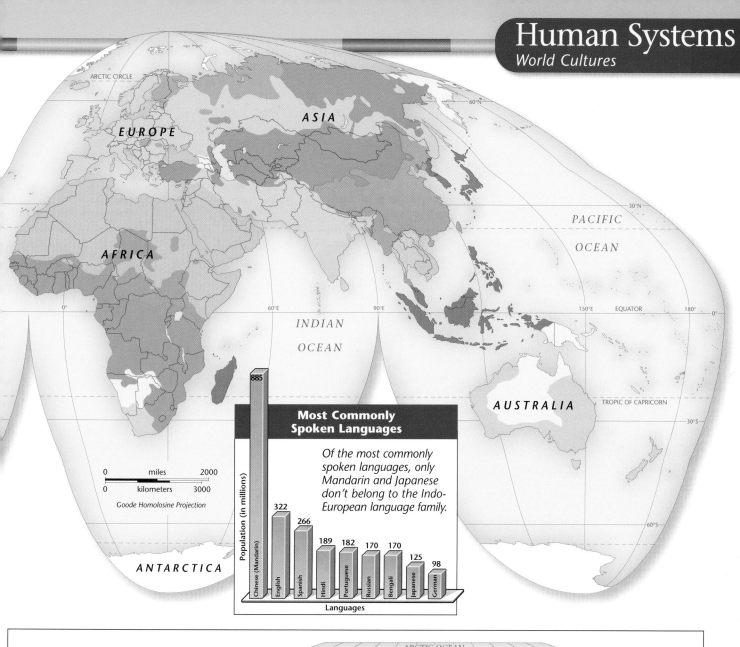

**Most Commonly Spoken Languages**

*Of the most commonly spoken languages, only Mandarin and Japanese don't belong to the Indo-European language family.*

Population (in millions)

| Language | Population |
|---|---|
| Chinese (Mandarin) | 885 |
| English | 322 |
| Spanish | 266 |
| Hindi | 189 |
| Portuguese | 182 |
| Russian | 170 |
| Bengali | 170 |
| Japanese | 125 |
| German | 98 |

Languages

0 — miles — 2000
0 — kilometers — 3000
Goode Homolosine Projection

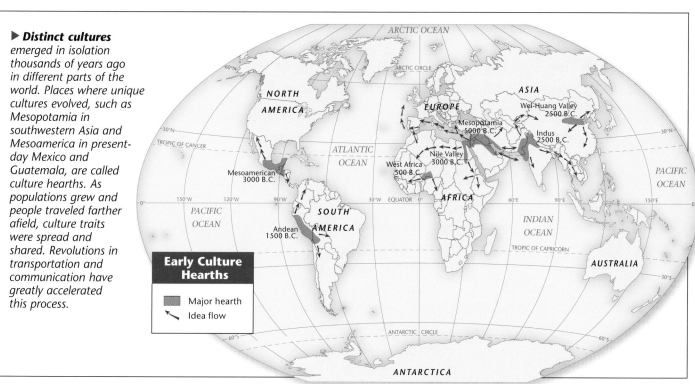

▶ **Distinct cultures** emerged in isolation thousands of years ago in different parts of the world. Places where unique cultures evolved, such as Mesopotamia in southwestern Asia and Mesoamerica in present-day Mexico and Guatemala, are called culture hearths. As populations grew and people traveled farther afield, culture traits were spread and shared. Revolutions in transportation and communication have greatly accelerated this process.

**Early Culture Hearths**

■ Major hearth
↙ Idea flow

Mesoamerican 3000 B.C.
Andean 1500 B.C.
West Africa 500 B.C.
Nile Valley 3000 B.C.
Mesopotamia 5000 B.C.
Indus 2500 B.C.
Wel-Huang Valley 2500 B.C.

# PREDOMINANT WORLD ECONOMIES

Economic activities are the many different ways that people create products and generate income to meet their needs and wants. Long ago most people lived by hunting and gathering. Today, most engage in a variety of other activities that are commonly grouped into the following categories. Primary activities: agriculture, fishing, forestry; secondary activities: manufacturing and processing industries; tertiary activities: services, such as finance, medicine, education; and quaternary activities: information exchange and e-commerce—buying and selling over the Internet. The more developed economies of the world have shifted from secondary activities toward tertiary and quaternary activities. Less developed economies continue to rely on primary activities. Web Link

**Predominant Economy**

- • Selected population center
- Agriculture
- Agriculture and forestry
- Fishing
- Forestry (lumber and pulpwood)
- Hunting, fishing and forestry
- Subsistence agriculture
- Little or no economic activity
- Manufacturing
- Nomadic herding
- Stock raising on ranges

▲ **Subsistence Agriculture.** *Many people in developing countries, such as these farmers in Peru, use traditional methods to grow crops for their daily food requirements rather than for commercial sale.*

◀ **Logging.** *Workers ready logs to float down the Columbia River in Washington State. Processing plants will turn the logs into paper products or cut them into lumber for the construction industry.*

▶ **Fishing.** *Tuna is one of the chief commercial fishes as well as a favorite among big game fishermen. Japan is the world's leading harvester of tuna. Albacore, shown here, is one of the top commercial varieties.*

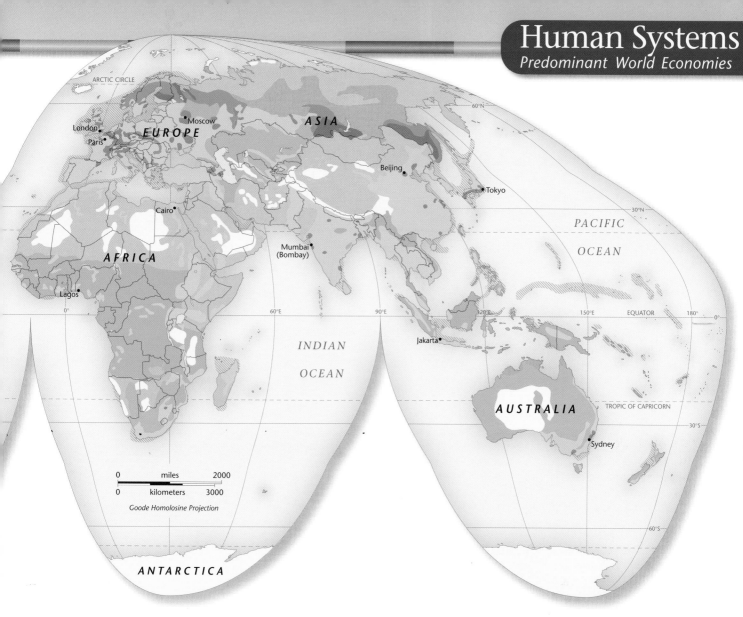

ARCTIC CIRCLE

EUROPE
London
Paris
Moscow

ASIA
Beijing
Tokyo

60°N

PACIFIC OCEAN

30°N

AFRICA
Cairo
Mumbai (Bombay)

Lagos

0°        60°E        90°E        120°E        150°E        EQUATOR        180°        0°

INDIAN OCEAN

Jakarta

AUSTRALIA
TROPIC OF CAPRICORN

30°S

Sydney

0        miles        2000
0        kilometers        3000
Goode Homolosine Projection

60°S

ANTARCTICA

▶ **Education and Communications.** *These services combine to allow students to interact with scientists working in the field. Here students explore the underwater ecology of California's Monterey Bay as part of renowned ocean explorer Robert Ballard's JASON Project.*

▲ **Manufacturing.** *This mill in Slovakia processes raw materials—coal and iron ore—to make steel, which in turn is used by other industries to produce cars, machinery, and other kinds of manufactured goods.*

▶ **The Internet.** *This has opened a whole new way of exchanging information. E-mail connects people in places near and far, while e-commerce allows them to buy and sell products without ever leaving home.*

# WORLD FOOD

**A**s the 20th century drew to a close, the world's population surpassed six billion—six billion hungry mouths to feed. Productive cropland, though, like other natural resources, is unevenly distributed. In addition, access to modern farming methods and technology varies from country to country. Some countries produce large surpluses; others struggle to feed their populations. Grains such as rice, corn, and wheat provide 80 percent of the world's food energy supply.

Web Link

NORTH AMERICA

30°N

TROPIC OF CANCER

ATLANTIC OCEAN

150°W        EQUATOR        120°W        90°W

0°

PACIFIC OCEAN

SOUTH AMERICA

30°S

**Major Types of Grain**

Corn
Wheat
Rice

60°S

ANTARCTIC CIR

▶ **Corn** originated in the Americas but was carried by Europeans to Europe, Asia, and Africa. Corn is an important food grain for both people and livestock.

▲ **Rice** is an important staple food crop, especially in eastern and southern Asia. Although China produces about one-third of the world's rice, it is also a major importer of rice to feed its population of more than a billion people.

◀ **Wheat** is the world's leading export grain. It is a main ingredient in bread and pasta and is grown on every inhabited continent. Each year trade in this grain exceeds 100 million tons.

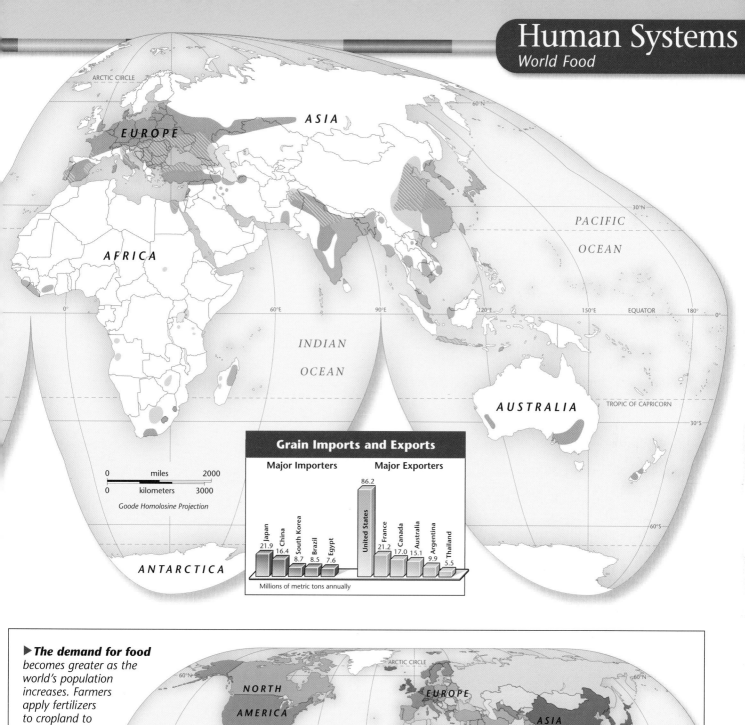

ARCTIC CIRCLE

EUROPE

ASIA

60°N

PACIFIC

OCEAN

30°N

AFRICA

60°E    90°E    EQUATOR    180°    0°

INDIAN

OCEAN

AUSTRALIA

TROPIC OF CAPRICORN

30°S

ANTARCTICA

60°S

miles    2000
0
0    kilometers    3000

Goode Homolosine Projection

### Grain Imports and Exports

**Major Importers**

| | |
|---|---|
| Japan | 21.9 |
| China | 16.4 |
| South Korea | 8.7 |
| Brazil | 8.5 |
| Egypt | 7.6 |

**Major Exporters**

| | |
|---|---|
| United States | 86.2 |
| France | 21.2 |
| Canada | 17.0 |
| Australia | 15.1 |
| Argentina | 9.9 |
| Thailand | 5.5 |

Millions of metric tons annually

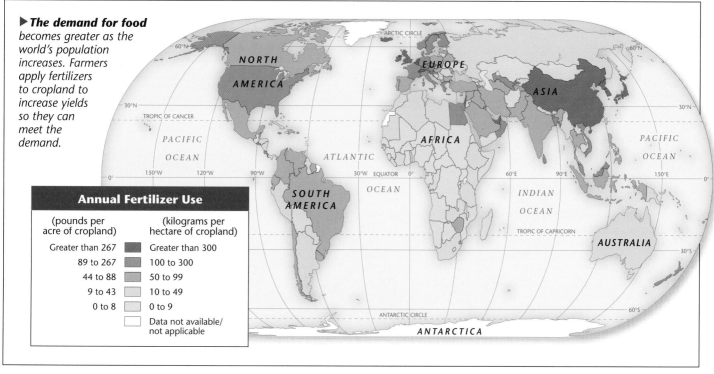

▶ **The demand for food** becomes greater as the world's population increases. Farmers apply fertilizers to cropland to increase yields so they can meet the demand.

ARCTIC CIRCLE

60°N    60°N

NORTH

AMERICA

EUROPE

ASIA

30°N    TROPIC OF CANCER    30°N

PACIFIC

OCEAN

AFRICA

PACIFIC

OCEAN

150°W    120°W    90°W    ATLANTIC    30°W    EQUATOR    0°    60°E    90°E    150°E    0°

SOUTH

AMERICA

OCEAN

INDIAN

OCEAN

TROPIC OF CAPRICORN

AUSTRALIA

30°S

### Annual Fertilizer Use

| (pounds per acre of cropland) | (kilograms per hectare of cropland) |
|---|---|
| Greater than 267 | Greater than 300 |
| 89 to 267 | 100 to 300 |
| 44 to 88 | 50 to 99 |
| 9 to 43 | 10 to 49 |
| 0 to 8 | 0 to 9 |
| | Data not available/ not applicable |

ANTARCTIC CIRCLE

60°S

ANTARCTICA

# WORLD WATER

Water is essential for life and is one of Earth's most valuable natural resources. It is even more important than food. More than 70 percent of Earth's surface is covered with water, but most of it—about 97 percent—is salty. Without treatment it is not usable for drinking or growing crops. The remaining 3 percent is fresh, but most of this is either trapped in glaciers or ice caps or lies too deep underground to be tapped economically.

Water is a renewable resource. We can use it over and over because the hydrologic, or water, cycle purifies water as it moves through the processes of evaporation, condensation, precipitation, runoff, and infiltration. But careless use can diminish the supply of usable fresh water. Water may become polluted as a result of runoff from industries, cultivated fields, and urban areas. In addition, water, like other natural resources, is unevenly distributed on Earth. Some countries have an abundance of water while others face serious water shortages, especially in parts of Asia and Africa. Web Link

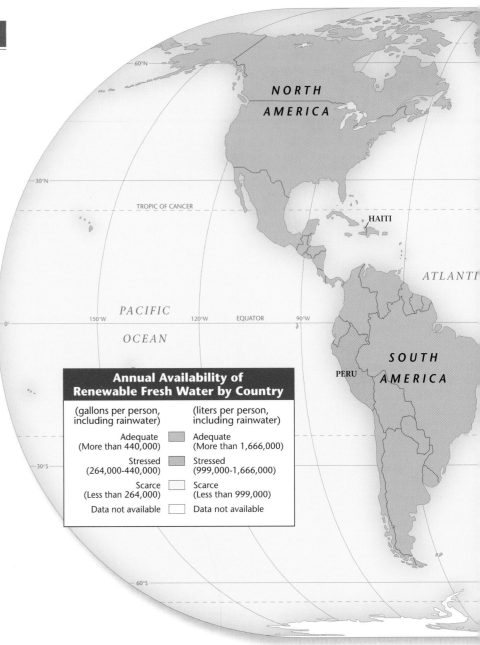

**Annual Availability of Renewable Fresh Water by Country**

| (gallons per person, including rainwater) | | (liters per person, including rainwater) | |
| --- | --- | --- | --- |
| Adequate (More than 440,000) | | Adequate (More than 1,666,000) | |
| Stressed (264,000-440,000) | | Stressed (999,000-1,666,000) | |
| Scarce (Less than 264,000) | | Scarce (Less than 999,000) | |
| Data not available | | Data not available | |

▲ *Domestic Water Use.* In much of the less developed world, people haul water daily for household use, as in this village in Central America.

▲ *Agricultural Water Use.* Irrigation has made agriculture possible in dry areas such as the San Pedro Valley in Arizona, shown here.

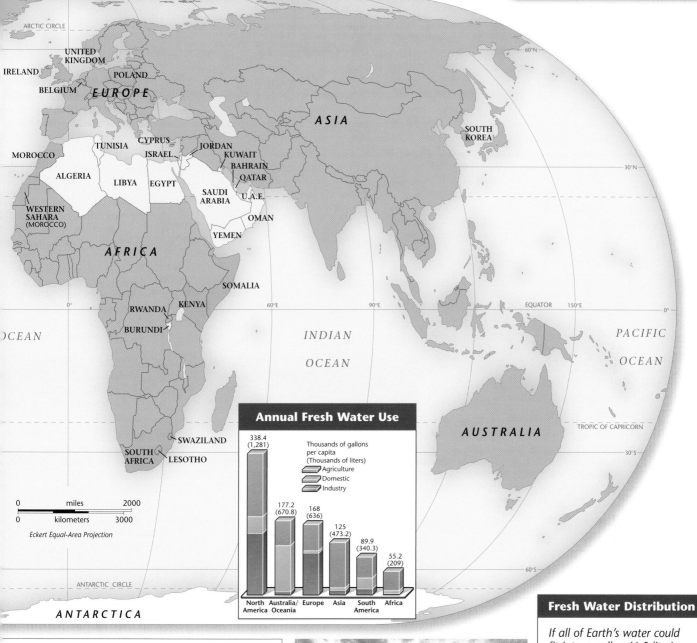

ARCTIC CIRCLE

IRELAND
UNITED KINGDOM
POLAND
BELGIUM
EUROPE
ASIA
SOUTH KOREA
60°N

MOROCCO
TUNISIA
CYPRUS
JORDAN
KUWAIT
ISRAEL
BAHRAIN
QATAR
30°N
ALGERIA
LIBYA
EGYPT
SAUDI ARABIA
U.A.E.
WESTERN SAHARA (MOROCCO)
OMAN
YEMEN

AFRICA
SOMALIA
0°
KENYA
60°E
90°E
EQUATOR
150°E
0°
RWANDA
BURUNDI
INDIAN OCEAN
PACIFIC OCEAN
OCEAN

SWAZILAND
AUSTRALIA
TROPIC OF CAPRICORN
SOUTH AFRICA
LESOTHO
30°S

| 0 | miles | 2000 |
| 0 | kilometers | 3000 |

*Eckert Equal-Area Projection*

60°S

ANTARCTIC CIRCLE

ANTARCTICA

### Annual Fresh Water Use

Thousands of gallons per capita
(Thousands of liters)
- Agriculture
- Domestic
- Industry

338.4 (1,281) North America
177.2 (670.8) Australia/ Oceania
168 (636) Europe
125 (473.2) Asia
89.9 (340.3) South America
55.2 (209) Africa

▲ **Industrial Water Use.** *Hydroelectric projects, such as South America's Itaipú Dam, harness running water to generate electricity that powers industry.*

▲ **Water Stress.** *By using groundwater faster than it is renewed, agriculture in dry areas puts stress on limited water supplies.*

### Fresh Water Distribution

*If all of Earth's water could fit into a gallon (4.5 liter) jug, only slightly more than a tablespoon of it would be available fresh water. This graph shows the sources of Earth's fresh water.*

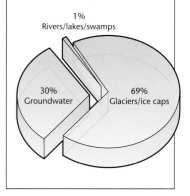

1% Rivers/lakes/swamps

30% Groundwater

69% Glaciers/ice caps

**37** ◄

# WORLD ENERGY & MINERAL RESOURCES

**B**eginning in the 19th century, as the Industrial Revolution spread across Europe and around the world, the demand for energy and mineral resources skyrocketed. Fossil fuels—first coal, then oil—provided the energy that kept the wheels of industry turning. Minerals such as iron ore, which is essential for the production of steel, and copper, which is used for electrical wiring, became increasingly important.

Energy and minerals, like all non-renewable resources, are in limited supply and are unevenly distributed. Countries with major deposits play an important role in the global economy. For example, the Organization of Petroleum Exporting Countries (OPEC) influences the world supply of oil and, therefore, fuel prices. Web Link

**Major fossil fuel deposits**

- Coal
- Natural gas
- Oil
- OPEC member

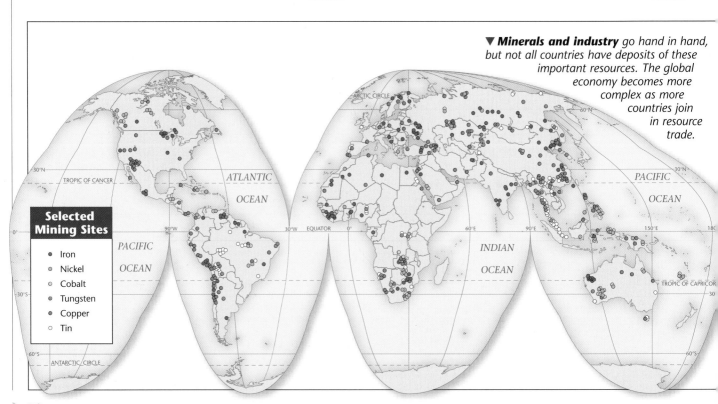

▼ **Minerals and industry** go hand in hand, but not all countries have deposits of these important resources. The global economy becomes more complex as more countries join in resource trade.

**Selected Mining Sites**

- Iron
- Nickel
- Cobalt
- Tungsten
- Copper
- Tin

38

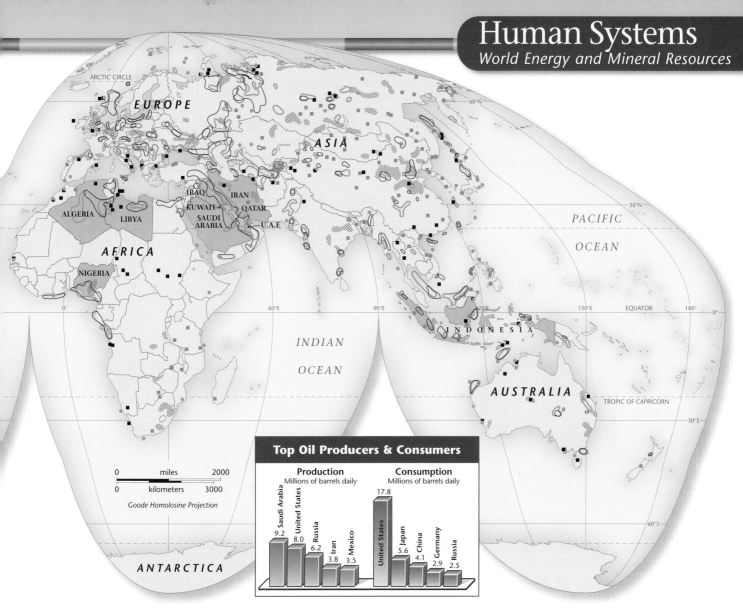

ARCTIC CIRCLE

EUROPE

ASIA

IRAQ
IRAN
ALGERIA    KUWAIT    QATAR
LIBYA    SAUDI
ARABIA    U.A.E

AFRICA

NIGERIA

PACIFIC
OCEAN

INDONESIA

INDIAN
OCEAN

AUSTRALIA

TROPIC OF CAPRICORN

ANTARCTICA

0    miles    2000
0    kilometers    3000
Goode Homolosine Projection

### Top Oil Producers & Consumers

| Production | Consumption |
| --- | --- |
| Millions of barrels daily | Millions of barrels daily |

Production:
- Saudi Arabia 9.2
- United States 8.0
- Russia 6.2
- Iran 3.8
- Mexico 3.5

Consumption:
- United States 17.8
- Japan 5.6
- China 4.1
- Germany 2.9
- Russia 2.5

▶ **Reactors** *near Sacramento, California, produce nuclear energy, and solar panels capture energy from the sun. These two sources of energy are important alternatives to nonrenewable fossil fuels.*

▲ **A wind energy farm** *near Tehachapi, California, uses windmills to capture the energy of winds blowing off the Pacific Ocean.*

◀ **A geothermal power plant,** *fueled by heat from deep within Earth, produces energy to heat homes in Iceland. Runoff creates a warm pool for bathers.*

▼ **Dependence on oil** *for motor vehicles, industries, and domestic power and heating makes the United States the world's leading consumer of this energy resource.*

# North America

**V**iewed from high above, North America stretches from the frozen expanses of the Arctic Ocean and Greenland to the lush green of Panama's tropical forests. Hudson Bay and the Great Lakes, fingerprints of long-departed glaciers, dominate the continent's east, while the brown landscapes of the west and southwest tell of dry lands where water is scarce.

## Facts & Figures

▶ **Land area:** 9,449,500 sq mi (24,474,000 sq km)

▶ **Population:** 479,326,000

▶ **Highest point:** Mount McKinley (Denali), Alaska: 20,320 ft (6,194 m)

▶ **Lowest point:** Death Valley, California: 282 ft (86 m) below sea level

▶ **Longest river:** Mississippi-Missouri, United States: 3,710 mi (5,971 km)

▶ **Largest lake:** Lake Superior, U.S.-Canada: 31,701 sq mi (82,100 sq km)

▶ **Number of Independent countries:** 23

▶ **Largest country:** Canada: 3,849,670 sq mi (9,970,610 sq km)

▶ **Smallest country:** St. Kitts and Nevis: 101 sq mi (261 sq km)

▶ **Most populous country:** United States: Pop. 275,600,000

▶ **Least populous country:** St. Kitts and Nevis: Pop. 43,000

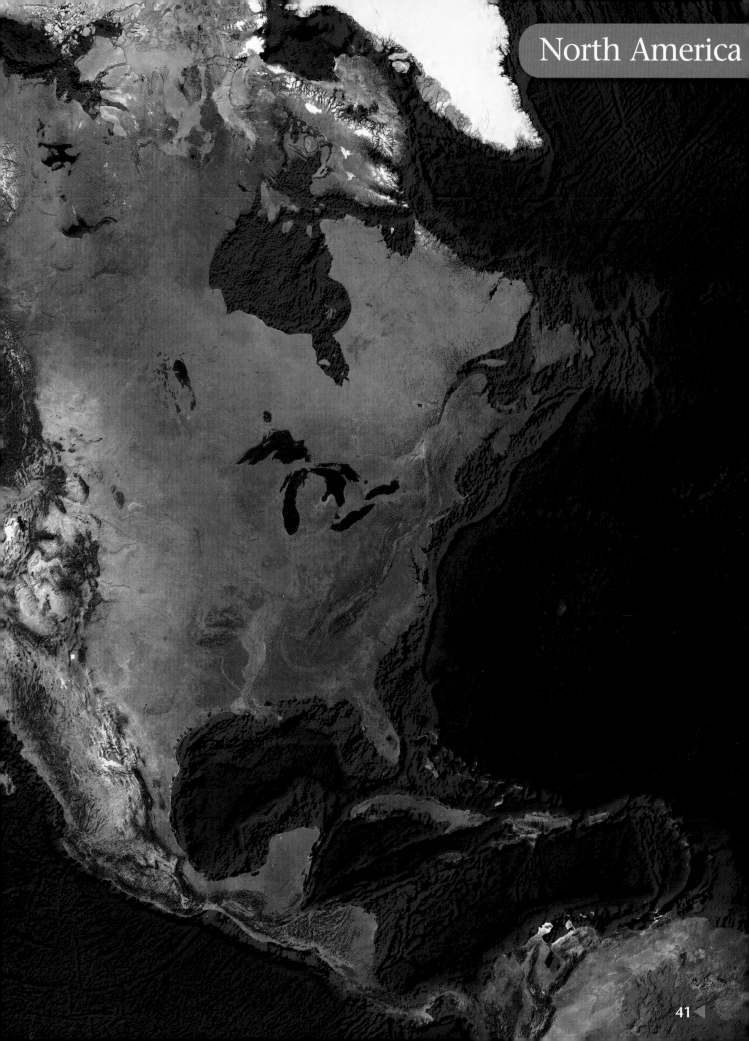

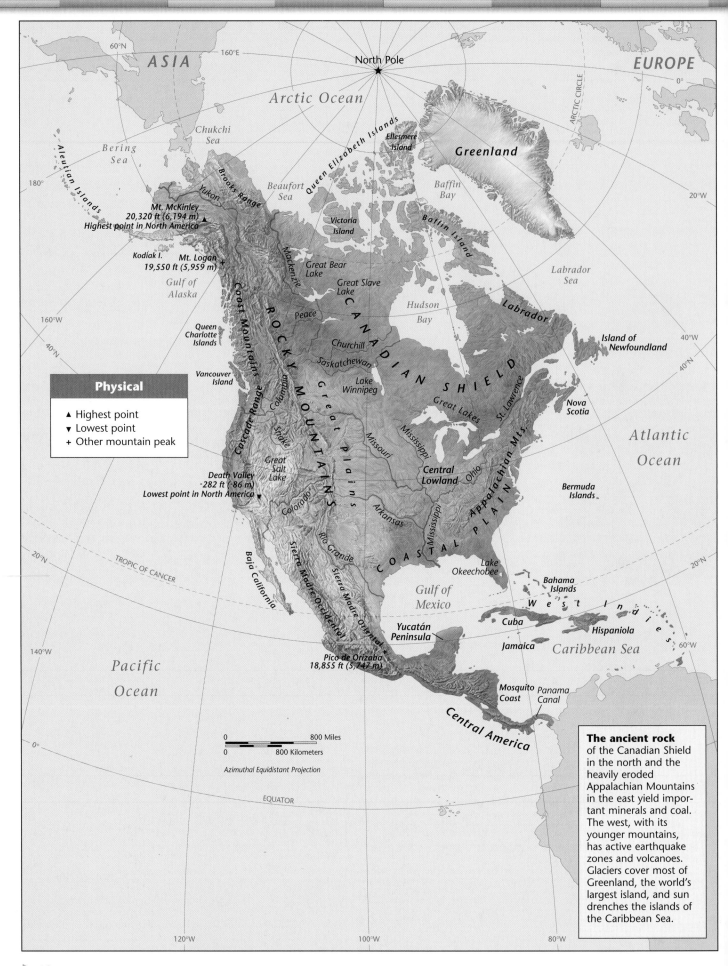

ASIA

EUROPE

60°N    160°E

North Pole

*Arctic Ocean*

160°E

*Chukchi Sea*

*Bering Sea*

180°

*Aleutian Islands*

*Brooks Range*

*Yukon*

Queen Elizabeth Islands

Ellesmere Island

**Greenland**

ARCTIC CIRCLE

0°

20°W

*Beaufort Sea*

*Baffin Bay*

**Mt. McKinley
20,320 ft (6,194 m)
Highest point in North America** ▲

*Mackenzie*

*Victoria Island*

*Baffin Island*

40°N

180°

Kodiak I.

**Mt. Logan
19,550 ft (5,959 m)** +

*Gulf of Alaska*

*Great Bear Lake*

*Great Slave Lake*

*Hudson Bay*

*Labrador Sea*

*Labrador*

Island of
Newfoundland

40°W

160°W

*Peace*

C A N A D I A N

40°N

40°N

Queen Charlotte Islands

*Churchill*

*Saskatchewan*

S H I E L D

St. Lawrence

Nova Scotia

Vancouver Island

*Lake Winnipeg*

*Great Lakes*

*Columbia*

*Snake*

*Missouri*

*Mississippi*

**Central
Lowland**

*Ohio*

*Appalachian Mts.*

*Atlantic
Ocean*

**Death Valley
-282 ft (-86 m)
Lowest point in North America** ▼

*Great Salt Lake*

*Colorado*

*Arkansas*

*Mississippi*

C
O
A
S
T
A
L

*Bermuda Islands*

*Rio Grande*

*Sierra Madre Occidental*

*Sierra Madre Oriental*

P
L
A
I
N

*Lake Okeechobee*

*Bahama Islands*

W e s t    I n d i e s

20°N

20°N

TROPIC OF CANCER

*Baja California*

**Yucatán Peninsula**

*Gulf of
Mexico*

Cuba

Hispaniola

60°W

140°W

Jamaica

*Caribbean Sea*

**Pico de Orizaba
18,855 ft (5,747 m)** +

*Pacific
Ocean*

**Mosquito
Coast**

Panama
Canal

0°

*Central America*

0      800 Miles

0      800 Kilometers

*Azimuthal Equidistant Projection*

EQUATOR

120°W          100°W          80°W

# North America

**Political**

⊛ National capital
• Other city

EUROPE

ASIA

Arctic Ocean

North Pole

Greenland
(Denmark)

Alaska
(U.S.)

•Anchorage

ARCTIC CIRCLE

C A N A D A

•Edmonton
•Calgary
Vancouver•
Victoria•     Winnipeg• •Thunder
•Seattle              Bay
•Portland                      Montréal
                                Ottawa⊛
                    Minneapolis• •St. Paul  Toronto•  •Boston
San Francisco•              Detroit•          •New York
  •San Jose    Omaha• Chicago• •Cleveland  •Philadelphia
•Sacramento            •St. Louis •Indianapolis •Washington, D.C.
Fresno•     Denver•                    Nashville
       U N I T E D   S T A T E S •Nashville
Los Angeles•  Las Vegas•  Oklahoma• •Tulsa •Memphis  •Charlotte
San Diego•  •Phoenix   City   •Birmingham •Atlanta
Tijuana•          El Paso• Fort •Dallas  •Jacksonville
       Ciudad         Worth •Austin  New
       Juárez  •San Antonio  Orleans•   Tampa•
Chihuahua•         •Houston        Miami•  BAHAMAS
       Monterrey•    Gulf of     Havana•  •Nassau
M E X I C O         Mexico             ⊛CUBA  W e s t   I n d i e s
       •San Luis Potosí
Guadalajara•                          Caribbean Sea
  México⊛ •Veracruz   BELIZE
Acapulco•  Guatemala  Belmopan⊛   HONDURAS
       GUATEMALA⊛    •Tegucigalpa  NICARAGUA
       San Salvador⊛       ⊛Managua
       EL SALVADOR
                       San José⊛  •Panamá
                       COSTA RICA  PANAMA
Central America                    SOUTH AMERICA

Pacific
Ocean

Atlantic
Ocean

Gulf of
Mexico

TROPIC OF CANCER

AREA ENLARGED

0        800 Miles
0        800 Kilometers
Azimuthal Equidistant Projection

### Inset map

80°W
20°N    CUBA
Cayman    HAITI  DOMINICAN
Islands      REPUBLIC   Virgin Islands
(U.K.)            (U.S.)  (U.K.)
       Port-au- ⊛Santo  San Juan  ST. KITTS
JAMAICA  Prince  Domingo       & NEVIS
  ⊛Kingston   Puerto Rico   St. John's
              (U.S.)  Basseterre⊛ ⊛
       Caribbean Sea   ANTIGUA & BARBUDA
                DOMINICA ⊛Roseau
15°N                    •Castries
              ST. LUCIA⊛
                Kingstown  BARBADOS
0      400 Miles   Aruba  Curaçao   ⊛Bridgetown
0      400 Kilometers (Neth.)  (Neth.)  ST. VINCENT &
Azimuthal Equidistant Projection  THE GRENADINES
              Bonaire  GRENADA ⊛St. George's
              (Neth.)  TRINIDAD & TOBAGO
10°N                       ⊛Port-of-
                             Spain

**Two countries—**
Canada and the United
States—dominate the
political map of North
America. But more
than two dozen other
countries and territories
make up that part of
North America referred
to as Middle America,
which includes Mexico,
Central America, and
the many islands of
the West Indies.

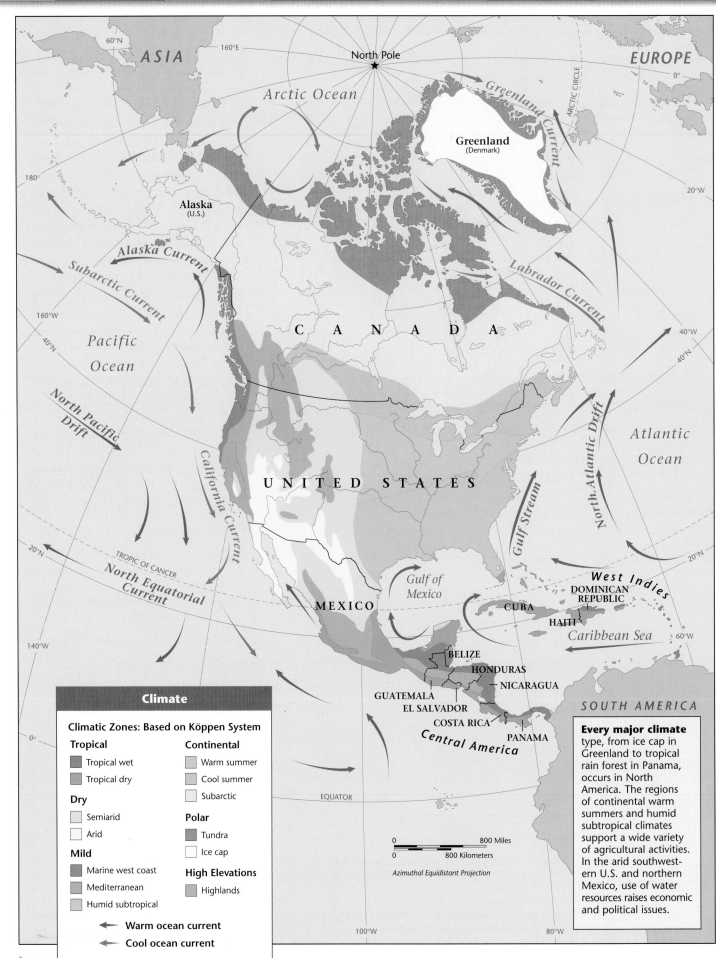

ASIA

EUROPE

*Arctic Ocean*

North Pole

*Greenland Current*

ARCTIC CIRCLE

Greenland
(Denmark)

20°W

Alaska
(U.S.)

160°E

180°

*Alaska Current*

*Subarctic Current*

*Labrador Current*

*Pacific Ocean*

C A N A D A

40°W

160°W

40°N

40°N

*North Pacific Drift*

U N I T E D   S T A T E S

*North Atlantic Drift*

*Gulf Stream*

*Atlantic Ocean*

*California Current*

20°N

TROPIC OF CANCER

*North Equatorial Current*

*Gulf of Mexico*

*West Indies*

DOMINICAN
REPUBLIC

20°N

140°W

M E X I C O

CUBA

HAITI

*Caribbean Sea*

60°W

BELIZE

HONDURAS

NICARAGUA

GUATEMALA

EL SALVADOR

COSTA RICA

PANAMA

*Central America*

SOUTH AMERICA

EQUATOR

0°

## Climate

### Climatic Zones: Based on Köppen System

**Tropical**
- Tropical wet
- Tropical dry

**Dry**
- Semiarid
- Arid

**Mild**
- Marine west coast
- Mediterranean
- Humid subtropical

**Continental**
- Warm summer
- Cool summer
- Subarctic

**Polar**
- Tundra
- Ice cap

**High Elevations**
- Highlands

← Warm ocean current

← Cool ocean current

0        800 Miles

0        800 Kilometers

*Azimuthal Equidistant Projection*

100°W

80°W

**Every major climate** type, from ice cap in Greenland to tropical rain forest in Panama, occurs in North America. The regions of continental warm summers and humid subtropical climates support a wide variety of agricultural activities. In the arid southwestern U.S. and northern Mexico, use of water resources raises economic and political issues.

# North America

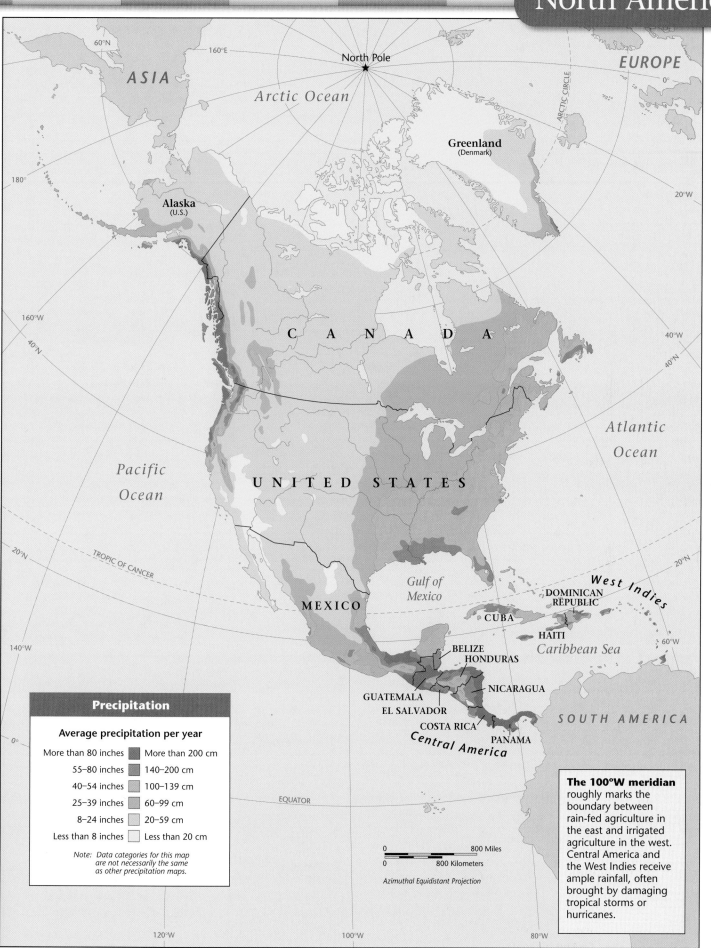

**ASIA**

60°N
160°E

North Pole

*Arctic Ocean*

ARCTIC CIRCLE

**EUROPE**

0°

Greenland
(Denmark)

20°W

180°

Alaska
(U.S.)

40°N

160°W

C A N A D A

40°W

40°N

*Pacific
Ocean*

U N I T E D   S T A T E S

*Atlantic
Ocean*

20°N

TROPIC OF CANCER

*Gulf of
Mexico*

*West Indies*

DOMINICAN
REPUBLIC

140°W

**MEXICO**

CUBA

HAITI

*Caribbean Sea*

60°W

BELIZE
HONDURAS

NICARAGUA

GUATEMALA
EL SALVADOR

**SOUTH AMERICA**

COSTA RICA

PANAMA

*Central America*

0°

EQUATOR

## Precipitation

**Average precipitation per year**

| | |
|---|---|
| More than 80 inches | More than 200 cm |
| 55–80 inches | 140–200 cm |
| 40–54 inches | 100–139 cm |
| 25–39 inches | 60–99 cm |
| 8–24 inches | 20–59 cm |
| Less than 8 inches | Less than 20 cm |

*Note: Data categories for this map
are not necessarily the same
as other precipitation maps.*

0        800 Miles

0        800 Kilometers

*Azimuthal Equidistant Projection*

**The 100°W meridian**
roughly marks the
boundary between
rain-fed agriculture in
the east and irrigated
agriculture in the west.
Central America and
the West Indies receive
ample rainfall, often
brought by damaging
tropical storms or
hurricanes.

120°W        100°W        80°W

**45**

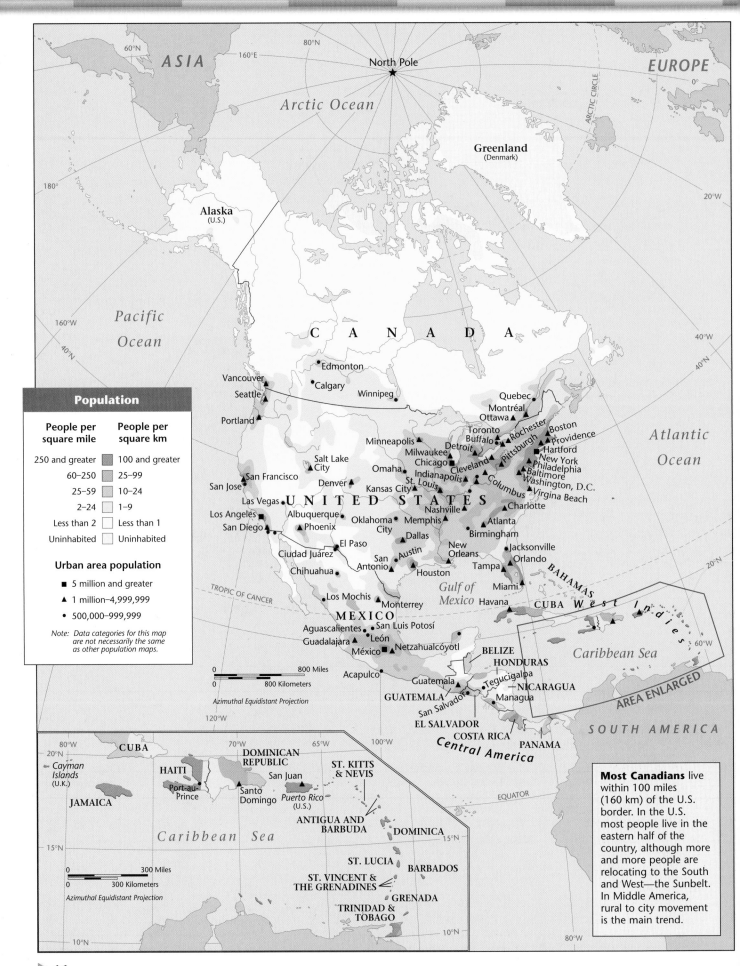

**Population**

| People per square mile | People per square km |
|---|---|
| 250 and greater | 100 and greater |
| 60–250 | 25–99 |
| 25–59 | 10–24 |
| 2–24 | 1–9 |
| Less than 2 | Less than 1 |
| Uninhabited | Uninhabited |

**Urban area population**

- ■ 5 million and greater
- ▲ 1 million–4,999,999
- • 500,000–999,999

*Note: Data categories for this map are not necessarily the same as other population maps.*

0    800 Miles
0    800 Kilometers
*Azimuthal Equidistant Projection*

0    300 Miles
0    300 Kilometers
*Azimuthal Equidistant Projection*

**Most Canadians** live within 100 miles (160 km) of the U.S. border. In the U.S. most people live in the eastern half of the country, although more and more people are relocating to the South and West—the Sunbelt. In Middle America, rural to city movement is the main trend.

# North America

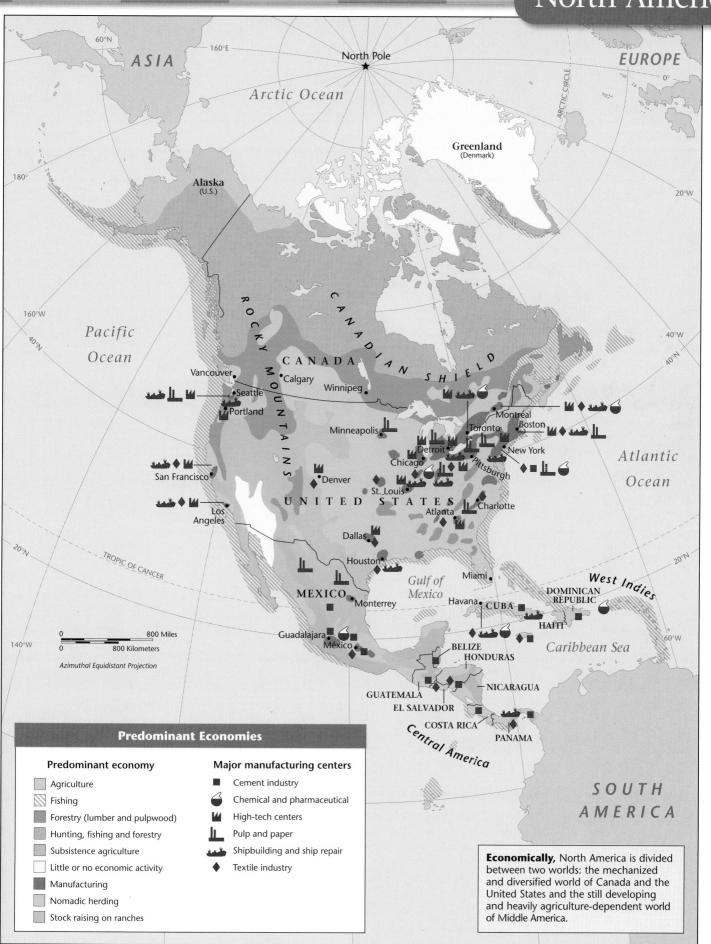

ASIA

EUROPE

Arctic Ocean

North Pole

Greenland
(Denmark)

Alaska
(U.S.)

Pacific
Ocean

CANADA

CANADIAN SHIELD

ROCKY MOUNTAINS

Vancouver
Calgary
Winnipeg
Seattle
Portland

Minneapolis

Montréal
Toronto
Boston

Detroit
Chicago
New York
Pittsburgh

San Francisco

Denver

St. Louis
UNITED STATES

Atlantic
Ocean

Los
Angeles

Atlanta
Charlotte

Dallas

Houston

MEXICO
Monterrey

Gulf of
Mexico

Miami

West Indies

Guadalajara
México

DOMINICAN
REPUBLIC

Havana
CUBA
HAITI

Caribbean Sea

BELIZE
HONDURAS

GUATEMALA
EL SALVADOR

NICARAGUA

COSTA RICA

PANAMA

Central America

SOUTH
AMERICA

800 Miles
800 Kilometers
*Azimuthal Equidistant Projection*

TROPIC OF CANCER

## Predominant Economies

### Predominant economy

- Agriculture
- Fishing
- Forestry (lumber and pulpwood)
- Hunting, fishing and forestry
- Subsistence agriculture
- Little or no economic activity
- Manufacturing
- Nomadic herding
- Stock raising on ranches

### Major manufacturing centers

- Cement industry
- Chemical and pharmaceutical
- High-tech centers
- Pulp and paper
- Shipbuilding and ship repair
- Textile industry

**Economically,** North America is divided between two worlds: the mechanized and diversified world of Canada and the United States and the still developing and heavily agriculture-dependent world of Middle America.

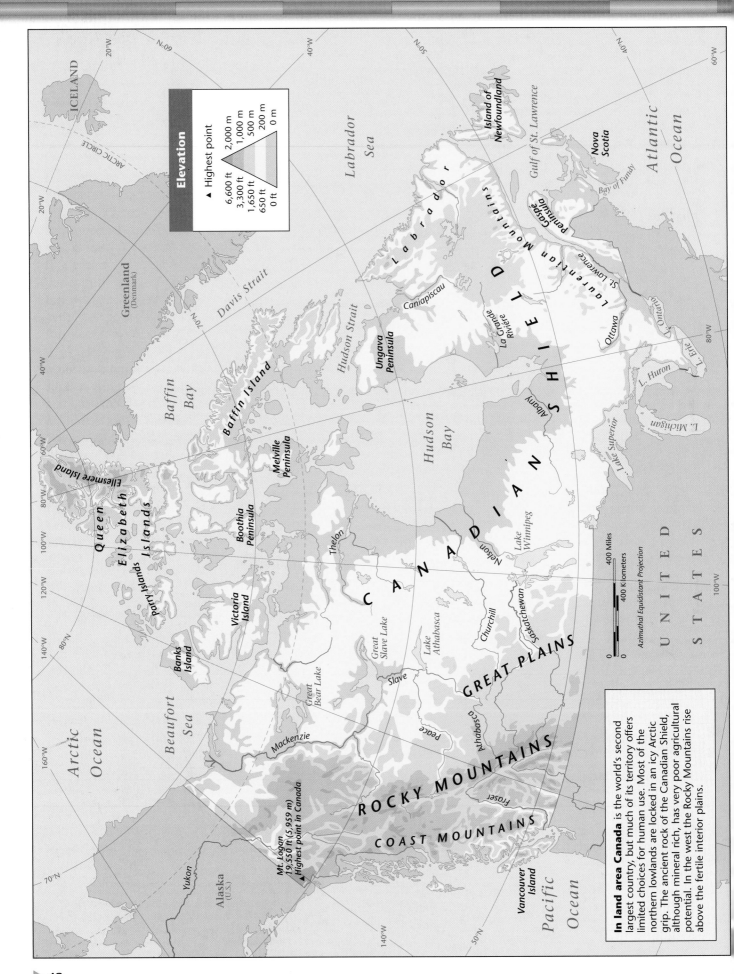

Elevation

▲ Highest point

2,000 m
1,000 m
500 m
200 m
0 m

6,600 ft
3,300 ft
1,650 ft
650 ft
0 ft

ICELAND

ARCTIC CIRCLE

Greenland
(Denmark)

Davis Strait

Labrador
Sea

Baffin
Bay

Island of
Newfoundland

Gulf of St. Lawrence

Nova
Scotia

Atlantic
Ocean

Bay of Fundy

Gaspé
Peninsula

St. Lawrence

Laurentian Mountains

Ottawa

L. Ontario

L. Erie

Caniapiscau

La Grande
Rivière

L. Huron

Baffin Island

Hudson Strait

Ungava
Peninsula

C A N A D I A N   S H I E L D

Albany

Lake Superior

L. Michigan

Hudson
Bay

Ellesmere Island

Melville
Peninsula

Queen
Elizabeth
Islands

Parry Islands

Boothia
Peninsula

Thelon

Nelson

Lake
Winnipeg

Churchill

Saskatchewan

GREAT PLAINS

Victoria
Island

Banks
Island

Great
Slave Lake

Lake
Athabasca

Great
Bear Lake

Slave

Athabasca

Peace

Beaufort
Sea

Mackenzie

ROCKY MOUNTAINS

Fraser

COAST MOUNTAINS

Vancouver
Island

Pacific
Ocean

Arctic
Ocean

Yukon

Alaska
(U.S.)

Mt. Logan
19,550 ft (5,959 m)
▲ Highest point in Canada

UNITED  STATES

0        400 Miles
0        400 Kilometers
Azimuthal Equidistant Projection

**In land area Canada** is the world's second largest country, but much of its territory offers limited choices for human use. Most of the northern lowlands are locked in an icy Arctic grip. The ancient rock of the Canadian Shield, although mineral rich, has very poor agricultural potential. In the west the Rocky Mountains rise above the fertile interior plains.

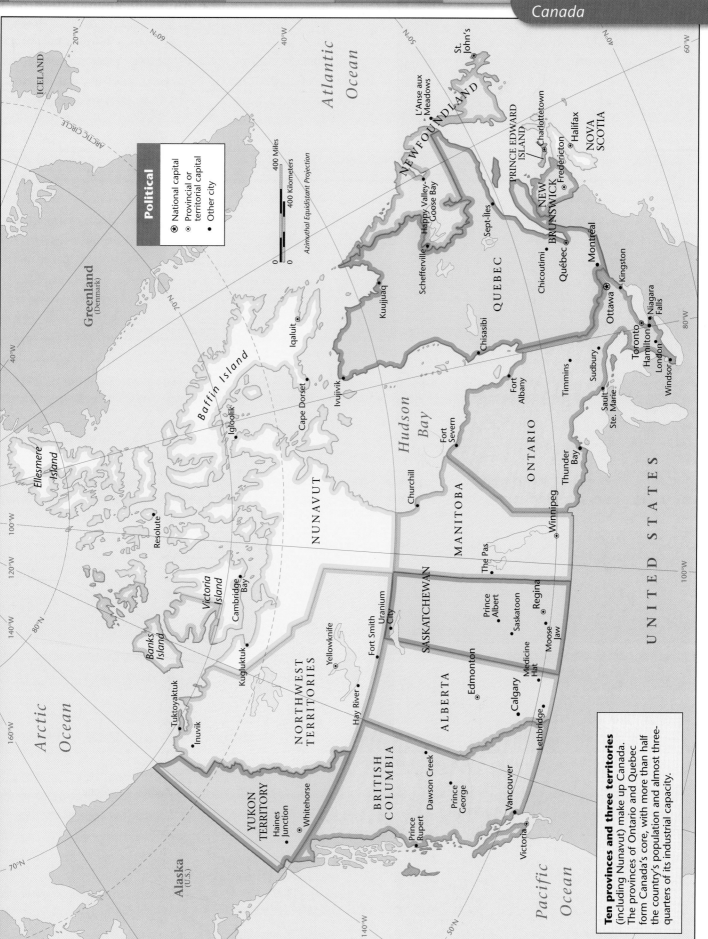

**Political**
⊕ National capital
⊙ Provincial or
territorial capital
• Other city

400 Miles
400 Kilometers
0
0
*Azimuthal Equidistant Projection*

ICELAND

ARCTIC CIRCLE

Greenland
(Denmark)

Ellesmere
Island

Baffin Island

Banks
Island

Victoria
Island

Arctic
Ocean

Atlantic
Ocean

Hudson
Bay

NEWFOUNDLAND

St.
John's

L'Anse aux
Meadows

Happy Valley-
Goose Bay

Schefferville

Sept-Îles

PRINCE EDWARD
ISLAND

Charlottetown

NEW
BRUNSWICK

Fredericton

Halifax

NOVA
SCOTIA

QUEBEC

Chicoutimi

Québec

Montréal

Kingston

Ottawa

Niagara
Falls

Toronto

Hamilton

London

Windsor

Sudbury

Sault
Ste. Marie

Timmins

Thunder
Bay

ONTARIO

Fort
Albany

Fort
Severn

Churchill

MANITOBA

Winnipeg

The Pas

Chisasibi

Kuujjuaq

Iqaluit

Cape Dorset

Ivujivik

Igloolik

Resolute

Cambridge
Bay

Kugluktuk

NUNAVUT

NORTHWEST
TERRITORIES

Yellowknife

Fort Smith

Uranium
City

SASKATCHEWAN

Prince
Albert

Saskatoon

Regina

Moose
Jaw

Medicine
Hat

ALBERTA

Edmonton

Calgary

Lethbridge

Hay River

Tuktoyaktuk

Inuvik

BRITISH
COLUMBIA

Dawson Creek

Prince
George

Prince
Rupert

Vancouver

Victoria

YUKON
TERRITORY

Haines
Junction

Whitehorse

Alaska
(U.S.)

Pacific
Ocean

UNITED STATES

**Ten provinces and three territories**
(including Nunavut) make up Canada.
The provinces of Ontario and Quebec
form Canada's core, with more than half
the country's population and almost three-
quarters of its industrial capacity.

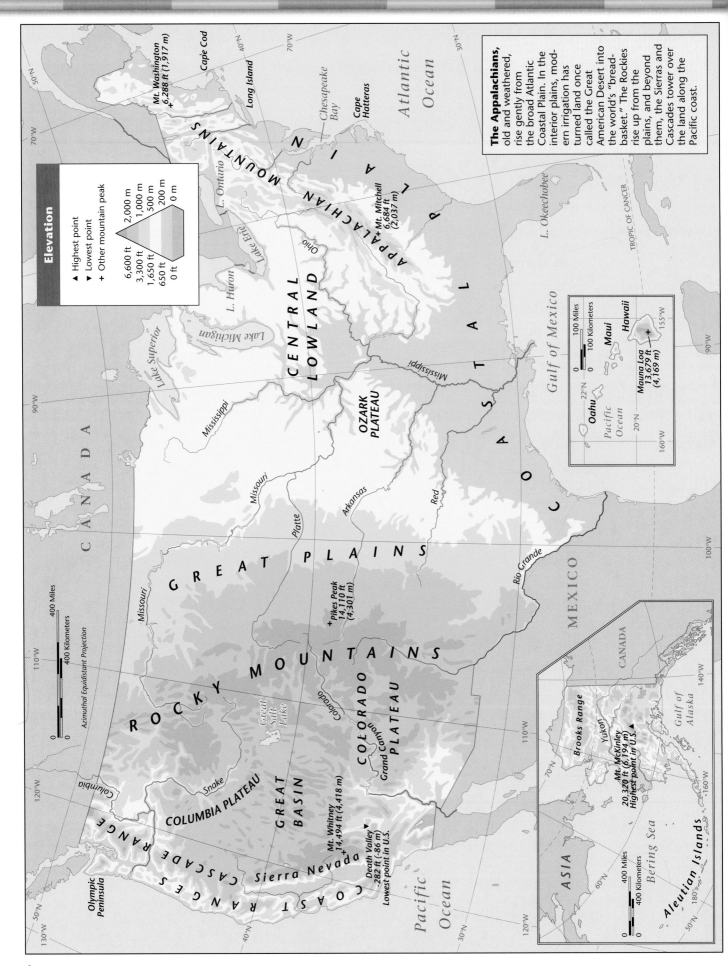

The **Appalachians,** old and weathered, rise gently from the broad Atlantic Coastal Plain. In the interior plains, modern irrigation has turned land once called the Great American Desert into the world's "bread-basket." The Rockies rise up from the plains, and beyond them, the Sierras and Cascades tower over the land along the Pacific coast.

**Elevation**

▲ Highest point
▼ Lowest point
+ Other mountain peak

6,600 ft — 2,000 m
3,300 ft — 1,000 m
1,650 ft — 500 m
650 ft — 200 m
0 ft — 0 m

Mt. Washington
6,288 ft (1,917 m)

Cape Cod

Long Island

Chesapeake Bay

Cape Hatteras

Atlantic Ocean

APPALACHIAN MOUNTAINS

Mt. Mitchell
6,684 ft
(2,037 m)

L. Ontario

Lake Erie

Ohio

C E N T R A L   L O W L A N D

Lake Superior

Lake Michigan

L. Huron

Mississippi

OZARK PLATEAU

Mississippi

Gulf of Mexico

L. Okeechobee

TROPIC OF CANCER

CANADA

Mississippi

Missouri

Platte

Arkansas

Red

Rio Grande

G R E A T   P L A I N S

+ Pikes Peak
14,110 ft
(4,301 m)

R O C K Y   M O U N T A I N S

Great Salt Lake

Colorado

COLORADO PLATEAU

Grand Canyon

GREAT BASIN

COLUMBIA PLATEAU

Snake

Columbia

Mt. Whitney
14,494 ft (4,418 m) ▼

Death Valley
-282 ft (-86 m)
Lowest point in U.S.

Sierra Nevada

COAST RANGES

CASCADE RANGE

Olympic Peninsula

Pacific Ocean

MEXICO

400 Miles
400 Kilometers
Azimuthal Equidistant Projection

**Hawaii**

Oahu

Maui

Mauna Loa
13,679 ft
(4,169 m) +

Pacific Ocean

100 Miles
100 Kilometers

22°N

20°N

160°W

155°W

90°W

Brooks Range

Yukon

Mt. McKinley
20,320 ft (6,194 m) ▲
Highest point in U.S.

Gulf of Alaska

CANADA

ASIA

Bering Sea

Aleutian Islands

400 Miles
400 Kilometers

# North America
## United States

**Fifty states,** ranging from tiny Rhode Island to giant Alaska; two Caribbean territories (Puerto Rico and the U.S. Virgin Islands); and 11 possessions in the Pacific, including Guam, American Samoa, and the Northern Mariana Islands, make up the political patchwork quilt of the United States.

**Political**
- ⊛ National capital
- ◉ State capital
- • Other city

*Atlantic Ocean*

MAINE
Augusta
NEW HAMPSHIRE
VERMONT
Montpelier
Concord
MASSACHUSETTS
Boston
Providence
RHODE ISLAND
CONNECTICUT
NEW JERSEY
Hartford
Albany
NEW YORK
Trenton
Philadelphia
DELAWARE
Dover
MARYLAND
Annapolis
Washington, D.C.
Newark
New York
Baltimore
Virginia Beach
Norfolk
PENNSYLVANIA
Harrisburg
Pittsburgh
Buffalo
Rochester
Lake Ontario
L. Erie
Cleveland
Columbus
OHIO
WEST VIRGINIA
Charleston
Richmond
VIRGINIA
Raleigh
NORTH CAROLINA
Greensboro
Charlotte
Columbia
SOUTH CAROLINA
Savannah
Jacksonville
Lansing
Detroit
Toledo
MICHIGAN
Lake Huron
Lake Superior
Lake Michigan
INDIANA
Indianapolis
Cincinnati
Louisville
Frankfort
KENTUCKY
Nashville
TENNESSEE
Memphis
Atlanta
GEORGIA
ALABAMA
Montgomery
Birmingham
Tallahassee
FLORIDA
Orlando
Tampa
St. Petersburg
Miami
TROPIC OF CANCER
Gulf of Mexico
WISCONSIN
Milwaukee
Madison
Chicago
ILLINOIS
Springfield
St. Louis
MISSOURI
Jefferson City
Kansas City
St. Paul
Minneapolis
MINNESOTA
IOWA
Des Moines
ARKANSAS
Little Rock
LOUISIANA
Jackson
MISSISSIPPI
Baton Rouge
New Orleans
Houston
CANADA
NORTH DAKOTA
Bismarck
SOUTH DAKOTA
Pierre
NEBRASKA
Omaha
Lincoln
KANSAS
Topeka
Wichita
Tulsa
Oklahoma City
OKLAHOMA
Dallas
Fort Worth
Austin
San Antonio
TEXAS
El Paso
MEXICO
MONTANA
Helena
WYOMING
Cheyenne
Denver
COLORADO
Santa Fe
Albuquerque
NEW MEXICO
IDAHO
Boise
UTAH
Salt Lake City
ARIZONA
Phoenix
Tucson
NEVADA
Carson City
Las Vegas
WASHINGTON
Seattle
Olympia
Portland
Salem
OREGON
Sacramento
San Francisco
San Jose
Fresno
Bakersfield
CALIFORNIA
Los Angeles
San Bernardino
Long Beach
San Diego
*Pacific Ocean*

400 Miles
400 Kilometers
Azimuthal Equidistant Projection

HAWAII
Honolulu
Hilo
Pacific Ocean
100 Miles
100 Kilometers

ALASKA
Barrow
Fairbanks
Nome
Anchorage
Juneau
Gulf of Alaska
CANADA
ASIA
Bering Sea
400 Miles
400 Kilometers

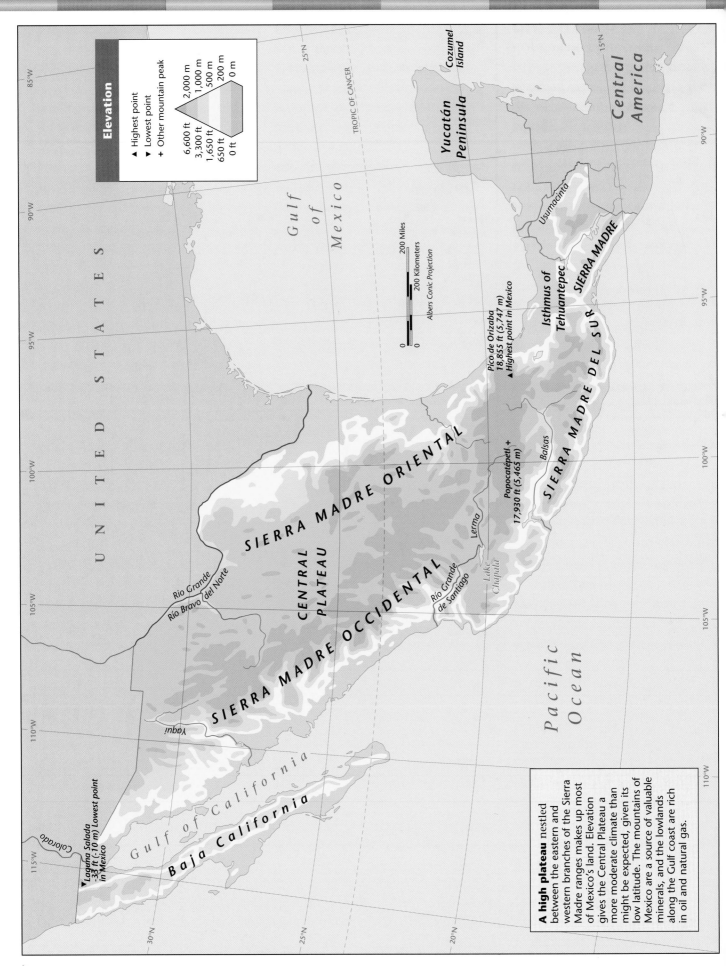

**Elevation**

▲ Highest point
▼ Lowest point
+ Other mountain peak

| | |
|---|---|
| 6,600 ft | 2,000 m |
| 3,300 ft | 1,000 m |
| 1,650 ft | 500 m |
| 650 ft | 200 m |
| 0 ft | 0 m |

UNITED STATES

Gulf *of* Mexico

TROPIC OF CANCER

Cozumel Island

Yucatán Peninsula

Central America

Usumacinta

SIERRA MADRE ORIENTAL

CENTRAL PLATEAU

SIERRA MADRE OCCIDENTAL

Rio Grande
Río Bravo del Norte

Río Grande de Santiago

Lerma

Lake Chapala

Yaqui

Balsas

Popocatépetl +
17,930 ft (5,465 m)

Pico de Orizaba
18,855 ft (5,747 m)
▲Highest point in Mexico

Isthmus of Tehuantepec

SIERRA MADRE

SIERRA MADRE DEL SUR

200 Miles
200 Kilometers
Albers Conic Projection
0
0

Pacific Ocean

Gulf of California

Baja California

Colorado

▲Laguna Salada
-33 ft (-10 m) Lowest point
in Mexico

**A high plateau** nestled between the eastern and western branches of the Sierra Madre ranges makes up most of Mexico's land. Elevation gives the Central Plateau a more moderate climate than might be expected, given its low latitude. The mountains of Mexico are a source of valuable minerals, and the lowlands along the Gulf coast are rich in oil and natural gas.

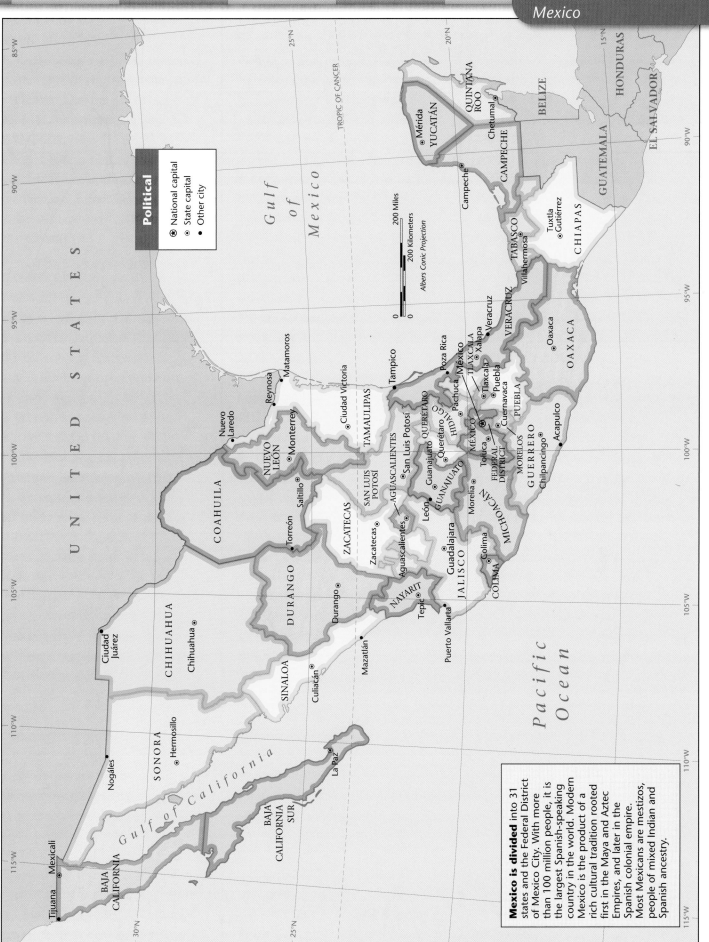

**Political**
⊛ National capital
⊙ State capital
• Other city

*Gulf of Mexico*

200 Miles
200 Kilometers
200
0
0
*Albers Conic Projection*

UNITED STATES

*Pacific Ocean*

*Gulf of California*

TROPIC OF CANCER

HONDURAS
EL SALVADOR
GUATEMALA
BELIZE

QUINTANA ROO
Chetumal

YUCATÁN
Mérida ⊙

CAMPECHE
Campeche •

CHIAPAS
Tuxtla
Gutiérrez ⊙

TABASCO
Villahermosa •

VERACRUZ
Veracruz •
Xalapa ⊙
Poza Rica •

OAXACA
Oaxaca ⊙

Matamoros •
Reynosa •
Nuevo Laredo •
Monterrey ⊙
NUEVO LEÓN

Ciudad Victoria ⊙
TAMAULIPAS

Tampico •

COAHUILA
Saltillo ⊙
Torreón •

SAN LUIS POTOSÍ
San Luis Potosí ⊙

ZACATECAS
Zacatecas ⊙

AGUASCALIENTES
Aguascalientes ⊙

GUANAJUATO
Guanajuato ⊙
León •

QUERÉTARO
Querétaro ⊙

HIDALGO
Pachuca ⊙

TLAXCALA
Tlaxcala ⊙

México
Toluca ⊙
MÉXICO
FEDERAL DISTRICT ⊛

MORELOS
Cuernavaca ⊙

PUEBLA
Puebla ⊙

GUERRERO
Chilpancingo ⊙
Acapulco •

MICHOACÁN
Morelia ⊙

JALISCO
Guadalajara ⊙

COLIMA
Colima ⊙

NAYARIT
Tepic ⊙

Puerto Vallarta •

DURANGO
Durango ⊙

SINALOA
Culiacán ⊙
Mazatlán •

CHIHUAHUA
Chihuahua ⊙
Ciudad Juárez •

SONORA
Hermosillo ⊙
Nogales •

BAJA CALIFORNIA
Mexicali ⊙
Tijuana •

BAJA CALIFORNIA SUR
La Paz ⊙

**Mexico is divided** into 31 states and the Federal District of Mexico City. With more than 100 million people, it is the largest Spanish-speaking country in the world. Modern Mexico is the product of a rich cultural tradition rooted first in the Maya and Aztec Empires, and later in the Spanish colonial empire. Most Mexicans are mestizos, people of mixed Indian and Spanish ancestry.

53

## Natural Hazards: *Selected Statistics*

### Hurricanes
This list names North America's eight strongest recorded hurricanes. In other parts of the world hurricanes are called cyclones and typhoons.

**1980** Allen: 165 mph/265 kmph*

**1979** Camille: 165 mph/265 kmph

**1950** Dog: 160 mph/257 kmph

**1988** Gilbert: 160 mph/257 kmph

**1977** Anita: 150 mph/241 kmph

**1961** Carla: 150 mph/241 kmph

**1979** David: 150 mph/241 kmph

**1955** Janet: 150 mph//241 kmph
*maximum wind speed recorded

### Tornadoes
The following states had the highest average annual number of tornadoes from 1961 to 1990.

**Texas:** 137

**Florida:** 52

**Oklahoma:** 47

**Kansas:** 36

**Nebraska:** 36

**Iowa:** 35

**South Dakota:** 28

**Illinois:** 27

**Louisiana:** 27

**Missouri:** 27

### Earthquakes
This list shows the number of earthquakes in North America in the 20th century that had a magnitude of 8.0 to 9.9 on the Richter scale.

**Mexico:** 8

**Alaska (U.S.):** 7

**Guatemala:** 2

**British Columbia (Canada):** 1

**California (U.S.):** 1

**Dominican Republic:** 1
(see map page 43)

**Panama:** 1

# Natural Hazards

The forces of nature inspire awe. They can also bring damage and destruction, especially when people locate homes and businesses in places that are at risk of experiencing violent storms, earthquakes, volcanoes, floods, wildfires, or other natural hazards.

Tornadoes, violent, swirling storms with winds that can exceed 200 miles (300 km) per hour, strike the U.S. more than 800 times each year. Hurricanes, massive low-pressure storms that form over warm ocean waters, bring destructive winds and rain primarily to the Gulf of Mexico and the southeastern mainland. Melting spring snows and heavy rains trigger flooding; periods of drought make other regions vulnerable to wildfires. These and other hazards of nature are not limited to this continent. Natural hazards pose serious threats to lives and property wherever people live.

▲ **Volcanoes.** *From deep inside Earth, molten rock, called magma, rises and breaks through the surface, sometimes quietly, but more often violently, shooting billowing ash clouds as shown here at Mount St. Helens, in Washington State.*

▼ **Wildfires.** *Putting lives and property at great risk, wildfires destroy millions of acres of forest each year. At the same time, fires help renew ecosystems by removing debris and encouraging seedling growth.*

▶ **Floods.** *Towns and farmland that occupy fertile plains along rivers are always in danger from floods. In 1993 the great Mississippi River floods devastated millions of people in the midwestern United States.*

*Web Link* for information on natural hazards: www.cindi.usgs.gov

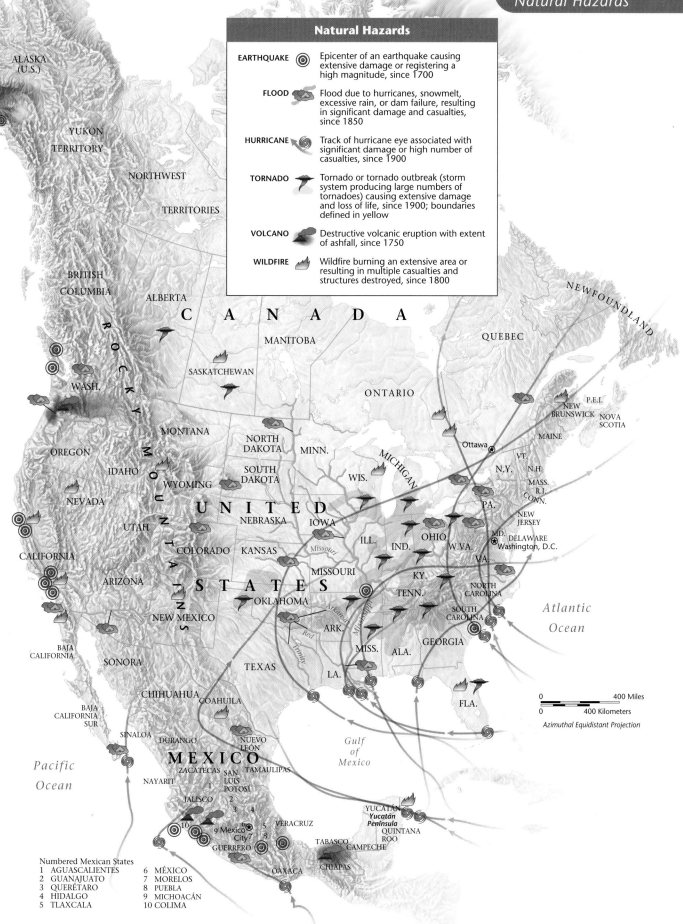

## Natural Hazards

**EARTHQUAKE** — Epicenter of an earthquake causing extensive damage or registering a high magnitude, since 1700

**FLOOD** — Flood due to hurricanes, snowmelt, excessive rain, or dam failure, resulting in significant damage and casualties, since 1850

**HURRICANE** — Track of hurricane eye associated with significant damage or high number of casualties, since 1900

**TORNADO** — Tornado or tornado outbreak (storm system producing large numbers of tornadoes) causing extensive damage and loss of life, since 1900; boundaries defined in yellow

**VOLCANO** — Destructive volcanic eruption with extent of ashfall, since 1750

**WILDFIRE** — Wildfire burning an extensive area or resulting in multiple casualties and structures destroyed, since 1800

ALASKA
(U.S.)

YUKON
TERRITORY

NORTHWEST
TERRITORIES

BRITISH
COLUMBIA

ALBERTA

C A N A D A

MANITOBA

SASKATCHEWAN

QUEBEC

NEWFOUNDLAND

ONTARIO

NEW
BRUNSWICK

P.E.I.

NOVA
SCOTIA

MAINE

Ottawa

WASH.

OREGON

IDAHO

MONTANA

NORTH
DAKOTA

SOUTH
DAKOTA

MINN.

MICHIGAN

WIS.

N.Y.

VT.

N.H.

MASS.
R.I.
CONN.

NEVADA

WYOMING

U N I T E D

NEBRASKA

IOWA

ILL.

IND.

OHIO

PA.

NEW
JERSEY

CALIFORNIA

UTAH

COLORADO

KANSAS

MISSOURI

KY.

W.VA.

VA.

MD.

DELAWARE
Washington, D.C.

ARIZONA

S T A T E S

OKLAHOMA

TENN.

NORTH
CAROLINA

ROCKY MOUNTAINS

NEW MEXICO

ARK.

MISS.

ALA.

GEORGIA

SOUTH
CAROLINA

Atlantic
Ocean

BAJA
CALIFORNIA

SONORA

TEXAS

LA.

FLA.

CHIHUAHUA

COAHUILA

BAJA
CALIFORNIA
SUR

SINALOA

DURANGO

NUEVO
LEÓN

Gulf
of
Mexico

Pacific
Ocean

M E X I C O

ZACATECAS

SAN
LUIS
POTOSÍ

TAMAULIPAS

NAYARIT

JALISCO

1

2

3

4

5

6

7

8

9 Mexico
City

10

VERACRUZ

YUCATÁN
Yucatán
Peninsula

QUINTANA
ROO

TABASCO

CAMPECHE

GUERRERO

CHIAPAS

OAXACA

Missouri

Arkansas

Red

Trinity

Mississippi

0        400 Miles
0        400 Kilometers

*Azimuthal Equidistant Projection*

Numbered Mexican States
1 AGUASCALIENTES
2 GUANAJUATO
3 QUERÉTARO
4 HIDALGO
5 TLAXCALA

6 MÉXICO
7 MORELOS
8 PUEBLA
9 MICHOACÁN
10 COLIMA

# South America

From the towering, snow-capped Andes in the west to the steamy rain forest of the Amazon Basin in the north, and from the fertile grasslands of the Pampas to the arid Atacama Desert along the Pacific coast, South America is a continent of extremes. North to south the continent extends from the tropical waters of the Caribbean Sea to the windblown islands of Tierra del Fuego. Its longest river, the Amazon, carries more water than any other river in the world.

## Facts & Figures

▶ **Land area:** 6,880,500 sq mi (17,819,000 sq km)

▶ **Population:** 344,790,000

▶ **Highest point:** Aconcagua, Argentina: 22,834 ft (6,960 m)

▶ **Lowest point:** Valdés Peninsula, Argentina: 131 ft (40 m) below sea level

▶ **Longest river:** Amazon: 4,000 mi (6,437 km)

▶ **Largest lake:** Lake Titicaca, Bolivia-Peru: 3,200 sq mi (8,287 sq km)

▶ **Number of independent countries:** 12

▶ **Largest country:** Brazil: 3,286,488 sq mi (8,511,965 sq km)

▶ **Smallest country:** Suriname: 63,037 sq mi (163,265 sq km)

▶ **Most populous country:** Brazil: Pop. 170,115,000

▶ **Least populous country:** Suriname: Pop. 434,000

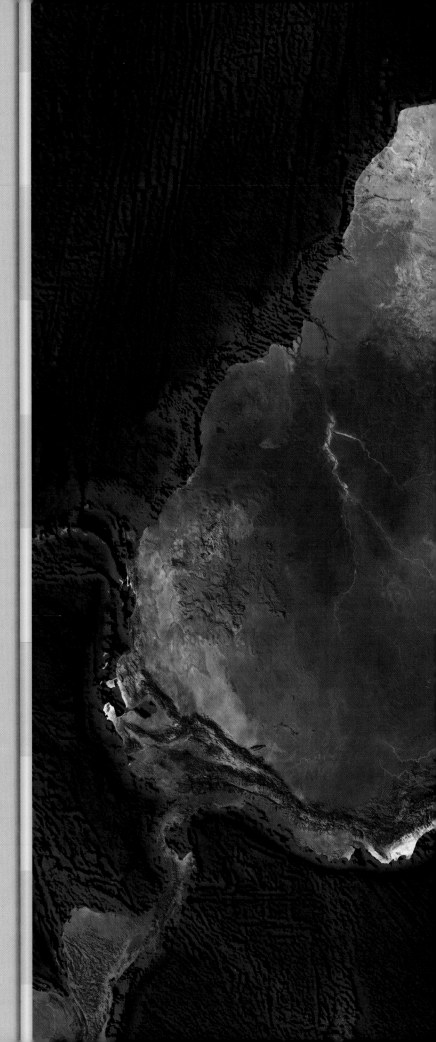

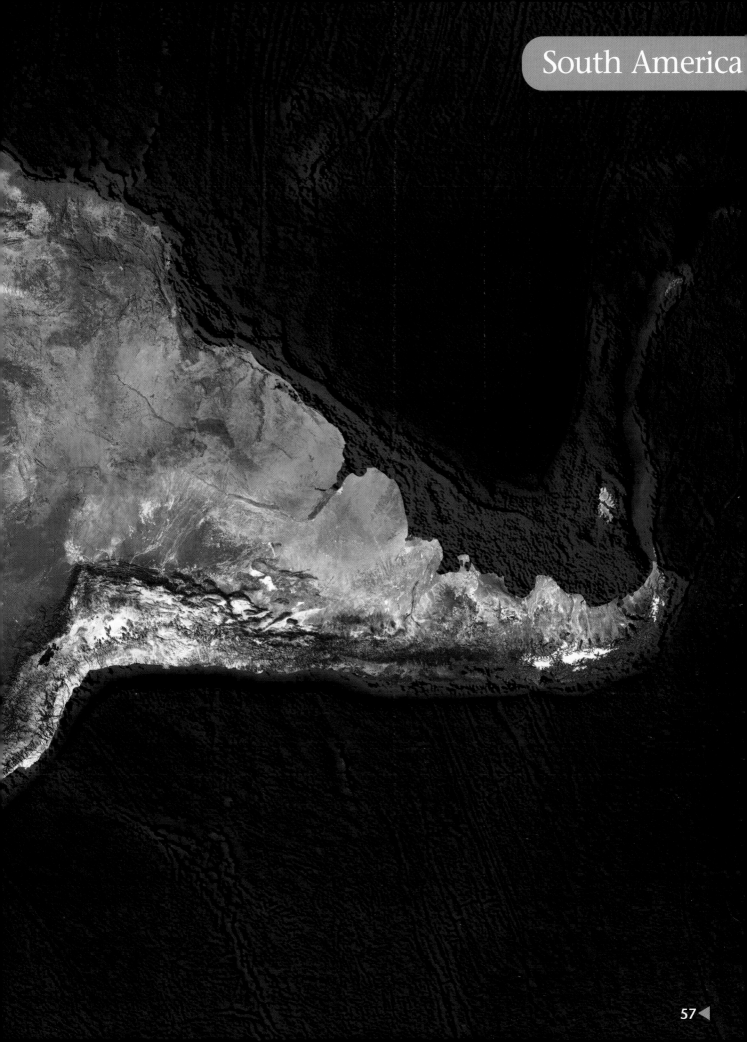

Caribbean Sea

Central America

Malpelo I.

80°W

70°W

60°W

50°W

EQUATOR

Lake Maracaibo

Orinoco

Llanos

GUIANA HIGHLANDS

Angel Falls

A N D E S

Negro

A M A Z O N

Amazon

Amazon

Marajó I.

0°

0°

B A S I N

Ucayali

Purus

Madeira

Tapajós

Xingu

Tocantins

São Francisco

10°S

10°S

Lake Titicaca

Mato Grosso Plateau

BRAZILIAN

Atacama Desert

HIGHLANDS

A N D E S

Paraguay

20°S

20°S

TROPIC OF CAPRICORN

Gran Chaco

Iguazú Falls

San Félix I.      San Ambrosio I.

Ojos del Salado
22,572 ft
(6,880 m)

Paraná

Uruguay

Atlantic Ocean

P A M P A S

Cerro Aconcagua
22,834 ft (6,960 m)
Highest point in South America

Juan Fernández Is.

Río de la Plata

30°S

30°S

Colorado

Pacific Ocean

Isla Grande de Chiloé

A N D E S

P A T A G O N I A

Valdés Peninsula
-131 ft (-40 m)
Lowest point in South America

40°S

40°S

Gulf of San Jorge

**Two physical features** dominate South America's landscape—the rugged Andes that stretch north to south from Colombia to Tierra del Fuego, and the Amazon Basin, the drainage area of the Amazon River and site of the world's largest tropical forest.

**Physical**

▲ Highest point
▼ Lowest point
+ Other mountain peak

0 ———— 600 Miles
0 ———— 600 Kilometers

*Azimuthal Equidistant Projection*

Falkland Islands

Strait of Magellan

Tierra del Fuego

Cape Horn

South Georgia

50°S

50°S

100°W      90°W      80°W      70°W      60°W      50°W      40°W      30°W      20°W

# South America

**Twelve countries** and one French territory (French Guiana) make up South America. The continent was under mainly Spanish and Portuguese control from the 16th to the 19th century. Colonial influence is still evident in the use of Spanish and Portuguese languages and in the widespread presence of the Roman Catholic church.

Central America

Caribbean Sea

Barranquilla
Maracaibo
Caracas
Barquisimeto
Valencia
VENEZUELA

Georgetown
Paramaribo
GUYANA
SURINAME
Cayenne
French Guiana
(France)

Medellín
Bogotá
Cali
COLOMBIA

EQUATOR

Quito
ECUADOR
Guayaquil

Manaus

Belém

EQUATOR

Fortaleza

Natal

Recife

PERU
Callao
Lima

B R A Z I L

BOLIVIA
La Paz

Salvador
(Bahia)

Goiânia
Brasília

Santa Cruz
Sucre

Belo
Horizonte

PARAGUAY

Nova Iguaçu
São Paulo
Rio de Janeiro
Santos
Curitiba

TROPIC OF CAPRICORN

Asunción

CHILE

San Miguel
de Tucumán

Pôrto Alegre

Atlantic
Ocean

Córdoba
Santa
Fe
Rosario
Buenos Aires
La Plata
URUGUAY
Montevideo

Valparaíso
Santiago

Pacific
Ocean

ARGENTINA

Mar del Plata

**Political**

⊛ National capital
• Other city

0        600 Miles
0     600 Kilometers

*Azimuthal Equidistant Projection*

Stanley
Falkland Islands
(U.K.)

South
Georgia
(U.K.)

**59** ◀

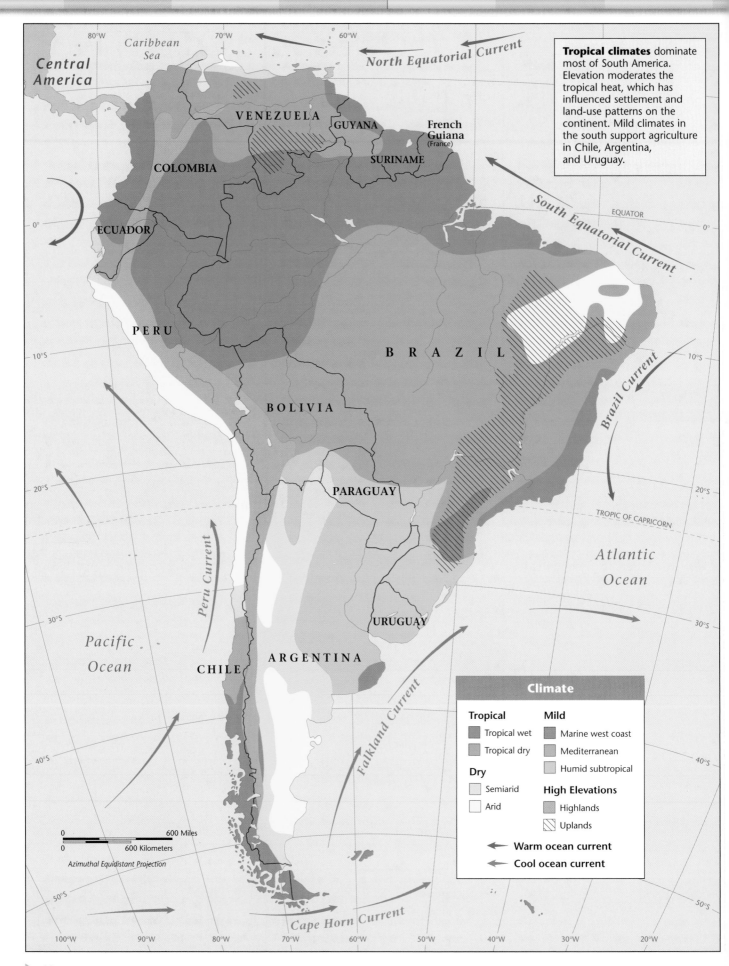

**Tropical climates** dominate most of South America. Elevation moderates the tropical heat, which has influenced settlement and land-use patterns on the continent. Mild climates in the south support agriculture in Chile, Argentina, and Uruguay.

Central America

Caribbean Sea

North Equatorial Current

VENEZUELA

GUYANA

French Guiana (France)

SURINAME

COLOMBIA

South Equatorial Current

EQUATOR

ECUADOR

PERU

B R A Z I L

Brazil Current

BOLIVIA

Peru Current

PARAGUAY

TROPIC OF CAPRICORN

Atlantic Ocean

URUGUAY

Pacific Ocean

ARGENTINA

CHILE

Falkland Current

**Climate**

**Tropical**
- Tropical wet
- Tropical dry

**Dry**
- Semiarid
- Arid

**Mild**
- Marine west coast
- Mediterranean
- Humid subtropical

**High Elevations**
- Highlands
- Uplands

← Warm ocean current
← Cool ocean current

0          600 Miles
0          600 Kilometers

*Azimuthal Equidistant Projection*

Cape Horn Current

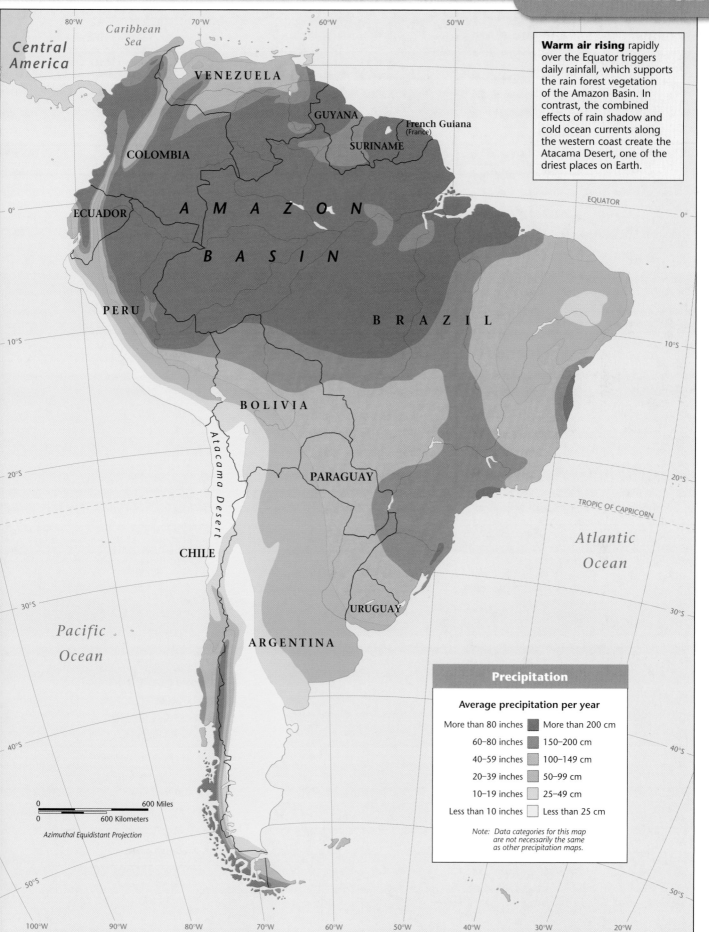

**Warm air rising** rapidly over the Equator triggers daily rainfall, which supports the rain forest vegetation of the Amazon Basin. In contrast, the combined effects of rain shadow and cold ocean currents along the western coast create the Atacama Desert, one of the driest places on Earth.

Central America

Caribbean Sea

VENEZUELA

GUYANA

French Guiana
(France)

COLOMBIA

SURINAME

ECUADOR

A M A Z O N

EQUATOR

B A S I N

PERU

B R A Z I L

BOLIVIA

*Atacama Desert*

PARAGUAY

TROPIC OF CAPRICORN

CHILE

*Atlantic Ocean*

URUGUAY

*Pacific Ocean*

ARGENTINA

0        600 Miles
0        600 Kilometers

*Azimuthal Equidistant Projection*

### Precipitation

**Average precipitation per year**

| | |
|---|---|
| More than 80 inches | More than 200 cm |
| 60–80 inches | 150–200 cm |
| 40–59 inches | 100–149 cm |
| 20–39 inches | 50–99 cm |
| 10–19 inches | 25–49 cm |
| Less than 10 inches | Less than 25 cm |

*Note: Data categories for this map are not necessarily the same as other precipitation maps.*

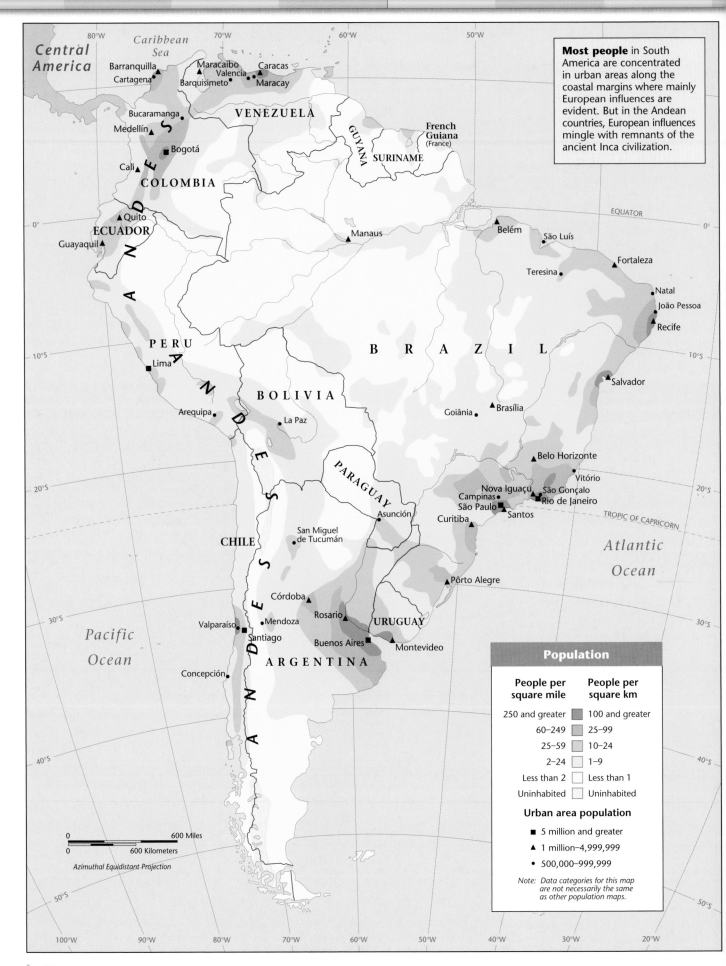

Central
America

Caribbean
Sea

Barranquilla
Cartagena
Maracaibo
Barquisimeto
Valencia
Caracas
Maracay

**VENEZUELA**

French
Guiana
(France)

GUYANA

SURINAME

Bucaramanga
Medellín
Bogotá
Cali

**COLOMBIA**

EQUATOR

Quito
**ECUADOR**
Guayaquil

Manaus

Belém
São Luís

Fortaleza

Teresina

Natal
João Pessoa
Recife

**PERU**
Lima

**B R A Z I L**

Salvador

Arequipa
**BOLIVIA**
La Paz

Goiânia
Brasília

Belo Horizonte
Vitório

**PARAGUAY**

Asunción

Nova Iguaçu
Campinas
São Paulo
São Gonçalo
Rio de Janeiro
Santos

TROPIC OF CAPRICORN

Atlantic
Ocean

San Miguel
de Tucumán

**CHILE**

Curitiba

Pôrto Alegre

Córdoba

Rosario
**URUGUAY**

Pacific
Ocean

Valparaíso
Mendoza
Santiago

Buenos Aires
Montevideo

Concepción

**ARGENTINA**

**Most people** in South
America are concentrated
in urban areas along the
coastal margins where mainly
European influences are
evident. But in the Andean
countries, European influences
mingle with remnants of the
ancient Inca civilization.

0        600 Miles
0      600 Kilometers

*Azimuthal Equidistant Projection*

### Population

| People per square mile | People per square km |
|---|---|
| 250 and greater | 100 and greater |
| 60–249 | 25–99 |
| 25–59 | 10–24 |
| 2–24 | 1–9 |
| Less than 2 | Less than 1 |
| Uninhabited | Uninhabited |

**Urban area population**

■ 5 million and greater
▲ 1 million–4,999,999
● 500,000–999,999

*Note: Data categories for this map
are not necessarily the same
as other population maps.*

# South America

**Plantation agriculture,** livestock raising, and mining are the base for much of South America's economy, although people in large areas of the Amazon Basin and the Andes still practice subsistence agriculture. Manufacturing centers have emerged near major cities.

Central America

Caribbean Sea

Cartagena
Maracaibo
Caracas

VENEZUELA

GUYANA

French Guiana (France)

SURINAME

Bogotá
Cali

COLOMBIA

Quito

ECUADOR

Guayaquil

PERU

A M A Z O N

B A S I N

B R A Z I L

EQUATOR

Belém

Lima

BOLIVIA

La Paz

PARAGUAY

Rio de Janeiro

São Paulo

TROPIC OF CAPRICORN

CHILE

Atlantic Ocean

Pacific Ocean

Santiago

Rosario

URUGUAY

Buenos Aires

Montevideo

Concepción

ARGENTINA

A N D E S

P A T A G O N I A

0      600 Miles
0      600 Kilometers

Azimuthal Equidistant Projection

## Predominant Economies

### Predominant economy

- Agriculture
- Fishing
- Forestry (lumber and pulpwood)
- Subsistence agriculture
- Little or no economic activity
- Manufacturing
- Stock raising on ranges

### Major manufacturing centers

- Cement industry
- Chemical and pharmaceutical
- High-tech centers
- Pulp and paper
- Shipbuilding and ship repair
- Textile industry

# Amazon Rain Forest

The Amazon rain forest, which covers approximately 2.7 million square miles (7 million sq km), is the world's largest tropical forest. Located mainly in Brazil, the Amazon rain forest accounts for more than 20 percent of all the world's tropical forests. Known in Brazil as the *selva*, the rain forest is a vast storehouse of biological diversity, filled with plants and animals both familiar and exotic. According to estimates, at least half of all species are found in tropical forests, but many of these species have not yet been identified.

Tropical forests contain many valuable resources, including cacao (chocolate), nuts, spices, rare hardwoods, and plant extracts used to make medicines. Some drugs used in treating cancer and heart disease come from plants found only in tropical forests. But human intervention—logging, mining, and clearing land for crops and grazing—has put tropical forests at great risk. In Brazil, roads cut into the rain forest have opened the way for settlers, who clear away the forest only to discover soil too poor in nutrients to sustain agriculture for more than a few years. Land usually is cleared by a method called slash-and-burn, which contributes to global warming by releasing great amounts of carbon dioxide into the atmosphere.

AREA ENLARGED

SOUTH AMERICA

Caracas

Lake Maracaibo

Orinoco

VENEZUELA

Angel Falls

Bogotá

COLOMBIA

EQUATOR

Quito

Negro

ECUADOR

Iquitos

Amazon

Marañón

B R

Ucayali

Purus

TRANS-AMAZ

PERU

Pôr Vel

Lima

BOLIVIA

Lake Titicáca

La Paz

Sucre

▶ **Tropical rain forests** grow in parts of every continent except Europe and Antarctica. Together, the tropical forests of South America and Africa make up three-quarters of the world's total. Brazil alone has more than 300 million acres (120 million hectares)—more than any other country.

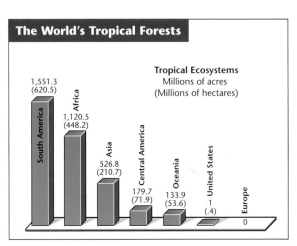

**The World's Tropical Forests**

Tropical Ecosystems
Millions of acres
(Millions of hectares)

South America 1,551.3 (620.5)
Africa 1,120.5 (448.2)
Asia 526.8 (210.7)
Central America 179.7 (71.9)
Oceania 133.9 (53.6)
United States 1 (.4)
Europe 0

## Price of Progress

CLEARING TREES to make way for expanding economic activities leads to widespread environmental destruction. Slash-and-burn agriculture exposes fragile soils to heat and torrential rains, and the runoff from mining operations pollutes streams and rivers. In an effort to reverse this trend, some countries and international organizations have set up national parks, reserves, and other protected areas.

*Web Link* for information on rain forests: www.wri.org

▶ **Dense canopy of the rain forest** stands in sharp contrast to the silt-laden waters of one of the Amazon's many tributaries. Although seemingly endless, the forest is rapidly decreasing in size at the rate of 200,000 acres (80,940 hectares) per day.

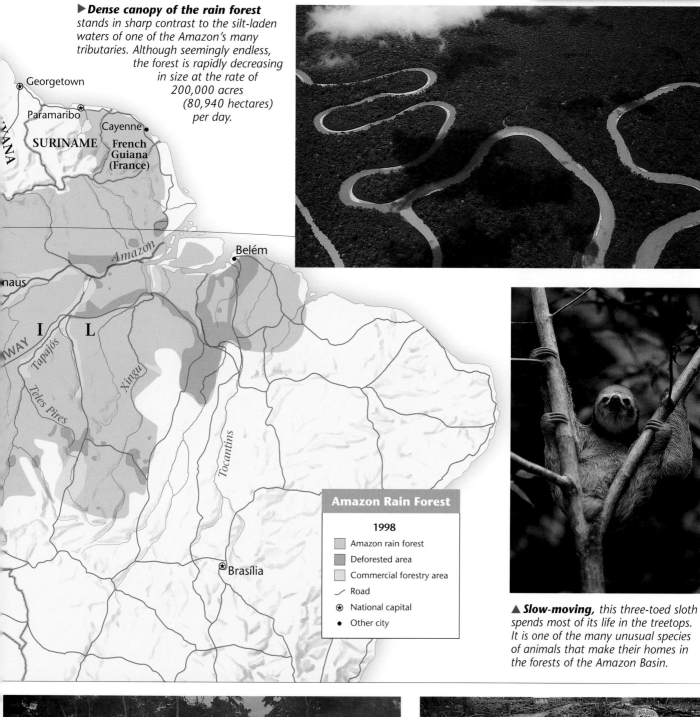

**Amazon Rain Forest**

**1998**

- Amazon rain forest
- Deforested area
- Commercial forestry area
- / Road
- ⊛ National capital
- • Other city

▲ **Slow-moving,** this three-toed sloth spends most of its life in the treetops. It is one of the many unusual species of animals that make their homes in the forests of the Amazon Basin.

▲ **Slash-and-burn** is a method used in the tropics for clearing land for farms. But the soil is poor in nutrients, and good yields are short-lived.

▲ **Mining operations,** such as this tin mine, remove forests to gain access to mineral deposits.

# Europe

**S**maller than every other continent except Australia, Europe is a mosaic of islands and peninsulas. In fact, Europe itself is one big peninsula, jutting westward from the huge land-mass of Asia and nearly touching Africa to the south. Europe's ragged coastline measures more than one and a half times the length of the Equator—37,877 miles (60,955 km) to be exact—giving 30 of its 43 countries direct access to the sea.

## Facts & Figures

▶ **Land area:** 3,837,400 sq mi
(9,938,000 sq km)

▶ **Population:** 727,758,000

▶ **Highest point:** Mount El'brus, Russia:
18,510 ft (5,642 m)

▶ **Lowest point:** Caspian Sea:
92 ft (28 m) below sea level

▶ **Longest river:** Volga, Russia:
2,290 mi (3,685 km)

▶ **Largest lake entirely in Europe:**
Ladoga, Russia: 6,853 sq mi (17,703 sq km)

▶ **Number of independent countries:**
43 (including Russia)

▶ **Largest country entirely in Europe:**
Ukraine 233,206 sq mi (604,001 sq km)

▶ **Smallest country:** Vatican City:
0.2 sq mi (0.4 sq km)

▶ **Most populous country entirely in
Europe:** Germany: Pop. 82,141,000

▶ **Least populous country:**
Vatican City: Pop. 1,000

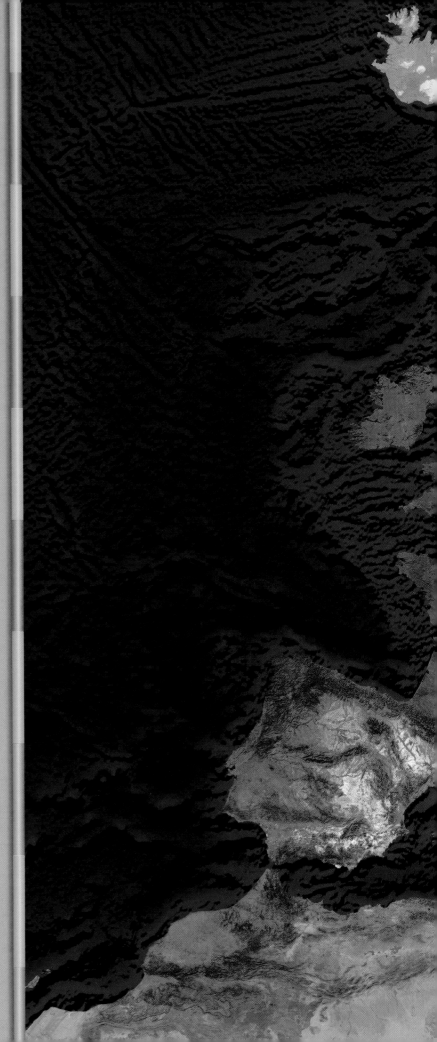

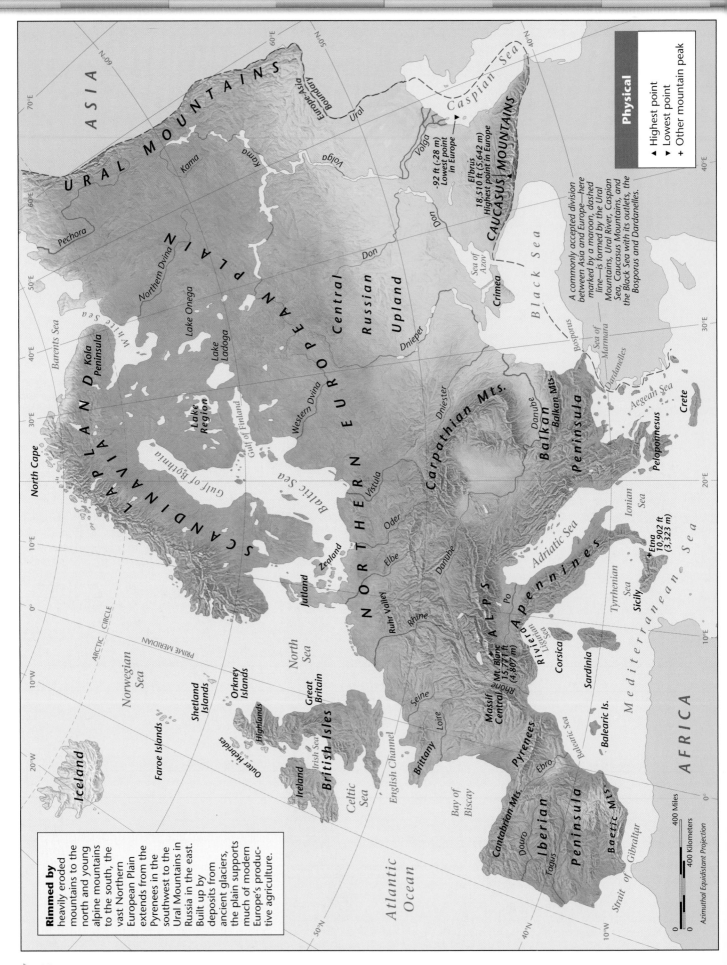

**Physical**

▲ Highest point
▼ Lowest point
+ Other mountain peak

ASIA

URAL MOUNTAINS

Europe-Asia Boundary

Ural

Pechora

Kama

Kama

Volga

Volga

Elbrus
18,510 ft (5,642 m)
Highest point in Europe

-92 ft (-28 m)
Lowest point in Europe

Caspian Sea

CAUCASUS MOUNTAINS

Northern Dvina

Lake Onega

Lake Ladoga

NORTHERN EUROPEAN PLAIN

Central

Russian

Upland

Don

Don

Dnieper

Crimea

Sea of Azov

Bosporus

Sea of Marmara

Dardanelles

Black Sea

A commonly accepted division between Asia and Europe—here marked by a maroon, dashed line—is formed by the Ural Mountains, Ural River, Caspian Sea, Caucasus Mountains, and the Black Sea with its outlets, the Bosporus and Dardanelles.

Barents Sea

White Sea

Kola Peninsula

Lake Region

Gulf of Finland

Western Dvina

Dniester

Carpathian Mts.

Danube

Balkan Mts.

Balkan Peninsula

Aegean Sea

Crete

Peloponnesus

North Cape

SCANDINAVIA

UPLAND

Gulf of Bothnia

Baltic Sea

Vistula

Oder

Vistula

Danube

Adriatic Sea

Ionian Sea

Etna
10,902 ft
(3,323 m)

Mediterranean Sea

Norwegian Sea

Faroe Islands

Shetland Islands

Orkney Islands

Highlands

Outer Hebrides

Great Britain

British Isles

Ireland

Irish Sea

Celtic Sea

North Sea

Zealand

Jutland

Ruhr Valley

Elbe

Rhine

ALPS

APENNINES

Po

Mt. Blanc
15,771 ft
(4,807 m)

Massif Central

Riviera

Rhône

Ligurian Sea

Corsica

Sardinia

Tyrrhenian Sea

Sicily

English Channel

Seine

Loire

Brittany

Bay of Biscay

Pyrenees

Ebro

Balearic Sea

Balearic Is.

Cantabrian Mts.

Douro

Tagus

Iberian Peninsula

Baetic Mts.

Strait of Gibraltar

AFRICA

Iceland

Atlantic Ocean

**Rimmed by** heavily eroded mountains to the north and young alpine mountains to the south, the vast Northern European Plain extends from the Pyrenees in the southwest to the Ural Mountains in Russia in the east. Built up by deposits from ancient glaciers, the plain supports much of modern Europe's productive agriculture.

400 Miles

400 Kilometers

Azimuthal Equidistant Projection

**Political**
- ⊛ National capital
- • Other city
- ▫ Small country

A commonly accepted division between Asia and Europe—here marked by a maroon, dashed line—is formed by the Ural Mountains, Ural River, Caspian Sea, Caucasus Mountains, and the Black Sea with its outlets, the Bosporus and Dardanelles.

**Europe has 43** independent countries that range in size from giant Russia to tiny Vatican City. Because Russia's capital is located in and most of its people live west of the Urals, the country is usually considered part of Europe. Iceland, United Kingdom, Ireland, and Malta are all island countries.

*Azimuthal Equidistant Projection*

400 Miles
400 Kilometers

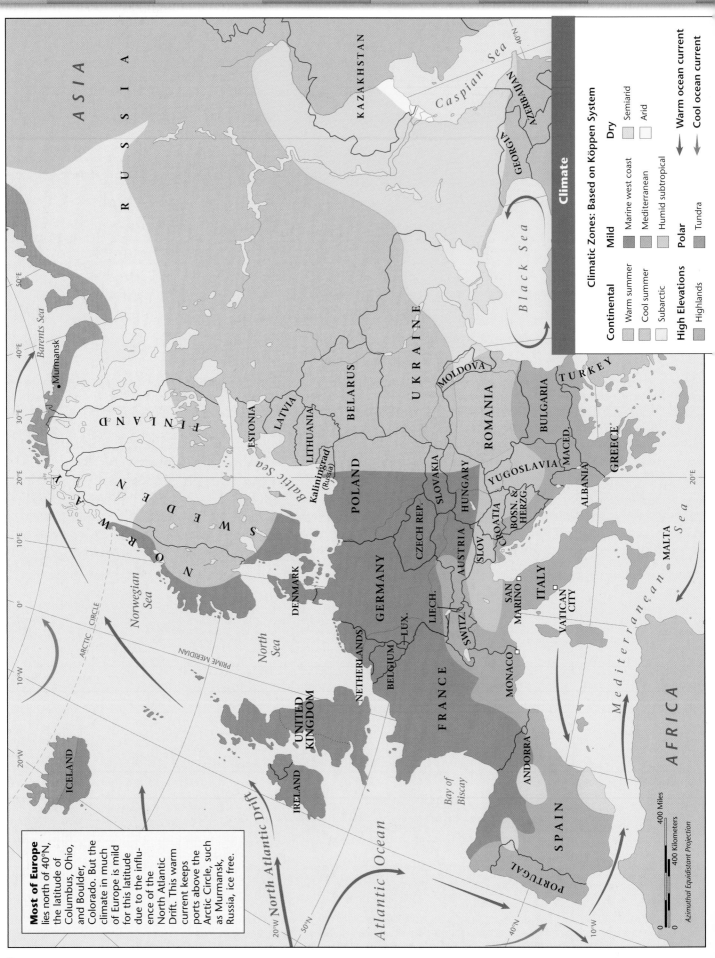

**Most of Europe** lies north of 40°N, the latitude of Columbus, Ohio, and Boulder, Colorado. But the climate in much of Europe is mild for this latitude due to the influence of the North Atlantic Drift. This warm current keeps ports above the Arctic Circle, such as Murmansk, Russia, ice free.

**Climate**

Climatic Zones: Based on Köppen System

**Continental**
- Warm summer
- Cool summer
- Subarctic

**High Elevations**
- Highlands

**Mild**
- Marine west coast
- Mediterranean
- Humid subtropical

**Polar**
- Tundra

**Dry**
- Semiarid
- Arid

→ Warm ocean current
→ Cool ocean current

Azimuthal Equidistant Projection

400 Miles
400 Kilometers

# Europe

**Precipitation**

**Average precipitation per year**

| | |
|---|---|
| More than 80 inches | More than 200 cm |
| 60–80 inches | 150–200 cm |
| 40–59 inches | 100–149 cm |
| 20–39 inches | 50–99 cm |
| 10–19 inches | 25–49 cm |
| Less than 10 inches | Less than 25 cm |

*Note: Data categories for this map are not necessarily the same as other precipitation maps.*

**Westerly winds** blowing off the Atlantic Ocean bring ample rainfall to Europe. This precipitation, combined with mild temperatures, supports a wide variety of agriculture. In the Mediterranean area, hot, dry summers favor orchards and vineyards.

ASIA

RUSSIA

KAZAKHSTAN

*Caspian Sea*

AZERBAIJAN

GEORGIA

*Barents Sea*

FINLAND

ESTONIA

LATVIA

LITHUANIA

Kaliningrad (Russia)

BELARUS

UKRAINE

MOLDOVA

ROMANIA

BULGARIA

*Black Sea*

TURKEY

MACED.

GREECE

ALBANIA

YUGOSLAVIA

BOSN. & HERZ.

CROATIA

SLOV.

HUNGARY

SLOVAKIA

CZECH REP.

POLAND

*Baltic Sea*

SWEDEN

NORWAY

DENMARK

GERMANY

NETH.

BELGIUM

LUX.

LIECH.

AUSTRIA

SWITZ.

SAN MARINO

ITALY

VATICAN CITY

MONACO

FRANCE

ANDORRA

MALTA

*Mediterranean Sea*

AFRICA

SPAIN

PORTUGAL

*Bay of Biscay*

UNITED KINGDOM

IRELAND

ICELAND

*Norwegian Sea*

*North Sea*

*Atlantic Ocean*

ARCTIC CIRCLE

PRIME MERIDIAN

40°N

40°N

50°N

60°N

30°E

20°E

20°E

10°E

0°

10°W

20°W

30°E

40°E

50°E

| 0 | 400 Miles |
|---|---|
| 0 | 400 Kilometers |

Azimuthal Equidistant Projection

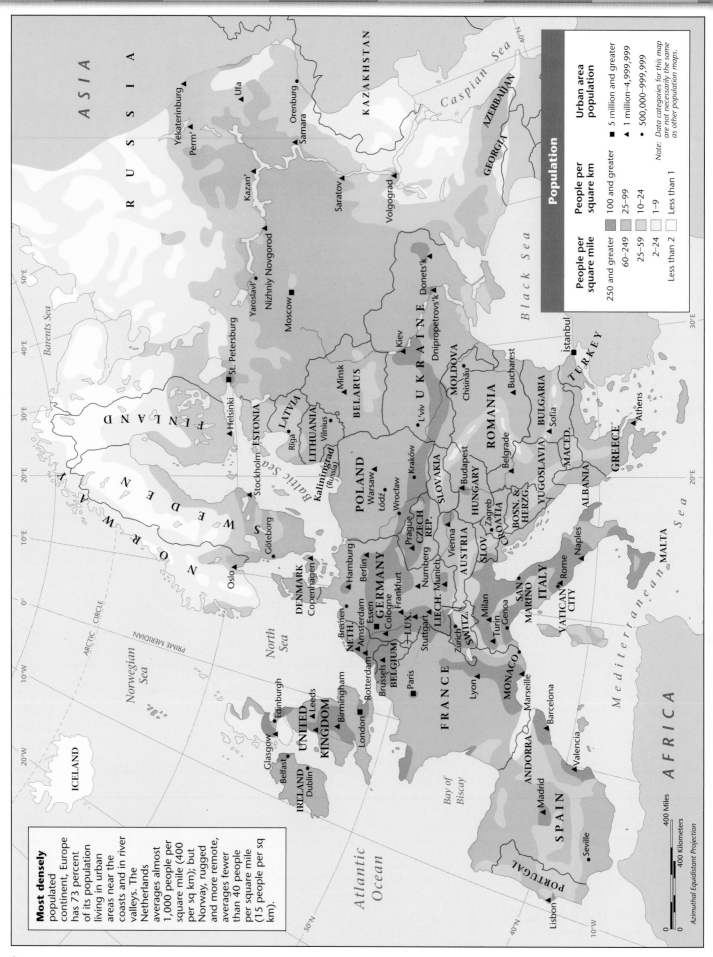

**Most densely** populated continent, Europe has 73 percent of its population living in urban areas near the coasts and in river valleys. The Netherlands averages almost 1,000 people per square mile (400 per sq km); but Norway, rugged and more remote, averages fewer than 40 people per square mile (15 people per sq km).

**Population**

| People per square mile | People per square km |
|---|---|
| 250 and greater | 100 and greater |
| 60–249 | 25–99 |
| 25–59 | 10–24 |
| 2–24 | 1–9 |
| Less than 2 | Less than 1 |

Urban area population
- ■ 5 million and greater
- ▲ 1 million–4,999,999
- • 500,000–999,999

Note: Data categories for this map are not necessarily the same as other population maps.

Azimuthal Equidistant Projection

# Europe

**The Industrial Revolution** had its beginnings in Europe, and manufacturing is still an important part of the continent's economy. Main industrial centers are in the United Kingdom and in Germany's Ruhr region are located near coal deposits, reflecting a time when coal was the main source of energy. Although agriculture is important, the region is not self-sufficient in food production.

## Predominant Economies

- Agriculture
- Agriculture and forestry
- Fishing
- Forestry (lumber and pulpwood)
- Hunting, fishing and forestry
- Subsistence agriculture
- Little or no economic activity
- Manufacturing
- Nomadic herding
- Stock raising on ranges

- ■ Cement industry
- ◒ Chemical and pharmaceutical
- ⚒ High-tech centers
- Pulp and paper
- Shipbuilding and ship repair
- ◆ Textile industry

### Place labels

ASIA
RUSSIA
KAZAKHSTAN
AZERBAIJAN
GEORGIA
Perm'
Yaroslavl'
Moscow
Volgograd
Kharkiv
UKRAINE
BELARUS
MOLDOVA
ROMANIA
BULGARIA
TURKEY
MACED.
GREECE
Athens
ALBANIA
YUGO.
BOSN. & HERZG.
CROATIA
HUNGARY
SLOVAKIA
Lviv
Warsaw
POLAND
LITHUANIA
Kaliningrad (Russia)
LATVIA
ESTONIA
FINLAND
SWEDEN
NORWAY
ARCTIC CIRCLE
PRIME MERIDIAN
ICELAND
IRELAND
UNITED KINGDOM
London
North Sea
DENMARK
Hamburg
Berlin
GERMANY
NETH.
BELGIUM
Paris
FRANCE
LUX.
CZECH REP.
AUSTRIA
SWITZ.
LIECH.
SLOV.
SAN MARINO
ITALY
VATICAN CITY
MONACO
ANDORRA
Barcelona
SPAIN
Madrid
PORTUGAL
Atlantic Ocean
AFRICA
MALTA

Azimuthal Equidistant Projection

400 Miles
400 Kilometers

## FOCUS ON

# European Union

In the years following World War II, the countries of Europe looked for ways to restore political stability to the continent while rebuilding their war-ravaged economies. The first step toward the European Union was taken in 1950 when France proposed creating common institutions to govern coal and steel production in Europe jointly. In 1951 France, West Germany, Italy, Belgium, Netherlands, and Luxembourg created the European Coal and Steel Community with the goal of bringing former adversaries together. In 1965 that organization became the European Community (EC).

The Maastricht Treaty took effect in 1993, establishing today's European Union (EU) and paving the way for a common foreign policy and a single European currency. The treaty also laid plans for the open flow of people, products, and services among the member countries. Since 1993, three more countries have joined the EU, bringing the total number of members to 15 (see map). As of the year 2000, 12 other countries were actively seeking admission: Bulgaria, Cypress, Czech Republic, Estonia, Hungary, Latvia, Lithuania, Poland, Romania, Slovakia, Slovenia, and Turkey.

▲ ***Main trade outlet*** *for Germany's heavily industrialized Ruhr Valley, the port of Rotterdam in the Netherlands accommodates massive supertankers and container ships.*

**Web Link** for information on the European Union: www.europa.eu.int

## European Union

- Member country
- Other European country
- 1957 Year of admission

ARCTIC CIRCLE

Norwegian Sea

FINLAND
1995

SWEDEN
1995

North Sea

Baltic Sea

UNITED KINGDOM
1973

IRELAND
1973

DENMARK
1973

NETHERLANDS
1957

Atlantic Ocean

English Channel

BELGIUM
1957

GERMANY
(WEST)    (EAST)
1957      1990

E U R O P E

LUXEMBOURG
1957

Bay of Biscay

FRANCE
1957

AUSTRIA
1995

E U R O P E

ITALY
1957

Adriatic Sea

PORTUGAL
1986

SPAIN
1986

ASIA

Mediterranean Sea

Aegean Sea

GREECE
1981

AFRICA

0        400 Miles
0        400 Kilometers
Azimuthal Equidistant Projection

## Symbols of New Unity

THE FLAG of the Council of Europe, a circle of gold stars on a field of blue, was adopted as a symbol of unity first by the EC and then by the EU. Another important step toward European unity came in 1999 with the introduction of a common currency—the euro—which is scheduled to begin circulating in January 2002.

## European Union's Share of World Trade

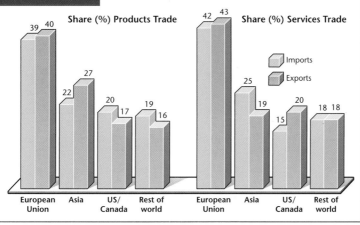

Acting as a trade bloc, the European Union is a major player in the global economy. With only a little more than six percent of the world's population, the EU accounts for about twice the trade of the U.S. and Canada combined or of Asia. The three regions together account for more than 80 percent of world trade in both products and services.

**Share (%) Products Trade**

| | European Union | Asia | US/Canada | Rest of world |
|---|---|---|---|---|
| Imports | 39 | 22 | 20 | 19 |
| Exports | 40 | 27 | 17 | 16 |

**Share (%) Services Trade**

| | European Union | Asia | US/Canada | Rest of world |
|---|---|---|---|---|
| Imports | 42 | 25 | 15 | 18 |
| Exports | 43 | 19 | 20 | 18 |

# Africa

From space, Africa appears divided into three regions: the northern third, dominated by the vast Sahara, largest hot desert in the world; a central green band of rain forests and tropical grasslands; and more dry lands to the south. Africa itself may be dividing literally: The Great Rift Valley, which runs from the Red Sea through the volcanic Afar Triangle to the lake district in the south (see map page 85), eventually may split apart the continent.

## Facts & Figures

- **Land area:** 11,609,000 sq mi (30,065,000 sq km)
- **Population:** 800,245,000
- **Highest point:** Mount Kilimanjaro, Tanzania: 19,340 ft (5,895 m)
- **Lowest point:** Lake Assal, Djibouti: 512 ft (156 m) below sea level
- **Longest river:** Nile: 4,241 mi (6,825 km)
- **Largest Lake:** Victoria: 26,836 sq mi (69,500 sq km)
- **Number of independent countries:** 53
- **Largest country:** Sudan: 963,600 sq mi (2,495,712 sq km)
- **Smallest country:** Seychelles: 175 sq mi (453 sq km)
- **Most populous country:** Nigeria: Pop. 123,338,000
- **Least populous country:** Seychelles: Pop. 82,000

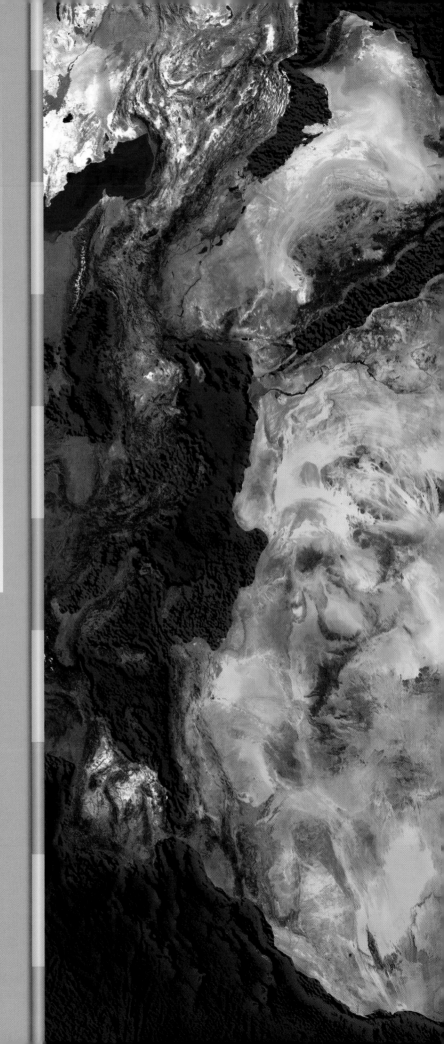

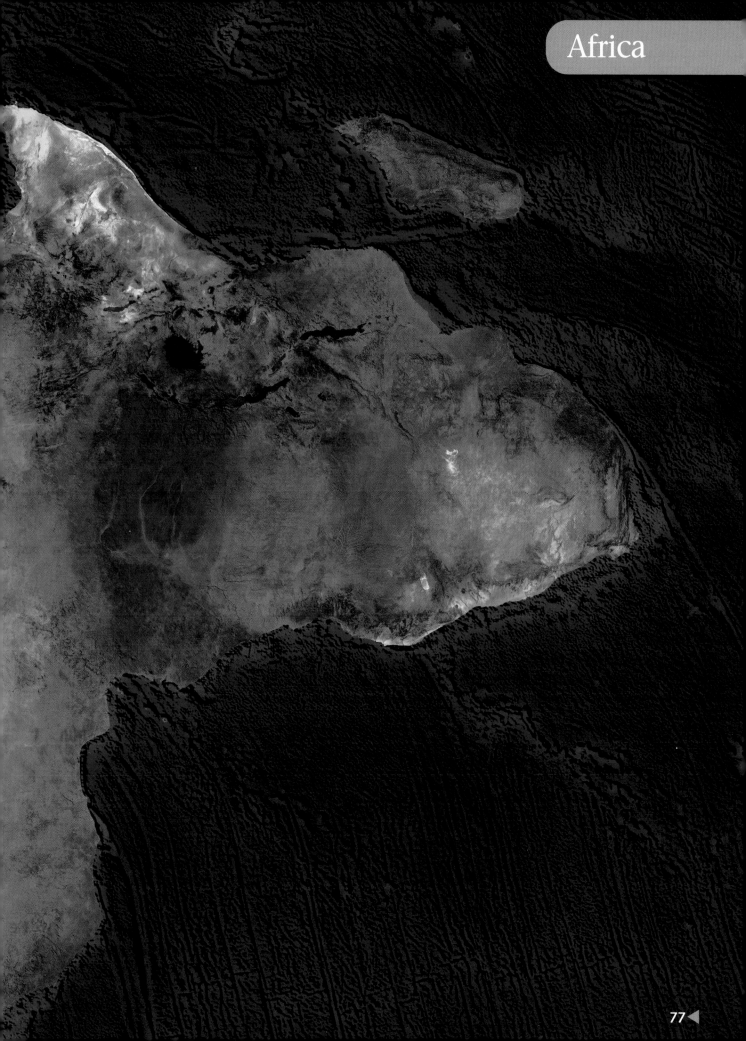

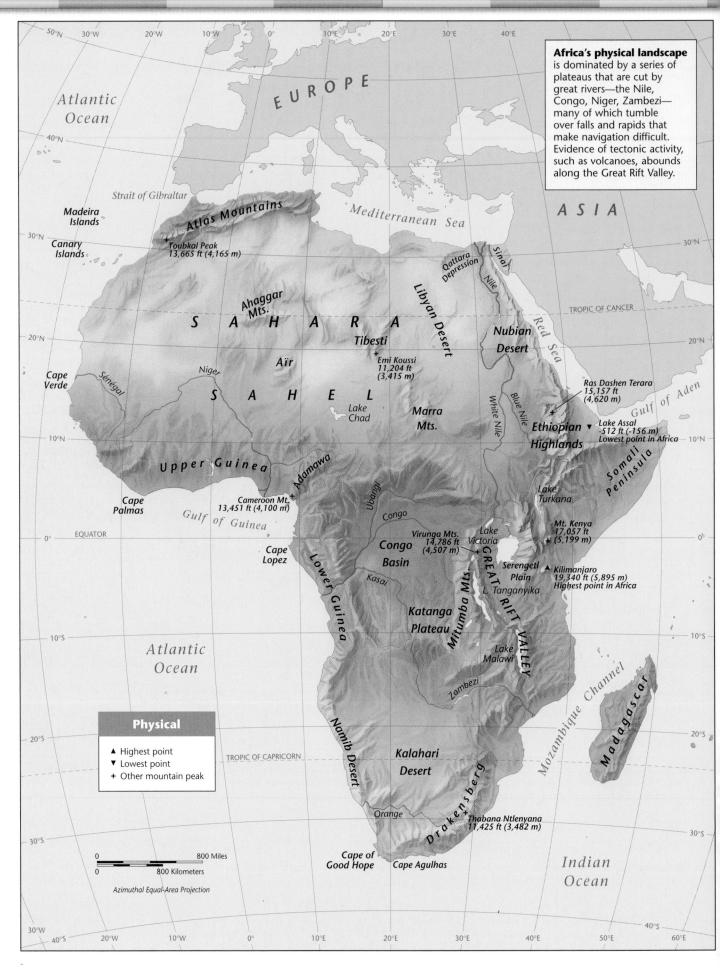

**Africa's physical landscape** is dominated by a series of plateaus that are cut by great rivers—the Nile, Congo, Niger, Zambezi— many of which tumble over falls and rapids that make navigation difficult. Evidence of tectonic activity, such as volcanoes, abounds along the Great Rift Valley.

EUROPE

ASIA

*Atlantic Ocean*

*Mediterranean Sea*

*Strait of Gibraltar*

Madeira Islands

Canary Islands

Atlas Mountains

+ Toubkal Peak 13,665 ft (4,165 m)

Qattara Depression

Sinai

Nile

Red Sea

TROPIC OF CANCER

S A H A R A

Ahaggar Mts.

Libyan Desert

Nubian Desert

Tibesti

+ Emi Koussi 11,204 ft (3,415 m)

Aïr

S A H E L

Cape Verde

Sénégal

Niger

Lake Chad

Marra Mts.

White Nile

Blue Nile

Ras Dashen Terara 15,157 ft (4,620 m) +

Gulf of Aden

Lake Assal -512 ft (-156 m) Lowest point in Africa ▼

Ethiopian Highlands

Somali Peninsula

*Upper Guinea*

Cape Palmas

Cameroon Mt. + 13,451 ft (4,100 m)

*Gulf of Guinea*

Adamawa

Ubangi

Congo

Lake Turkana

Mt. Kenya 17,057 ft (5,199 m) +

EQUATOR

Cape Lopez

Congo Basin

Kasai

Virunga Mts. 14,786 ft (4,507 m) +

Lake Victoria

GREAT RIFT VALLEY

Serengeti Plain

▲ Kilimanjaro 19,340 ft (5,895 m) Highest point in Africa

*Lower Guinea*

Katanga Plateau

Mitumba Mts.

L. Tanganyika

Lake Malawi

Zambezi

Mozambique Channel

Madagascar

*Atlantic Ocean*

**Physical**

▲ Highest point
▼ Lowest point
+ Other mountain peak

Namib Desert

TROPIC OF CAPRICORN

Kalahari Desert

Drakensberg

Orange

Thabana Ntlenyana + 11,425 ft (3,482 m)

*Indian Ocean*

0 — 800 Miles
0 — 800 Kilometers

*Azimuthal Equal-Area Projection*

Cape of Good Hope

Cape Agulhas

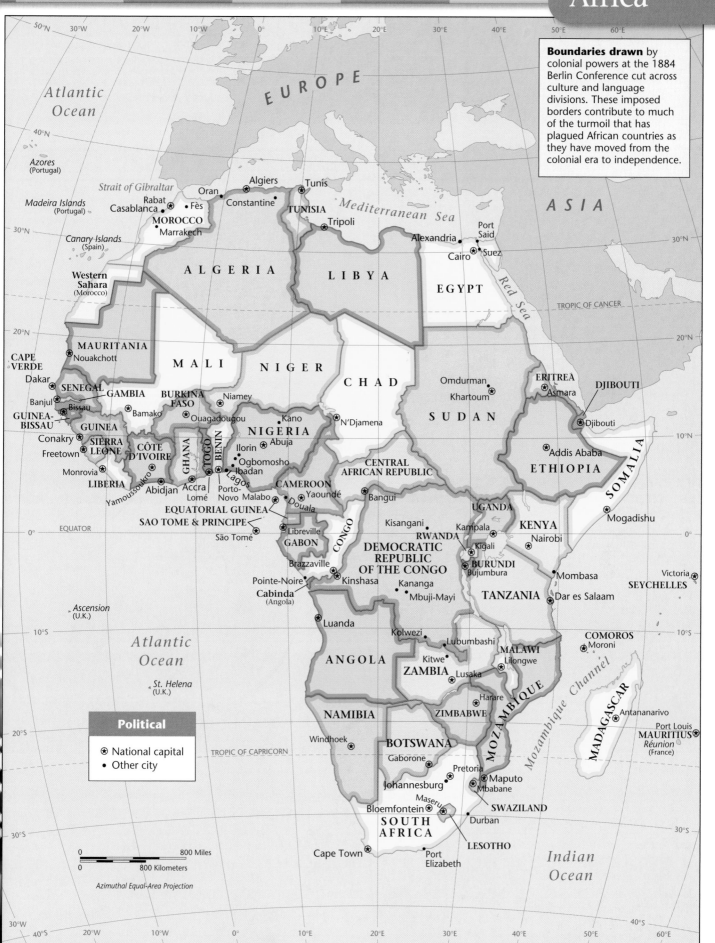

**Boundaries drawn** by colonial powers at the 1884 Berlin Conference cut across culture and language divisions. These imposed borders contribute to much of the turmoil that has plagued African countries as they have moved from the colonial era to independence.

**Political**

⊛ National capital
• Other city

0   800 Miles
0   800 Kilometers

Azimuthal Equal-Area Projection

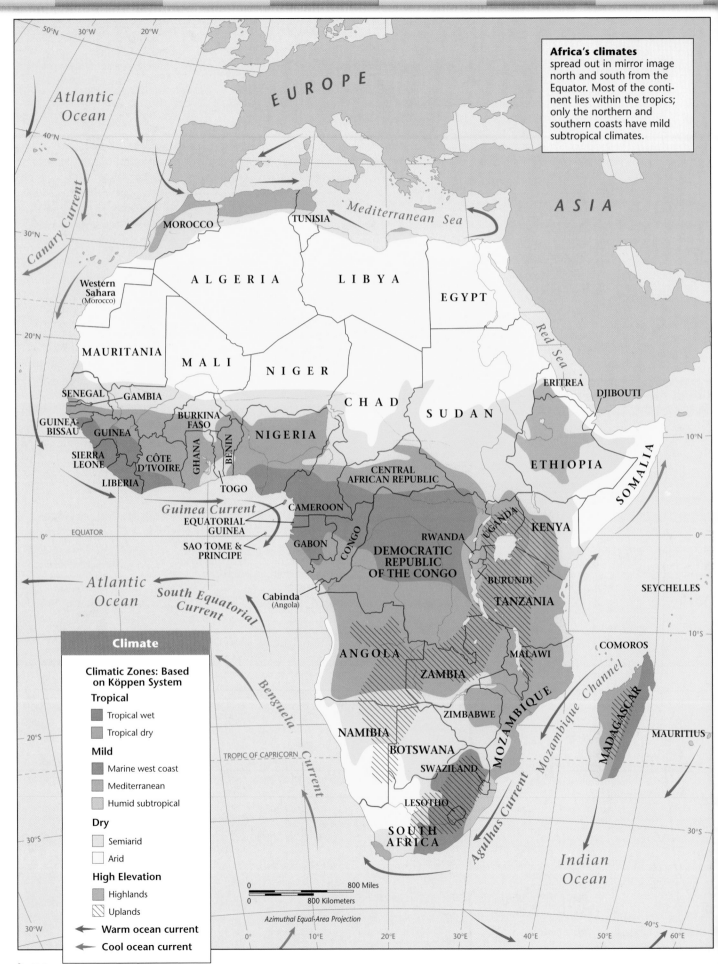

**Africa's climates**
spread out in mirror image north and south from the Equator. Most of the continent lies within the tropics; only the northern and southern coasts have mild subtropical climates.

EUROPE

ASIA

*Atlantic Ocean*

*Mediterranean Sea*

MOROCCO

TUNISIA

ALGERIA

LIBYA

EGYPT

Western Sahara (Morocco)

MAURITANIA

MALI

NIGER

CHAD

SUDAN

ERITREA

DJIBOUTI

SENEGAL

GAMBIA

GUINEA-BISSAU

GUINEA

BURKINA FASO

NIGERIA

ETHIOPIA

SOMALIA

SIERRA LEONE

CÔTE D'IVOIRE

GHANA

BENIN

CENTRAL AFRICAN REPUBLIC

LIBERIA

TOGO

*Guinea Current*

CAMEROON

EQUATORIAL GUINEA

SAO TOME & PRINCIPE

GABON

CONGO

DEMOCRATIC REPUBLIC OF THE CONGO

RWANDA

UGANDA

KENYA

BURUNDI

TANZANIA

SEYCHELLES

Cabinda (Angola)

EQUATOR

*Atlantic Ocean*

*South Equatorial Current*

ANGOLA

MALAWI

COMOROS

ZAMBIA

ZIMBABWE

MOZAMBIQUE

MADAGASCAR

MAURITIUS

NAMIBIA

BOTSWANA

SWAZILAND

*Mozambique Channel*

*Benguela Current*

TROPIC OF CAPRICORN

LESOTHO

SOUTH AFRICA

*Agulhas Current*

*Indian Ocean*

*Canary Current*

### Climate

**Climatic Zones: Based on Köppen System**

**Tropical**
- Tropical wet
- Tropical dry

**Mild**
- Marine west coast
- Mediterranean
- Humid subtropical

**Dry**
- Semiarid
- Arid

**High Elevation**
- Highlands
- Uplands

→ Warm ocean current
→ Cool ocean current

0        800 Miles
0        800 Kilometers

*Azimuthal Equal-Area Projection*

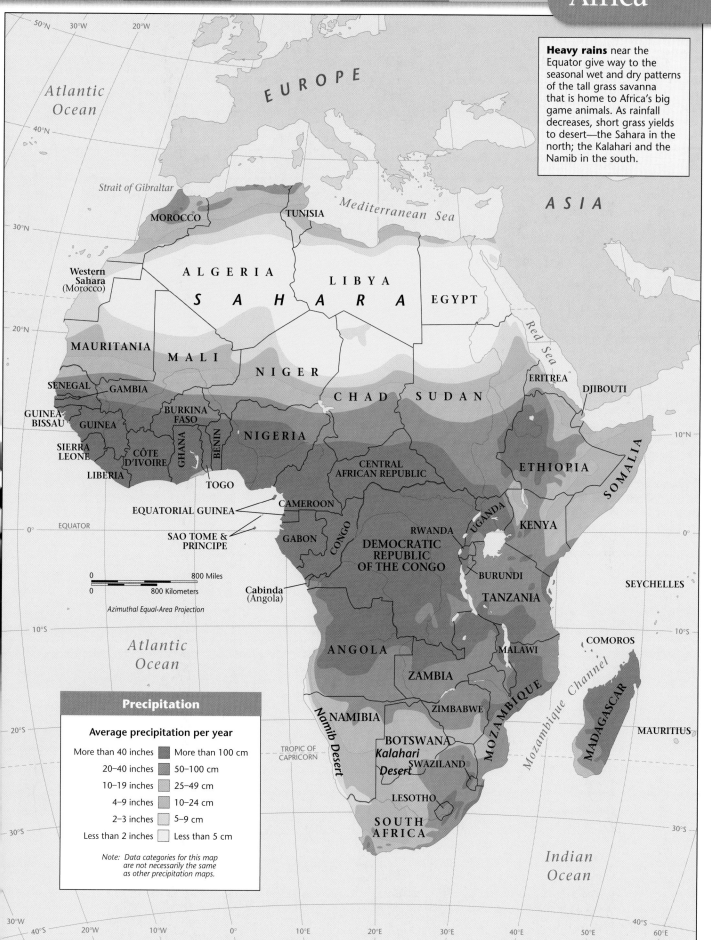

**Heavy rains** near the Equator give way to the seasonal wet and dry patterns of the tall grass savanna that is home to Africa's big game animals. As rainfall decreases, short grass yields to desert—the Sahara in the north; the Kalahari and the Namib in the south.

Atlantic Ocean

EUROPE

ASIA

Strait of Gibraltar

Mediterranean Sea

MOROCCO

TUNISIA

Western Sahara (Morocco)

ALGERIA

LIBYA

EGYPT

S A H A R A

Red Sea

MAURITANIA

MALI

NIGER

CHAD

SUDAN

ERITREA

DJIBOUTI

SENEGAL

GAMBIA

GUINEA-BISSAU

GUINEA

BURKINA FASO

NIGERIA

CENTRAL AFRICAN REPUBLIC

ETHIOPIA

SOMALIA

SIERRA LEONE

CÔTE D'IVOIRE

GHANA

BENIN

LIBERIA

TOGO

EQUATORIAL GUINEA

CAMEROON

SAO TOME & PRINCIPE

GABON

CONGO

DEMOCRATIC REPUBLIC OF THE CONGO

RWANDA

UGANDA

KENYA

BURUNDI

TANZANIA

SEYCHELLES

EQUATOR

Cabinda (Angola)

800 Miles

800 Kilometers

Azimuthal Equal-Area Projection

ANGOLA

MALAWI

COMOROS

ZAMBIA

Atlantic Ocean

Namib Desert

NAMIBIA

ZIMBABWE

MOZAMBIQUE

Mozambique Channel

MADAGASCAR

MAURITIUS

BOTSWANA

Kalahari Desert

SWAZILAND

TROPIC OF CAPRICORN

LESOTHO

SOUTH AFRICA

Indian Ocean

**Precipitation**

Average precipitation per year

| | |
|---|---|
| More than 40 inches | More than 100 cm |
| 20–40 inches | 50–100 cm |
| 10–19 inches | 25–49 cm |
| 4–9 inches | 10–24 cm |
| 2–3 inches | 5–9 cm |
| Less than 2 inches | Less than 5 cm |

*Note: Data categories for this map are not necessarily the same as other precipitation maps.*

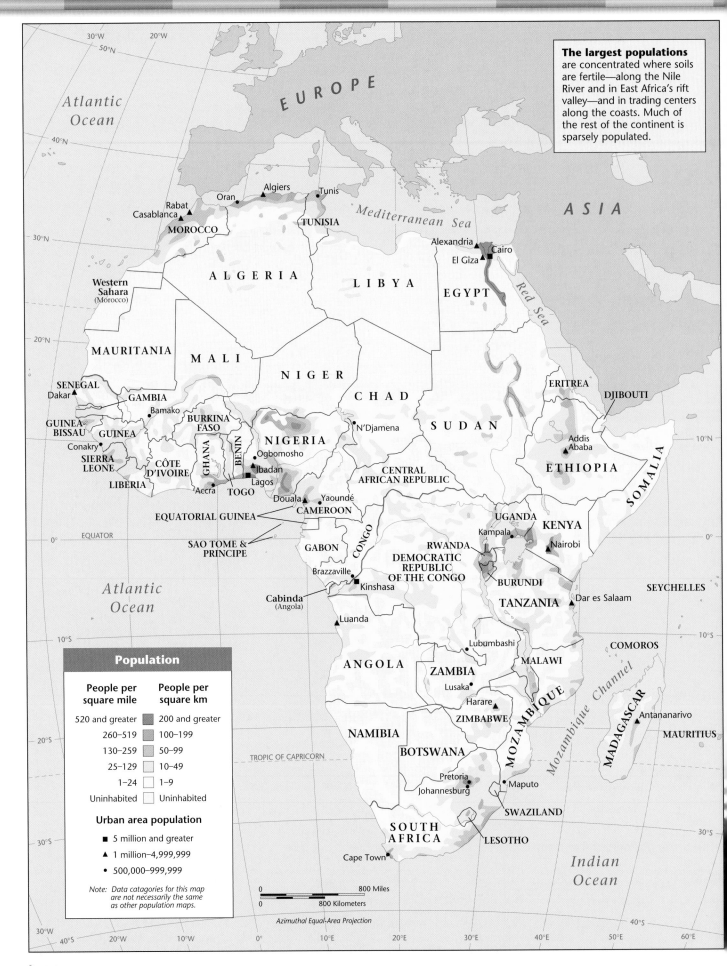

The largest populations are concentrated where soils are fertile—along the Nile River and in East Africa's rift valley—and in trading centers along the coasts. Much of the rest of the continent is sparsely populated.

**Population**

| People per square mile | | People per square km |
|---|---|---|
| 520 and greater | | 200 and greater |
| 260–519 | | 100–199 |
| 130–259 | | 50–99 |
| 25–129 | | 10–49 |
| 1–24 | | 1–9 |
| Uninhabited | | Uninhabited |

**Urban area population**

■ 5 million and greater
▲ 1 million–4,999,999
• 500,000–999,999

*Note: Data catagories for this map are not necessarily the same as other population maps.*

0   800 Miles
0   800 Kilometers

*Azimuthal Equal-Area Projection*

# Africa

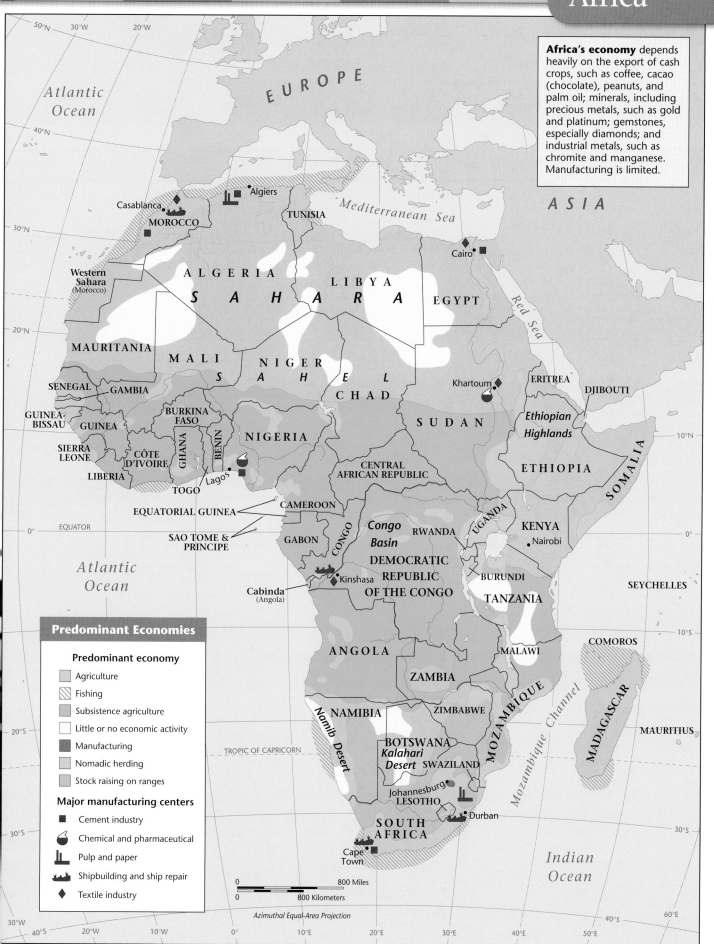

**Africa's economy** depends heavily on the export of cash crops, such as coffee, cacao (chocolate), peanuts, and palm oil; minerals, including precious metals, such as gold and platinum; gemstones, especially diamonds; and industrial metals, such as chromite and manganese. Manufacturing is limited.

Atlantic Ocean

EUROPE

ASIA

Mediterranean Sea

Algiers

Casablanca
MOROCCO

TUNISIA

Cairo

Western Sahara (Morocco)

ALGERIA

LIBYA

EGYPT

S A H A R A

Red Sea

MAURITANIA

MALI

NIGER

CHAD

SUDAN

ERITREA

DJIBOUTI

Khartoum

S A H E L

SENEGAL

GAMBIA

GUINEA-BISSAU

GUINEA

BURKINA FASO

*Ethiopian Highlands*

SIERRA LEONE

LIBERIA

CÔTE D'IVOIRE

GHANA

BENIN

NIGERIA

TOGO

Lagos

CAMEROON

CENTRAL AFRICAN REPUBLIC

ETHIOPIA

SOMALIA

EQUATORIAL GUINEA

SAO TOME & PRINCIPE

GABON

CONGO

*Congo Basin*

RWANDA

UGANDA

KENYA

Nairobi

EQUATOR

Atlantic Ocean

DEMOCRATIC REPUBLIC OF THE CONGO

BURUNDI

Kinshasa

Cabinda (Angola)

TANZANIA

SEYCHELLES

ANGOLA

MALAWI

COMOROS

ZAMBIA

MOZAMBIQUE

MADAGASCAR

NAMIBIA

ZIMBABWE

*Namib Desert*

BOTSWANA

*Kalahari Desert*

SWAZILAND

MAURITIUS

Mozambique Channel

TROPIC OF CAPRICORN

Johannesburg

LESOTHO

Durban

SOUTH AFRICA

Cape Town

Indian Ocean

## Predominant Economies

### Predominant economy

- Agriculture
- Fishing
- Subsistence agriculture
- Little or no economic activity
- Manufacturing
- Nomadic herding
- Stock raising on ranges

### Major manufacturing centers

- Cement industry
- Chemical and pharmaceutical
- Pulp and paper
- Shipbuilding and ship repair
- Textile industry

0 — 800 Miles
0 — 800 Kilometers

*Azimuthal Equal-Area Projection*

**30 million years before present**

**The Arabian Peninsula** and Africa were joined as one landmass 30 million years ago.

**7 million years before present**

ASIA

AFRICA

**Fiery-hot magma** rising from within Earth caused rifting that began to push apart the land along what is now the Red Sea.

**30 million years in the future**

ASIA

AFRICA

**Long, narrow lakes** could become a single channel if rifting continues and causes the Somali Plate to break away.

## FOCUS ON

# The Great Rift Valley

**M**ore than a hundred million years ago, Gondwana, the southern part of the supercontinent Pangaea, began to break apart. Landmasses that we know today as South America, Antarctica, Australia, and the Indian subcontinent slowly moved away, propelled by tectonic forces originating deep within Earth (see map page 14). The part of Gondwana that was left behind is what we know as Africa.

The forces that tore apart Gondwana continue today, especially in East Africa where the Great Rift Valley marks the boundary of what many earth scientists believe eventually will be a new sea that will separate part of eastern and southern Africa from the rest of the continent.

▶ **Volcanic cones,** *in the tiny country of Djibouti, mark the area where active tectonic rifting may someday result in the formation of a new ocean.*

▼ **Colorful flamingos** *are attracted to rift valley lakes, where high evaporation rates help create alkaline waters. The birds feed on brine shrimp and various kinds of algae.*

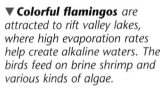

▶ **Subsistence farmers,** *many of them women, grow staple crops of maize (corn) and beans in the fertile volcanic soils. Large commercial farms produce cash crops, such as coffee and sisal.*

**Web Link** for information on the Great Rift: www.robinsonresearch.com/AFRICA/THE_LAND/Rift_Val.htm

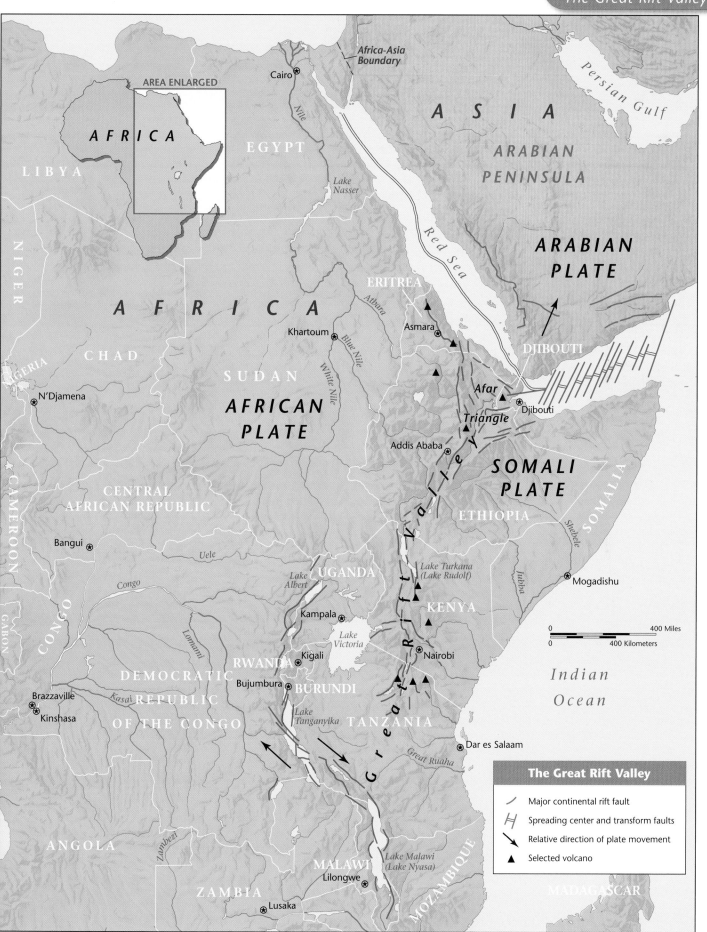

AREA ENLARGED

AFRICA

Africa-Asia Boundary

Cairo

Persian Gulf

LIBYA

EGYPT

ASIA

ARABIAN PENINSULA

NIGER

Nile

Lake Nasser

Red Sea

ARABIAN PLATE

AFRICA

Athara

ERITREA

Khartoum

Blue Nile

White Nile

Asmara

DJIBOUTI

CHAD

SUDAN

AFRICAN PLATE

Afar
Triangle

Djibouti

NIGERIA

N'Djamena

Addis Ababa

SOMALI PLATE

CAMEROON

CENTRAL AFRICAN REPUBLIC

ETHIOPIA

SOMALIA

Shebele

Bangui

Uele

Jubba

Mogadishu

CONGO

Congo

Lomami

Lake Albert

UGANDA

Lake Turkana (Lake Rudolf)

KENYA

GABON

Kampala

Lake Victoria

Kigali

Nairobi

RWANDA

Indian Ocean

Brazzaville

Kasai

DEMOCRATIC REPUBLIC

Bujumbura

BURUNDI

Kinshasa

OF THE CONGO

Lake Tanganyika

TANZANIA

Great Ruaha

Dar es Salaam

ANGOLA

Zambezi

MALAWI

Lake Malawi (Lake Nyasa)

MOZAMBIQUE

MADAGASCAR

ZAMBIA

Lilongwe

Lusaka

Great Rift Valley

| 0 | | | | 400 Miles |
| 0 | | | | 400 Kilometers |

### The Great Rift Valley

- Major continental rift fault
- Spreading center and transform faults
- Relative direction of plate movement
- ▲ Selected volcano

# Asia

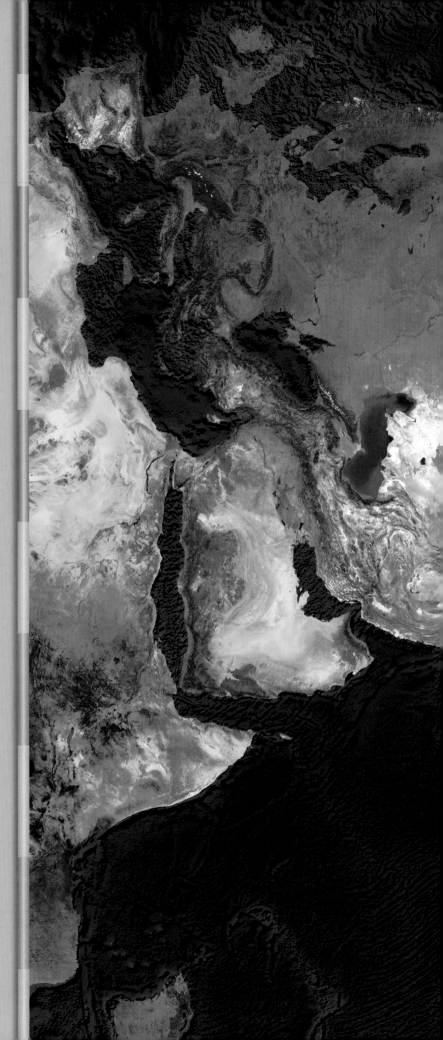

From the frozen shores of the Arctic Ocean to the equatorial islands of Indonesia, Asia stretches across 90 degrees of latitude. From the Ural Mountains to the Pacific Ocean it covers more than 150 degrees of longitude. Here, three of history's great culture hearths emerged in the valleys of the Tigris-Euphrates, the Indus, and the Yellow (Huang) Rivers. Today, Asia is home to more than 60 percent of Earth's people and some of the world's fastest growing economies.

## Facts & Figures

▶ **Land area:** 17,213,300 sq mi (44,579,000 sq km)

▶ **Population:** 3,684,490,000

▶ **Highest point:** Mount Everest, China-Nepal: 29,035 ft (8,850 m)

▶ **Lowest point:** Dead Sea, Israel-Jordan: 1,349 ft (411 m) below sea level

▶ **Longest river:** Yangtze (Chang), China: 3,964 mi (6,380 km)

▶ **Largest lake entirely in Asia:** Baikal, Russia: 12,163 sq mi (31,500 sq km)

▶ **Number of independent countries:** 46 (excluding Russia)

▶ **Largest country entirely in Asia:** China: 3,705,820 sq mi (9,598,032 sq km)

▶ **Smallest country:** Maldives: 115 sq mi (298 sq km)

▶ **Most populous country:** China: Pop. 1,264,536,000

▶ **Least populous country:** Maldives: Pop. 286,000

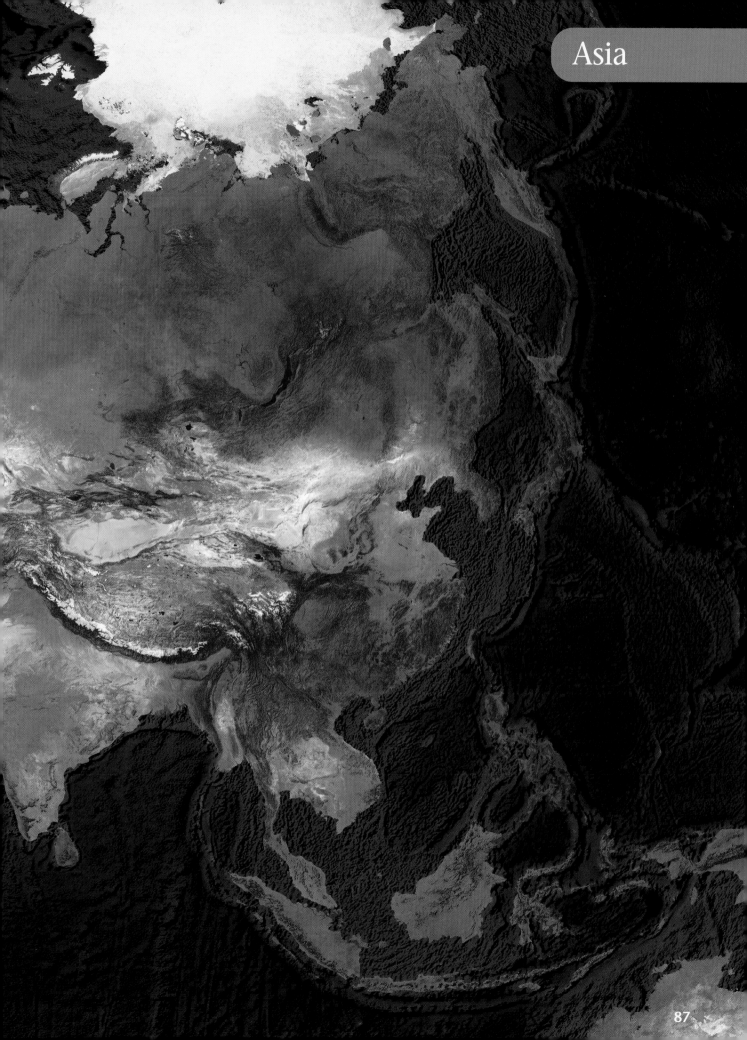

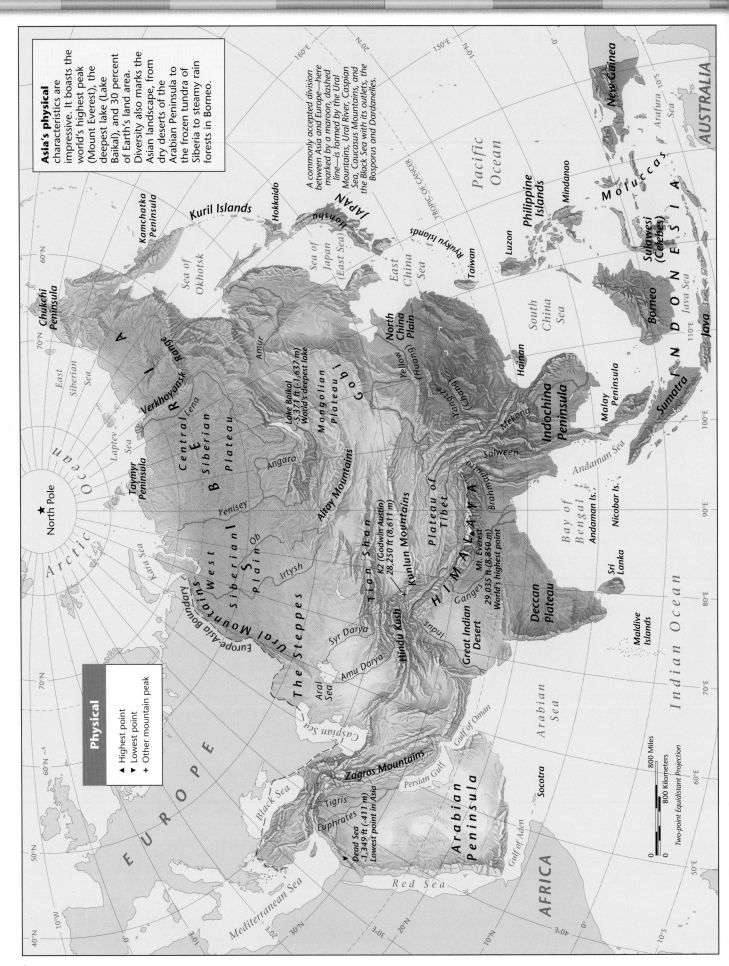

**Asia's physical** characteristics are impressive. It boasts the world's highest peak (Mount Everest), the deepest lake (Lake Baikal), and 30 percent of Earth's land area. Diversity also marks the Asian landscape, from dry deserts of the Arabian Peninsula to the frozen tundra of Siberia to steamy rain forests in Borneo.

A commonly accepted division between Asia and Europe—here marked by a maroon, dashed line—is formed by the Ural Mountains, Ural River, Caspian Sea, Caucasus Mountains, and the Black Sea with its outlets, the Bosporus and Dardanelles.

**Physical**

▲ Highest point
▼ Lowest point
+ Other mountain peak

800 Miles

800 Kilometers

Two-point Equidistant Projection

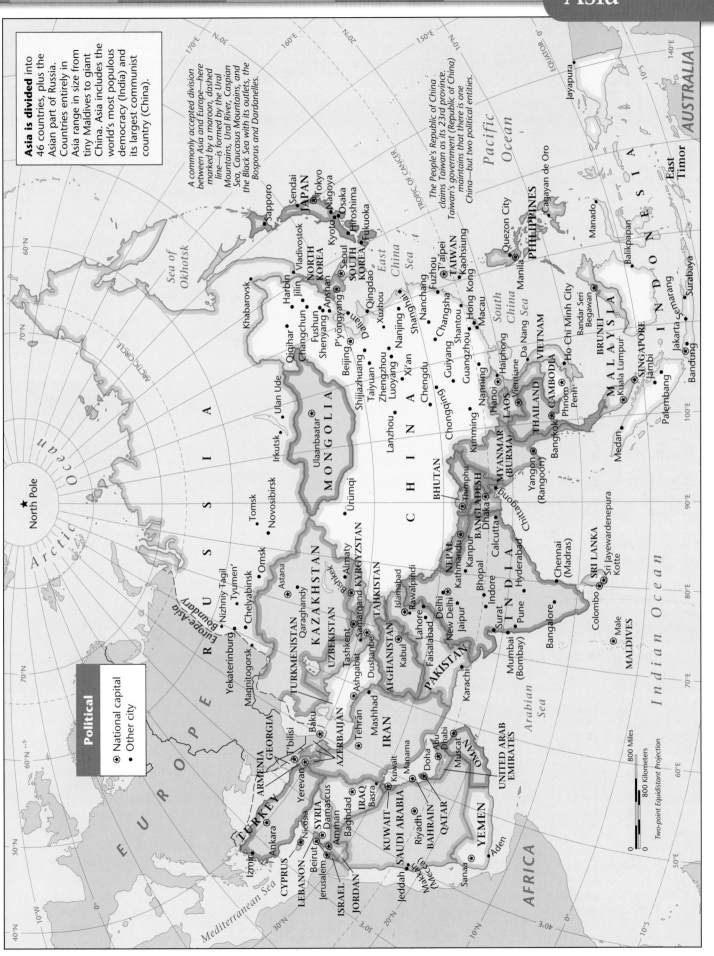

Asia is divided into 46 countries, plus the Asian part of Russia. Countries entirely in Asia range in size from tiny Maldives to giant China. Asia includes the world's most populous democracy (India) and its largest communist country (China).

A commonly accepted division between Asia and Europe—here marked by a maroon, dashed line—is formed by the Ural Mountains, Ural River, Caspian Sea, Caucasus Mountains, and the Black Sea with its outlets, the Bosporus and Dardanelles.

The People's Republic of China claims Taiwan as its 23rd province. Taiwan's government (Republic of China) maintains that there is one China—but two political entities.

**Political**

⊛ National capital
• Other city

North Pole

Two-point Equidistant Projection

800 Miles
800 Kilometers

89

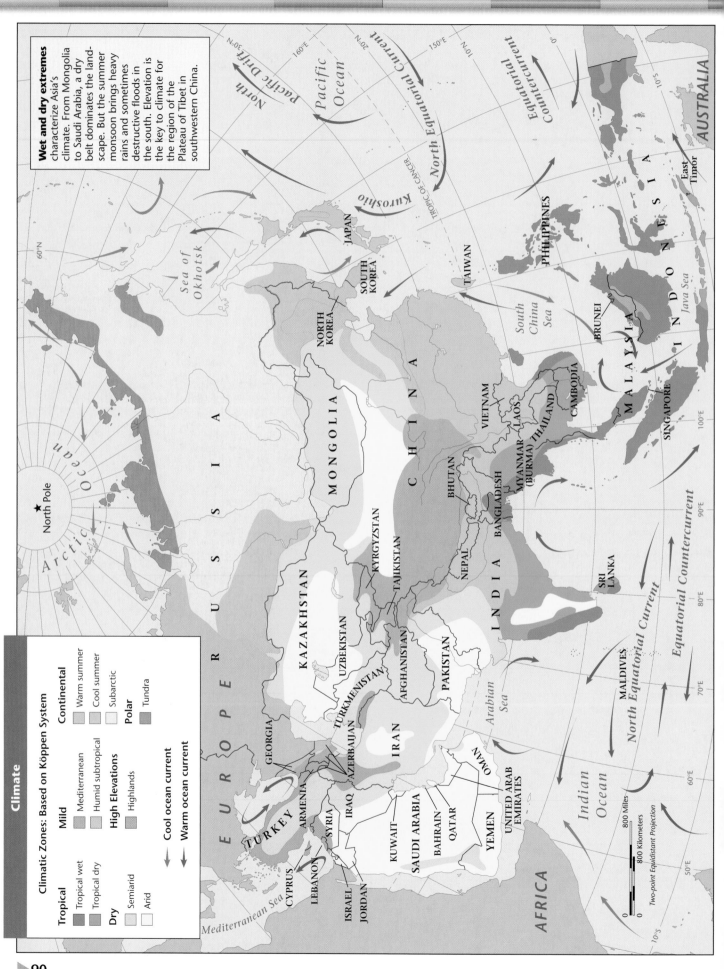

## Climate

### Climatic Zones: Based on Köppen System

**Tropical**
- Tropical wet
- Tropical dry

**Dry**
- Semiarid
- Arid

**Mild**
- Mediterranean
- Humid subtropical

**High Elevations**
- Highlands

**Continental**
- Warm summer
- Cool summer
- Subarctic

**Polar**
- Tundra

→ Cool ocean current
→ Warm ocean current

**Wet and dry extremes** characterize Asia's climate. From Mongolia to Saudi Arabia, a dry belt dominates the landscape. But the summer monsoon brings heavy rains and sometimes destructive floods in the south. Elevation is the key to climate for the region of the Plateau of Tibet in southwestern China.

Precipitation

**Abstract rainfall,** especially in summer, is typical of southern and southeastern Asia. Mawsynram, Assam, in eastern India, averages almost 470 inches (1,194 cm) of rain each year. In contrast, large areas of southwestern and interior Asia average less than 10 inches (25 cm) annually.

**Average precipitation per year**

- 39 inches and greater / 100 cm and greater
- 20–39 inches / 50–99 cm
- 10–19 inches / 25–49 cm
- 4–9 inches / 10–24 cm
- 2–3 inches / 5–9 cm
- Less than 2 inches / Less than 5 cm

*Note: Data categories for this map are not necessarily the same as other precipitation maps.*

North Pole

Arctic Ocean

Sea of Okhotsk

RUSSIA

EUROPE

JAPAN

SOUTH KOREA

NORTH KOREA

East China Sea

TAIWAN

Pacific Ocean

TROPIC OF CANCER

South China Sea

PHILIPPINES

MONGOLIA

BRUNEI

KAZAKHSTAN

CHINA

VIETNAM

CAMBODIA

LAOS

MYANMAR (BURMA)

THAILAND

MALAYSIA

INDONESIA

Java Sea

East Timor

AUSTRALIA

KYRGYZSTAN

TAJIKISTAN

UZBEKISTAN

BHUTAN

BANGLADESH

Mawsynram

SINGAPORE

NEPAL

INDIA

SRI LANKA

TURKMENISTAN

AFGHANISTAN

PAKISTAN

MALDIVES

GEORGIA

AZERBAIJAN

IRAN

Arabian Sea

ARMENIA

OMAN

Indian Ocean

TURKEY

SYRIA

IRAQ

KUWAIT

BAHRAIN

QATAR

UNITED ARAB EMIRATES

SAUDI ARABIA

YEMEN

CYPRUS

LEBANON

ISRAEL

JORDAN

Mediterranean Sea

AFRICA

800 Miles

800 Kilometers

Two-point Equidistant Projection

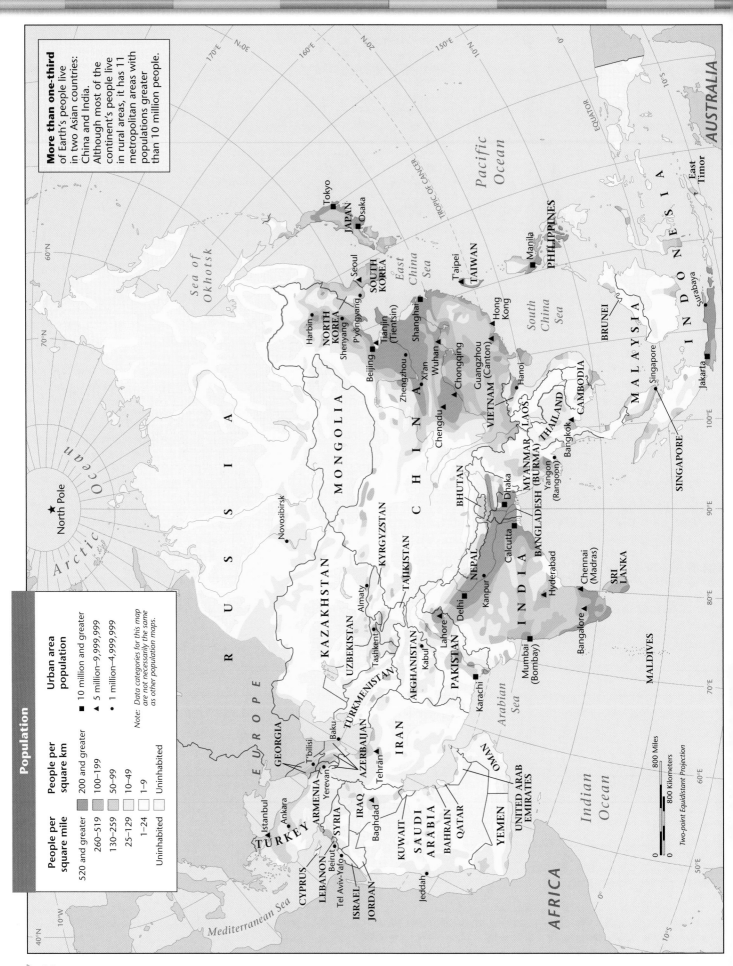

## Population

**People per square mile**

- 520 and greater
- 260–519
- 130–259
- 25–129
- 1–24
- Uninhabited

**People per square km**

- 200 and greater
- 100–199
- 50–99
- 10–49
- 1–9
- Uninhabited

**Urban area population**

- ■ 10 million and greater
- ▲ 5 million–9,999,999
- • 1 million–4,999,999

*Note: Data categories for this map are not necessarily the same as other population maps.*

**More than one-third** of Earth's people live in two Asian countries: China and India. Although most of the continent's people live in rural areas, it has 11 metropolitan areas with populations greater than 10 million people.

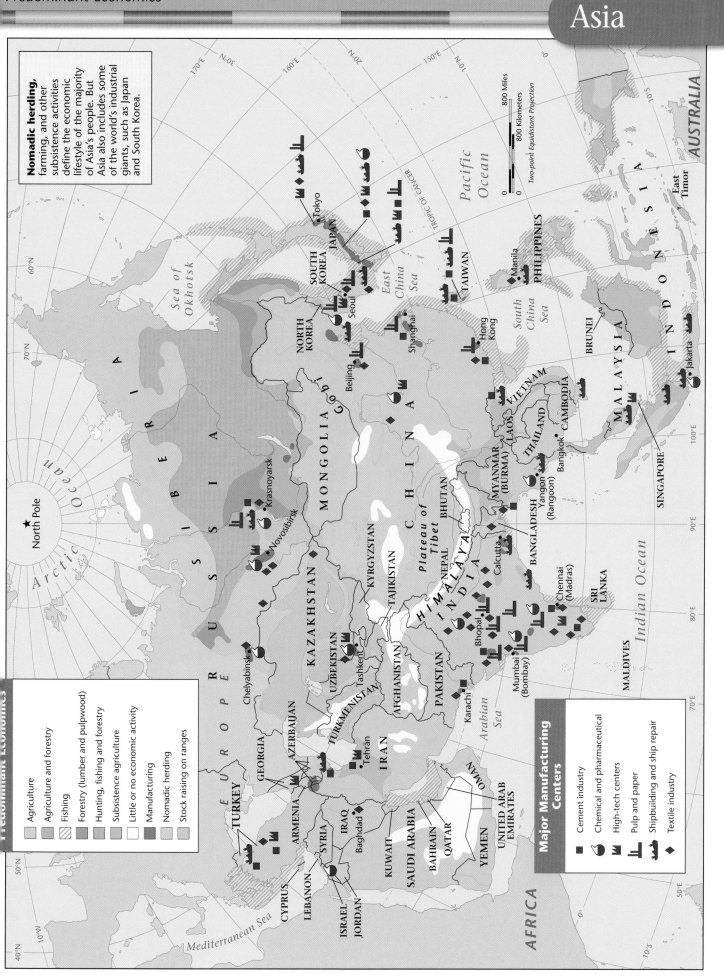

**Nomadic herding,** farming, and other subsistence activities define the economic lifestyle of the majority of Asia's people. But Asia also includes some of the world's industrial giants, such as Japan and South Korea.

800 Miles
800 Kilometers
Two-point Equidistant Projection

**Predominant Economies**

- Agriculture
- Agriculture and forestry
- Fishing
- Forestry (lumber and pulpwood)
- Hunting, fishing and forestry
- Subsistence agriculture
- Little or no economic activity
- Manufacturing
- Nomadic herding
- Stock raising on ranges

**Major Manufacturing Centers**

- Cement industry
- Chemical and pharmaceutical
- High-tech centers
- Pulp and paper
- Shipbuilding and ship repair
- Textile industry

North Pole

Arctic Ocean

SIBERIA

RUSSIA

Sea of Okhotsk

MONGOLIA

Gobi

KAZAKHSTAN

UZBEKISTAN

TURKMENISTAN

KYRGYZSTAN

TAJIKISTAN

AFGHANISTAN

PAKISTAN

CHINA

Plateau of Tibet

HIMALAYA

NEPAL

BHUTAN

INDIA

BANGLADESH

Calcutta

Chennai (Madras)

SRI LANKA

MALDIVES

Indian Ocean

MYANMAR (BURMA)

Yangon (Rangoon)

LAOS

THAILAND

Bangkok

CAMBODIA

VIETNAM

MALAYSIA

SINGAPORE

BRUNEI

INDONESIA

Jakarta

East Timor

AUSTRALIA

PHILIPPINES

Manila

Hong Kong

South China Sea

TAIWAN

East China Sea

Shanghai

Beijing

NORTH KOREA

SOUTH KOREA

Seoul

JAPAN

Tokyo

Pacific Ocean

TROPIC OF CANCER

Krasnoyarsk

Novosibirsk

Chelyabinsk

Tashkent

Karachi

Mumbai (Bombay)

Bhopal

Arabian Sea

Tehrān

IRAN

OMAN

UNITED ARAB EMIRATES

YEMEN

QATAR

BAHRAIN

SAUDI ARABIA

KUWAIT

IRAQ

Baghdad

JORDAN

ISRAEL

LEBANON

CYPRUS

SYRIA

TURKEY

ARMENIA

AZERBAIJAN

GEORGIA

EUROPE

Mediterranean Sea

AFRICA

# World Heritage Sites

In 1972, the United Nations Educational, Scientific and Cultural Organization (UNESCO) adopted a treaty, signed by more than 150 countries, dedicated to the preservation of cultural and natural sites of "outstanding universal value" that are "testimonies to an enduring past." These sites are designated as World Heritage Sites because they are part of the universal heritage of people everywhere.

Since much of human history is rooted in Asia, the continent is home to many of the best known World Heritage Sites, including the Taj Mahal, in India, and the temple complex at Angkor in Cambodia. Some of the world's endangered and vulnerable animals, such as the tiger and the komodo dragon, are native to Asia, and their habitats also are preserved as World Heritage Sites.

In December 1999, the World Heritage List included 630 sites in 118 countries. Among these, 148 sites are in Asian countries, including four in the part of Russia that lies east of the Ural Mountains.

▲ **Cappadocia,** a centuries-old complex of caves, dwellings, and Christian churches carved into ancient volcanic rock in central Turkey, is an example of a mixed World Heritage Site.

## World Heritage Sites

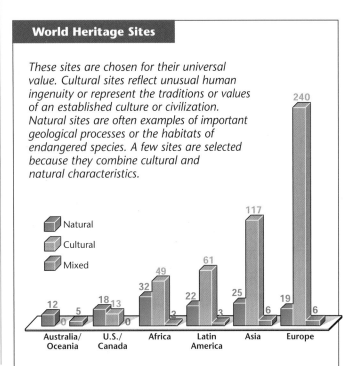

These sites are chosen for their universal value. Cultural sites reflect unusual human ingenuity or represent the traditions or values of an established culture or civilization. Natural sites are often examples of important geological processes or the habitats of endangered species. A few sites are selected because they combine cultural and natural characteristics.

Natural / Cultural / Mixed

Australia/Oceania 12, 5, 0; U.S./Canada 18, 13, 0; Africa 32, 49, 2; Latin America 22, 61, 3; Asia 25, 117, 6; Europe 19, 240, 6

▲ **Angkor Wat,** which is part of a cultural site in Cambodia, honors the Hindu god Vishnu. Nearby temples at Angkor Thom are Buddhist.

*Web Link* for information on World Heritage Sites: www.unesco.org/whc/

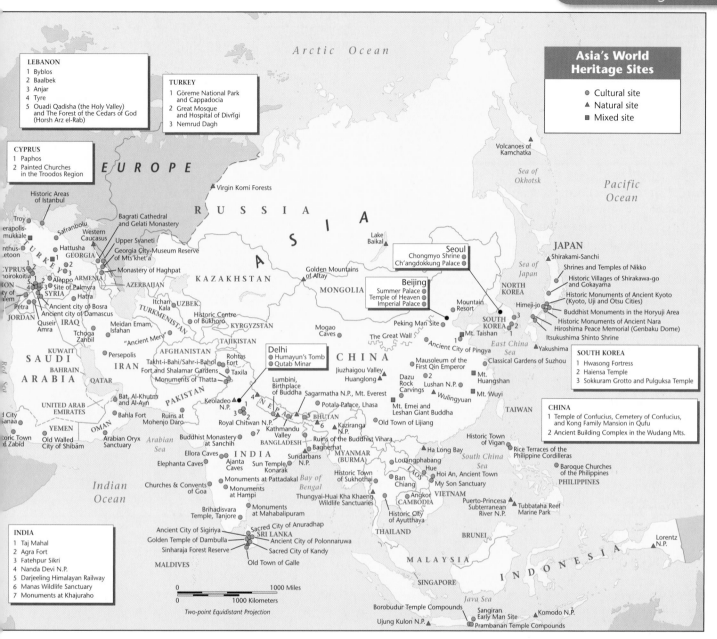

*Arctic Ocean*

**Asia's World Heritage Sites**
- ● Cultural site
- ▲ Natural site
- ■ Mixed site

**LEBANON**
1 Byblos
2 Baalbek
3 Anjar
4 Tyre
5 Ouadi Qadisha (the Holy Valley) and The Forest of the Cedars of God (Horsh Arz el-Rab)

**TURKEY**
1 Göreme National Park and Cappadocia
2 Great Mosque and Hospital of Divriği
3 Nemrud Dagh

**CYPRUS**
1 Paphos
2 Painted Churches in the Troodos Region

EUROPE

Virgin Komi Forests

Historic Areas of Istanbul

Troy
erapolis-mukkale
Hattusha
Safranbolu
Western Caucasus
Bagrati Cathedral and Gelati Monastery
Upper Svaneti
Georgia City-Museum Reserve of Mts'khet'a
Monastery of Haghpat

RUSSIA

ASIA

Lake Baikal

Golden Mountains of Altay

KAZAKHSTAN

MONGOLIA

**Seoul**
Chongmyo Shrine
Ch'angdokkung Palace

**Beijing**
Summer Palace
Temple of Heaven
Imperial Palace

JAPAN

Shirakami-Sanchi
Shrines and Temples of Nikko
Historic Villages of Shirakawa-go and Gokayama
Historic Monuments of Ancient Kyoto (Kyoto, Uji and Otsu Cities)
Buddhist Monuments in the Horyuji Area
Historic Monuments of Ancient Nara
Hiroshima Peace Memorial (Genbaku Dome)
Itsukushima Shinto Shrine

Sea of Japan

NORTH KOREA

SOUTH KOREA

Himeji-jo

Yakushima

Volcanoes of Kamchatka

Sea of Okhotsk

Pacific Ocean

**SOUTH KOREA**
1 Hwasong Fortress
2 Haiensa Temple
3 Sokkuram Grotto and Pulguksa Temple

GEORGIA
ARMENIA
CYPRUS
noirokoitia
AZERBAIJAN
Aleppo
SYRIA
Hatra
Ancient city of Bosra
Ancient city of Damascus

TURKMENISTAN
"Ancient Mery"
Itchan Kala
UZBEK.
Historic Centre of Bukhoro
KYRGYZSTAN
TAJIKISTAN

Mogao Caves
The Great Wall

Peking Man Site
Mountain Resort

Mt. Taishan
Ancient City of Pingya

Mausoleum of the First Qin Emperor
Classical Gardens of Suzhou

Mt. Huangshan

East China Sea

**CHINA**
1 Temple of Confucius, Cemetery of Confucius, and Kong Family Mansion in Qufu
2 Ancient Building Complex in the Wudang Mts.

Meidan Emam, Isfahan
Tchoga Zanbil
IRAQ

SAUDI ARABIA
KUWAIT
BAHRAIN
QATAR
IRAN
Persepolis

AFGHANISTAN
Takht-i-Bahi/Sahr-i-Bahol
Fort and Shalamar Gardens
Monuments of Thatta

Rohtas Fort
Taxila

**Delhi**
Humayun's Tomb
Qutab Minar

CHINA

Jiuzhaigou Valley
Huanglong
Dazu Rock Carvings
Lushan N.P.
Wulingyuan
Mt. Wuyi

Mt. Huangshan

TAIWAN

UNITED ARAB EMIRATES
Bat, Al-Khutm and Al-Ayn
Bahla Fort
QATAR

PAKISTAN
Keoladeo N.P.
Lumbini, Birthplace of Buddha
Sagarmatha N.P., Mt. Everest
Potala Palace, Lhasa

Mt. Emei and Leshan Giant Buddha

Old Town of Lijiang

Historic Town of Vigan

Rice Terraces of the Philippine Cordilleras

YEMEN
OMAN
Arabian Oryx Sanctuary
Old Walled City of Shibām

Ruins at Mohenjo Daro
Royal Chitwan N.P.

NEPAL

Buddhist Monastery at Sanchi

Kathmandu Valley

BHUTAN

Kaziranga N.P.

Ruins of the Buddhist Vihara
Bagerhat

BANGLADESH

Ha Long Bay
Louangphrabang

South China Sea

Baroque Churches of the Philippines

PHILIPPINES

Indian Ocean

Ellora Caves
Elephanta Caves
Churches & Convents of Goa

Ajanta Caves

INDIA

Sun Temple, Konarak

Monuments at Pattadakal
Monuments at Hampi

Sundarbans N.P.

MYANMAR (BURMA)

Bay of Bengal

Historic Town of Sukhothai
Ban Chiang

Hoi An, Ancient Town
My Son Sanctuary

Hue

LAOS

VIETNAM

Puerto-Princesa Subterranean River N.P.

Tubbataha Reef Marine Park

**INDIA**
1 Taj Mahal
2 Agra Fort
3 Fatehpur Sikri
4 Nanda Devi N.P.
5 Darjeeling Himalayan Railway
6 Manas Wildlife Sanctuary
7 Monuments at Khajuraho

Brihadisvara Temple, Tanjore
Monuments at Mahabalipuram

Ancient City of Sigiriya
Golden Temple of Dambulla
Sinharaja Forest Reserve

Thungyai-Huai Kha Khaeng Wildlife Sanctuaries
CAMBODIA
Angkor

Historic City of Ayutthaya

THAILAND

BRUNEI

Lorentz N.P.

SRI LANKA
Ancient City of Polonnaruwa
Sacred City of Anuradhap
Sacred City of Kandy
Old Town of Galle

MALDIVES

MALAYSIA

SINGAPORE

INDONESIA

Java Sea

Borobudur Temple Compounds
Ujung Kulon N.P.
Sangiran Early Man Site
Prambanan Temple Compounds
Komodo N.P.

0 ___ 1000 Miles
0 ___ 1000 Kilometers
*Two-point Equidistant Projection*

▲ **The Taj Mahal,** a cultural site in India, is an outstanding example of Muslim architecture in a country most often associated with Hinduism.

▲ **Tubbataha Reef Marine Park,** a natural site in the Philippines, is habitat for birds, sea turtles, and fish.

# Australia & Oceania

**S**mallest of Earth's great landmasses, Australia is the only continent that is both a continent and a country. It is part of the greater region of Oceania, which includes New Zealand, the eastern part of New Guinea, and hundreds of smaller islands scattered across the Pacific Ocean. Although Hawaii is politically part of the United States, geographically and culturally it is part of Oceania.

## Facts & Figures

- ▶ **Land area:** 3,284,000 sq mi (8,505,000 sq km)

- ▶ **Population:** 30,663,000

- ▶ **Highest point:** Mount Wilhelm, Papua New Guinea: 14,793 ft (4,509 m)

- ▶ **Lowest point:** Lake Eyre, Australia: 52 ft (16 m) below sea level

- ▶ **Longest river:** Murray-Darling, Australia: 2,911 mi (4,685 km)

- ▶ **Largest lake:** Lake Eyre, Australia: 3,430 sq mi (8,884 sq km)

- ▶ **Number of independent countries:** 14

- ▶ **Largest country:** Australia: 2,968,000 sq mi (7,687,000 sq km)

- ▶ **Smallest country:** Nauru: 8 sq mi (21 sq km)

- ▶ **Most populous country:** Australia: Pop. 19,195,000

- ▶ **Least populous country:** Nauru: Pop. 12,000

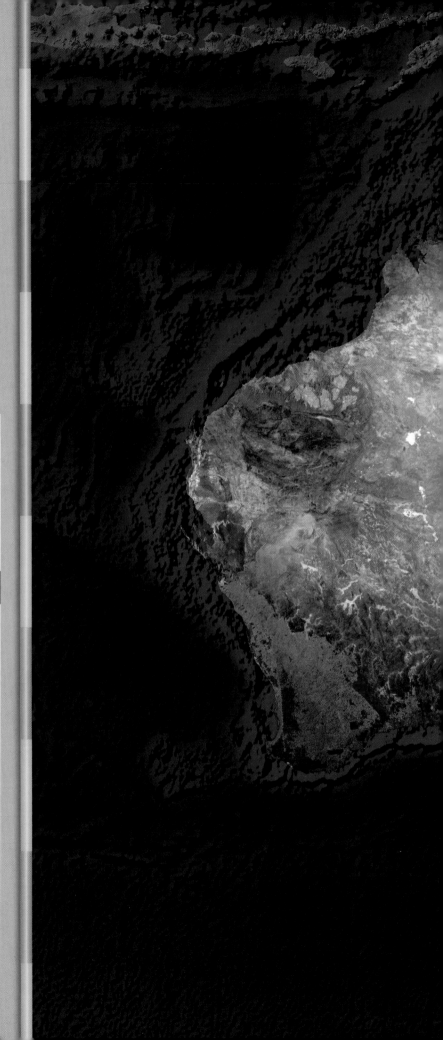

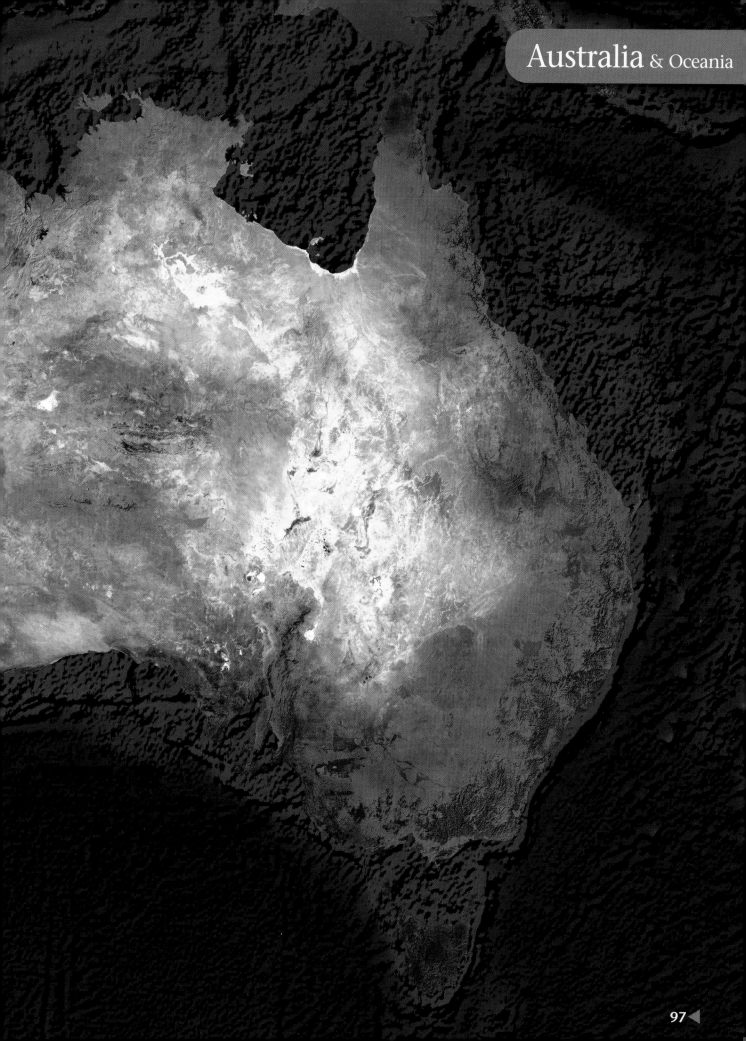

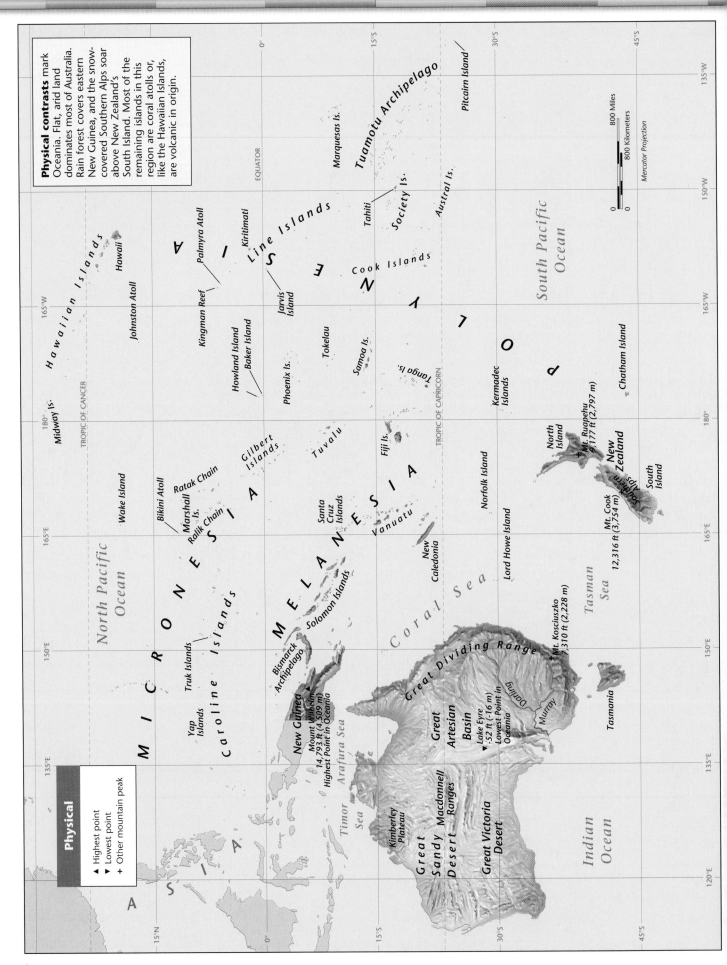

**Physical contrasts** mark Oceania. Flat, arid land dominates most of Australia. Rain forest covers eastern New Guinea, and the snow-covered Southern Alps soar above New Zealand's South Island. Most of the remaining islands in this region are coral atolls or, like the Hawaiian Islands, are volcanic in origin.

**Physical**

▲ Highest point
▼ Lowest point
+ Other mountain peak

800 Miles
800 Kilometers
Mercator Projection

EQUATOR

TROPIC OF CANCER

TROPIC OF CAPRICORN

North Pacific Ocean

South Pacific Ocean

Indian Ocean

Coral Sea

Tasman Sea

Arafura Sea

Timor Sea

MICRONESIA

MELANESIA

POLYNESIA

ASIA

Hawaiian Islands
Hawaii
Midway Is.
Johnston Atoll
Palmyra Atoll
Kingman Reef
Kiritimati
Line Islands
Marquesas Is.
Tuamotu Archipelago
Society Is.
Tahiti
Austral Is.
Pitcairn Island
Jarvis Island
Howland Island
Baker Island
Phoenix Is.
Tokelau
Cook Islands
Samoa Is.
Tonga Is.
Kermadec Islands
Wake Island
Bikini Atoll
Ratak Chain
Marshall Is.
Ralik Chain
Gilbert Islands
Tuvalu
Fiji Is.
Vanuatu
Santa Cruz Islands
Solomon Islands
New Caledonia
Norfolk Island
Lord Howe Island
Yap Islands
Truk Islands
Caroline Islands
Bismarck Archipelago
New Guinea
Mount Wilhelm
14,793 ft (4,509 m)
Highest Point in Oceania
North Island
Mt. Ruapehu
9,177 ft (2,797 m)
New Zealand
Southern Alps
South Island
Mt. Cook
12,316 ft (3,754 m)
Chatham Island
Tasmania
Great Dividing Range
Mt. Kosciuszko
7,310 ft (2,228 m)
Great Artesian Basin
Lake Eyre
-52 ft (-16 m)
Lowest Point in Oceania
Murray
Darling
Macdonnell Ranges
Great Sandy Desert
Great Victoria Desert
Kimberley Plateau

120°E  135°E  150°E  165°E  180°  165°W  150°W  135°W
15°N  0°  15°S  30°S  45°S

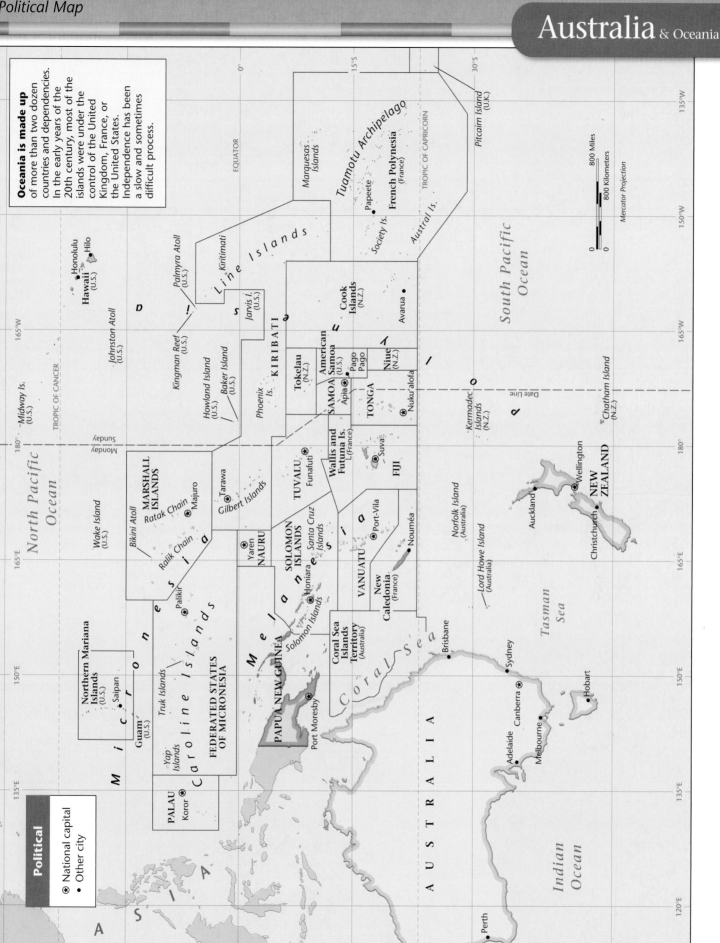

**Oceania is made up** of more than two dozen countries and dependencies. In the early years of the 20th century, most of the islands were under the control of the United Kingdom, France, or the United States. Independence has been a slow and sometimes difficult process.

**Political**

⊛ National capital
• Other city

North Pacific Ocean

South Pacific Ocean

Indian Ocean

Tasman Sea

Coral Sea

EQUATOR

TROPIC OF CANCER

TROPIC OF CAPRICORN

Date Line

Sunday / Monday

Monday / Sunday

800 Miles

800 Kilometers

Mercator Projection

M i c r o n e s i a

M e l a n e s i a

P o l y n e s i a

Hawaii (U.S.)
Honolulu
Hilo

Midway Is. (U.S.)

Johnston Atoll (U.S.)

Palmyra Atoll (U.S.)

Kingman Reef (U.S.)

Line Islands

Kiritimati

Jarvis I. (U.S.)

KIRIBATI

Howland Island (U.S.)

Baker Island (U.S.)

Phoenix Is.

Marquesas Islands

Tuamotu Archipelago

Papeete
Society Is.
French Polynesia (France)

Australis.

Austral Is.

Cook Islands (N.Z.)
Avarua

Niue (N.Z.)

American Samoa (U.S.)
Pago Pago

Tokelau (N.Z.)

SAMOA
Apia

TONGA
Nuku'alofa

Wallis and Futuna Is. (France)

TUVALU
Funafuti

FIJI
Suva

Wake Island (U.S.)

Bikini Atoll
Ratak Chain
Majuro
MARSHALL ISLANDS
Ralik Chain

Tarawa
Gilbert Islands

NAURU
Yaren

Pitcairn Island (U.K.)

Chatham Island (N.Z.)

Kermadec Islands (N.Z.)

NEW ZEALAND
Wellington
Auckland
Christchurch

Northern Mariana Islands (U.S.)
Saipan

Truk Islands

Guam (U.S.)

Yap Islands

Caroline Islands

FEDERATED STATES OF MICRONESIA

Palikir

PALAU
Koror

PAPUA NEW GUINEA
Port Moresby

Solomon Islands

SOLOMON ISLANDS
Honiara

Santa Cruz Islands

VANUATU
Port-Vila

New Caledonia (France)
Nouméa

Norfolk Island (Australia)

Lord Howe Island (Australia)

Coral Sea Islands Territory (Australia)

AUSTRALIA

Perth

Adelaide

Canberra
Melbourne
Sydney
Brisbane

Hobart

A S I A

135°E  150°E  165°E  180°  165°W  150°W  135°W

15°N  0°  15°S  30°S  45°S

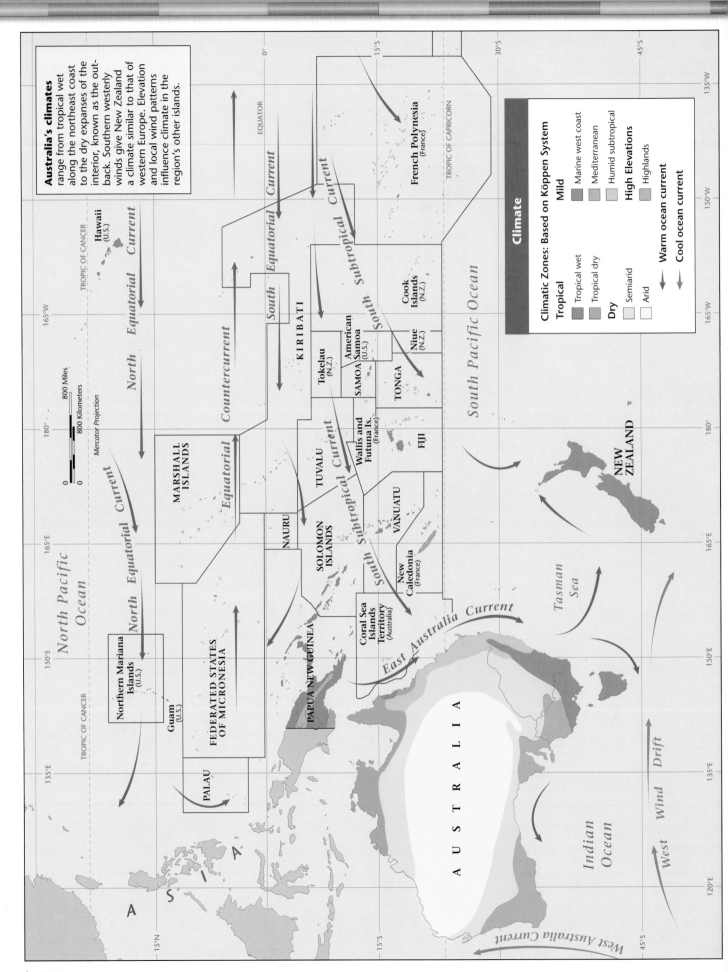

**Australia's climates** range from tropical wet along the northeast coast to the dry expanses of the interior, known as the outback. Southern westerly winds give New Zealand a climate similar to that of western Europe. Elevation and local wind patterns influence climate in the region's other islands.

**Climate**

Climatic Zones: Based on Köppen System

**Tropical**
- Tropical wet
- Tropical dry

**Dry**
- Semiarid
- Arid

**Mild**
- Marine west coast
- Mediterranean
- Humid subtropical

**High Elevations**
- Highlands

→ Warm ocean current
→ Cool ocean current

Mercator Projection

0    800 Miles
0    800 Kilometers

TROPIC OF CANCER

EQUATOR

TROPIC OF CAPRICORN

*North Pacific Ocean*

*South Pacific Ocean*

*Indian Ocean*

*Tasman Sea*

Hawaii (U.S.)

French Polynesia (France)

Cook Islands (N.Z.)

Niue (N.Z.)

KIRIBATI

Tokelau (N.Z.)

American Samoa (U.S.)

SAMOA

TONGA

TUVALU

Wallis and Futuna Is. (France)

FIJI

MARSHALL ISLANDS

NAURU

SOLOMON ISLANDS

VANUATU

New Caledonia (France)

Coral Sea Islands Territory (Australia)

PAPUA NEW GUINEA

FEDERATED STATES OF MICRONESIA

Guam (U.S.)

Northern Mariana Islands (U.S.)

PALAU

A S I A

AUSTRALIA

NEW ZEALAND

*North Equatorial Current*

*North Equatorial Current*

*Equatorial Countercurrent*

*South Equatorial Current*

*South Equatorial Current*

*South Subtropical Current*

*South Subtropical Current*

*South Subtropical Current*

*East Australia Current*

*West Australia Current*

*West Wind Drift*

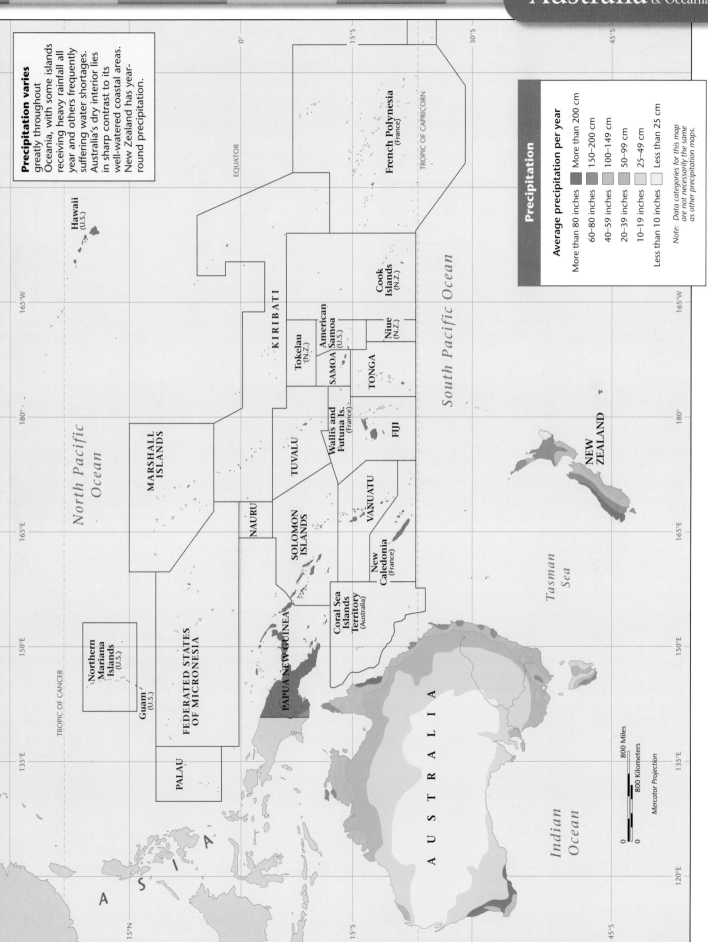

**Precipitation varies** greatly throughout Oceania, with some islands receiving heavy rainfall all year and others frequently suffering water shortages. Australia's dry interior lies in sharp contrast to its well-watered coastal areas. New Zealand has year-round precipitation.

**Precipitation**

**Average precipitation per year**

| | |
|---|---|
| More than 80 inches | More than 200 cm |
| 60–80 inches | 150–200 cm |
| 40–59 inches | 100–149 cm |
| 20–39 inches | 50–99 cm |
| 10–19 inches | 25–49 cm |
| Less than 10 inches | Less than 25 cm |

*Note: Data categories for this map are not necessarily the same as other precipitation maps.*

EQUATOR

TROPIC OF CAPRICORN

TROPIC OF CANCER

Hawaii (U.S.)

French Polynesia (France)

Cook Islands (N.Z.)

KIRIBATI

American Samoa (U.S.)

Tokelau (N.Z.)

SAMOA

Niue (N.Z.)

TONGA

Wallis and Futuna Is. (France)

FIJI

TUVALU

MARSHALL ISLANDS

NAURU

SOLOMON ISLANDS

VANUATU

New Caledonia (France)

Northern Mariana Islands (U.S.)

Guam (U.S.)

FEDERATED STATES OF MICRONESIA

Coral Sea Islands Territory (Australia)

PAPUA NEW GUINEA

PALAU

ASIA

North Pacific Ocean

South Pacific Ocean

NEW ZEALAND

Tasman Sea

AUSTRALIA

Indian Ocean

800 Miles

800 Kilometers

Mercator Projection

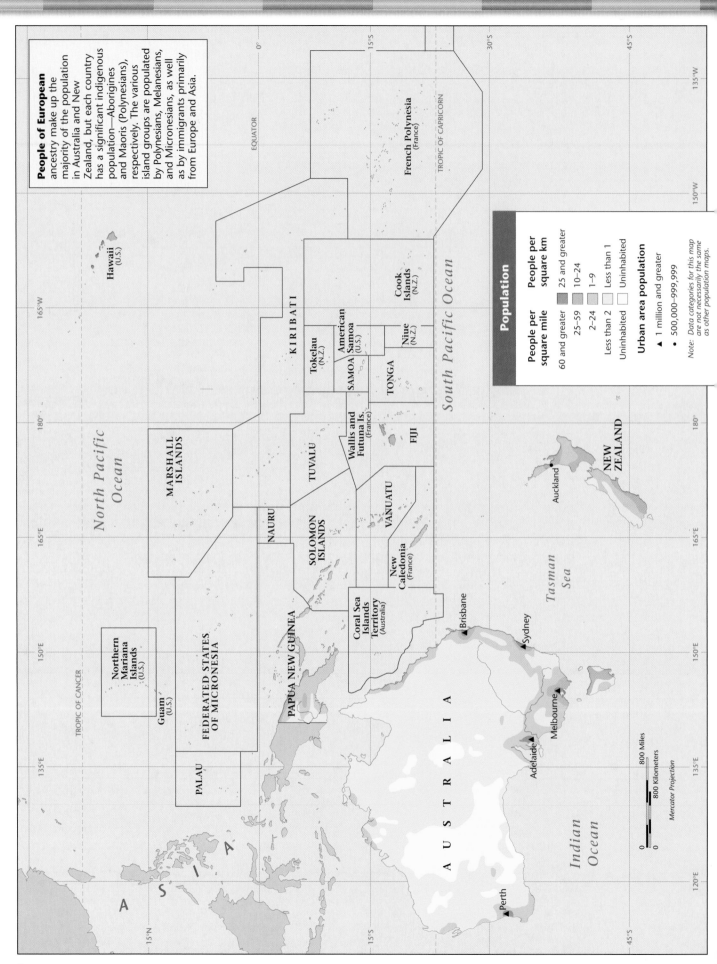

**People of European** ancestry make up the majority of the population in Australia and New Zealand, but each country has a significant indigenous population—Aborigines and Maoris (Polynesians), respectively. The various island groups are populated by Polynesians, Melanesians, and Micronesians, as well as by immigrants primarily from Europe and Asia.

Hawaii (U.S.)

KIRIBATI

Tokelau (N.Z.)

American Samoa (U.S.)

SAMOA

TONGA

Niue (N.Z.)

Cook Islands (N.Z.)

French Polynesia (France)

TROPIC OF CAPRICORN

South Pacific Ocean

MARSHALL ISLANDS

TUVALU

Wallis and Futuna Is. (France)

FIJI

VANUATU

NAURU

SOLOMON ISLANDS

New Caledonia (France)

NEW ZEALAND

Auckland

North Pacific Ocean

Northern Mariana Islands (U.S.)

Guam (U.S.)

FEDERATED STATES OF MICRONESIA

PALAU

PAPUA NEW GUINEA

Coral Sea Islands Territory (Australia)

Tasman Sea

Brisbane

Sydney

Melbourne

Adelaide

ASIA

A U S T R A L I A

Perth

Indian Ocean

**Population**

**People per square mile**
- 60 and greater
- 25–59
- 2–24
- Less than 2
- Uninhabited

**People per square km**
- 25 and greater
- 10–24
- 1–9
- Less than 1
- Uninhabited

**Urban area population**
- ▲ 1 million and greater
- ● 500,000–999,999

*Note: Data categories for this map are not necessarily the same as other population maps.*

0          800 Miles
0          800 Kilometers
Mercator Projection

TROPIC OF CANCER

EQUATOR

# Australia & Oceania

**Primary economic** products make up much of the market in Oceania. New Zealand and Australia account for almost two-thirds of world wool exports and more than one-fifth of beef exports. Plantation agriculture, fishing, tourism, or mining form the economic base in most of the small island countries. For example, New Caledonia is a leading exporter of nickel, and Fiji exports sugar and gold.

## Predominant Economies

**Predominant economy**

- Agriculture
- Fishing
- Hunting, fishing and forestry
- Subsistence agriculture
- Little or no economic activity
- Manufacturing
- Stock raising on ranges

**Major manufacturing centers**

- High-tech centers
- Pulp and paper
- Shipbuilding and ship repair

EQUATOR

TROPIC OF CANCER

TROPIC OF CAPRICORN

North Pacific Ocean

South Pacific Ocean

Indian Ocean

Tasman Sea

Coral Sea Islands Territory (Australia)

Hawaii (U.S.)

French Polynesia (France)

Cook Islands (N.Z.)

KIRIBATI

Tokelau (N.Z.)

American Samoa (U.S.)

SAMOA

Niue (N.Z.)

TONGA

Wallis and Futuna Is. (France)

FIJI

TUVALU

MARSHALL ISLANDS

NAURU

SOLOMON ISLANDS

VANUATU

New Caledonia (France)

Northern Mariana Islands (U.S.)

Guam (U.S.)

FEDERATED STATES OF MICRONESIA

PALAU

PAPUA NEW GUINEA

Port Moresby

A S I A

A U S T R A L I A

Perth

Adelaide

Melbourne

Canberra

Sydney

Brisbane

NEW ZEALAND

Auckland

Wellington

800 Miles

800 Kilometers

Mercator Projection

165°W

180°

165°E

150°E

135°E

120°E

135°W

180°

150°E

135°E

0°

15°S

30°S

15°N

15°S

45°S

103

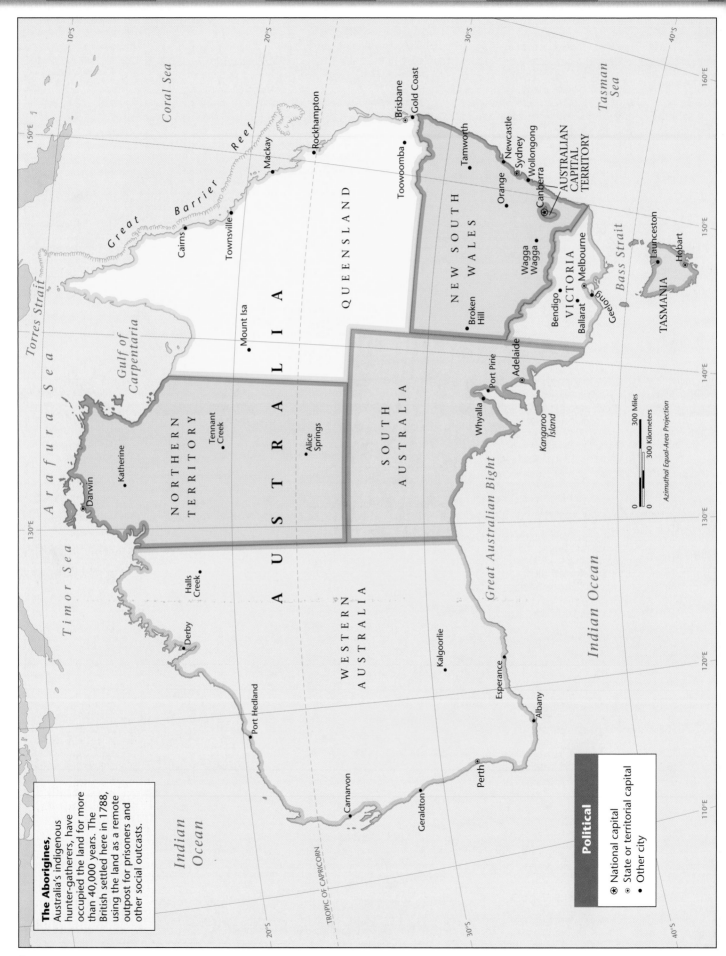

**The Aborigines,** Australia's indigenous hunter-gatherers, have occupied the land for more than 40,000 years. The British settled here in 1788, using the land as a remote outpost for prisoners and other social outcasts.

Coral Sea

Great Barrier Reef

Torres Strait

Arafura Sea

Gulf of Carpentaria

Timor Sea

Tasman Sea

Bass Strait

Great Australian Bight

Indian Ocean

Indian Ocean

Rockhampton
Mackay
Cairns
Townsville
Mount Isa
Brisbane
Gold Coast
Toowoomba
Tamworth
Newcastle
Sydney
Wollongong
Orange
Canberra

AUSTRALIAN CAPITAL TERRITORY

NEW SOUTH WALES

QUEENSLAND

Wagga Wagga
Broken Hill
Bendigo
Ballarat
Melbourne
Geelong

VICTORIA

Launceston
Hobart

TASMANIA

Adelaide
Port Pirie
Whyalla

SOUTH AUSTRALIA

Kangaroo Island

Katherine
Darwin

NORTHERN TERRITORY

Tennant Creek
Alice Springs

A U S T R A L I A

Halls Creek
Derby

WESTERN AUSTRALIA

Kalgoorlie
Esperance
Albany
Port Hedland
Carnarvon
Geraldton
Perth

TROPIC OF CAPRICORN

300 Miles
300 Kilometers
*Azimuthal Equal-Area Projection*

**Political**

⊛ National capital
⊙ State or territorial capital
• Other city

10°S · 20°S · 30°S · 40°S

150°E · 160°E · 130°E · 120°E · 110°E · 140°E

▶ **104**

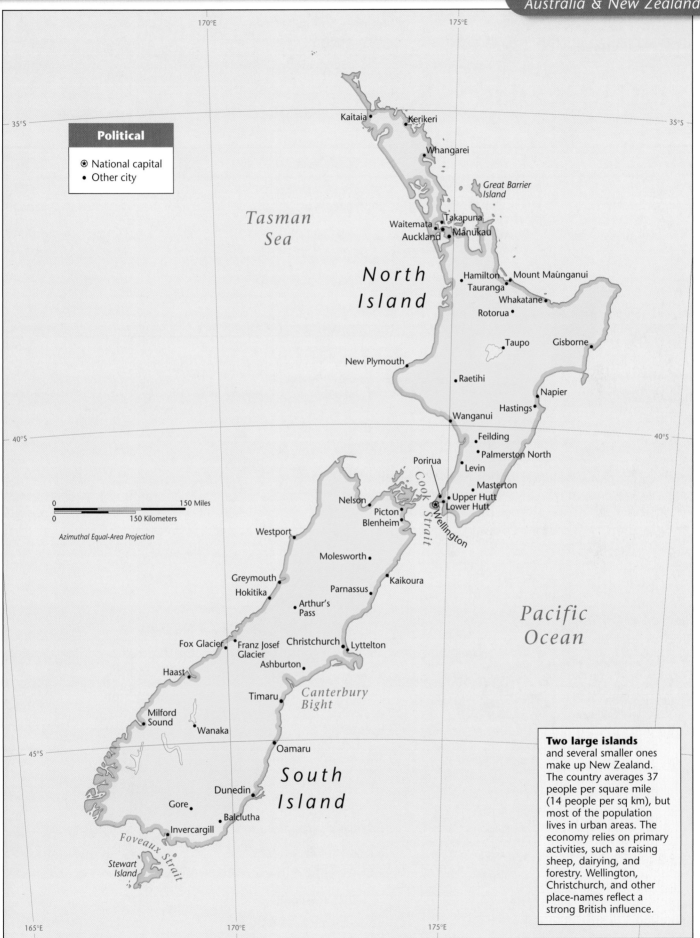

**Political**

⊛ National capital
• Other city

Tasman
Sea

Kaitaia
Kerikeri

Whangarei

Great Barrier
Island

Takapuna
Waitemata
Auckland    Manukau

North
Island

Hamilton    Mount Maunganui
Tauranga
Whakatane
Rotorua

Taupo    Gisborne

New Plymouth

Raetihi

Napier
Hastings

Wanganui

Feilding

Palmerston North

Porirua    Levin

Masterton

Cook Strait

Nelson    Upper Hutt
Lower Hutt
Picton
Blenheim    Wellington

Westport

Molesworth

Greymouth    Kaikoura
Hokitika    Parnassus

Arthur's
Pass

Pacific
Ocean

Fox Glacier    Christchurch    Lyttelton
Franz Josef
Glacier
Ashburton

Haast

Timaru    Canterbury
Bight

Milford
Sound
Wanaka

Oamaru

South
Island

Dunedin
Gore
Balclutha
Invercargill

Foveaux Strait

Stewart
Island

0                    150 Miles
0              150 Kilometers

Azimuthal Equal-Area Projection

35°S    35°S

40°S    40°S

45°S

170°E    175°E

165°E    170°E    175°E

**Two large islands**
and several smaller ones
make up New Zealand.
The country averages 37
people per square mile
(14 people per sq km), but
most of the population
lives in urban areas. The
economy relies on primary
activities, such as raising
sheep, dairying, and
forestry. Wellington,
Christchurch, and other
place-names reflect a
strong British influence.

# Time Zones & the Date Line

The *Fiji Times,* a newspaper published in Suva, capital of the Fiji Islands, carries the message "The First Newspaper Published in the World Today" on the front page of each edition. How can this newspaper from a small island country make such a claim? Fiji and most of the other islands that make up Oceania, including Australia and New Zealand, lie west of the date line, an invisible boundary designated to mark the beginning of each new day. The date line is just part of the system we have adopted to keep track of the passage of days.

For most of human history, people determined time by observing the position of the sun in the sky. Slight differences in time did not matter until, in the mid-19th century, the spread of railroads and telegraph lines changed forever the importance of time. High-speed transportation and communications required schedules, and schedules required that everyone agree on the time.

In 1884, an international conference, convened in Washington, D.C., established an international system of 24 time zones based on the fact that Earth turns from west to east 15 degrees of longitude every hour. Each time zone has a central meridian and is 15 degrees wide, 7½ degrees to either side of the named central meridian.

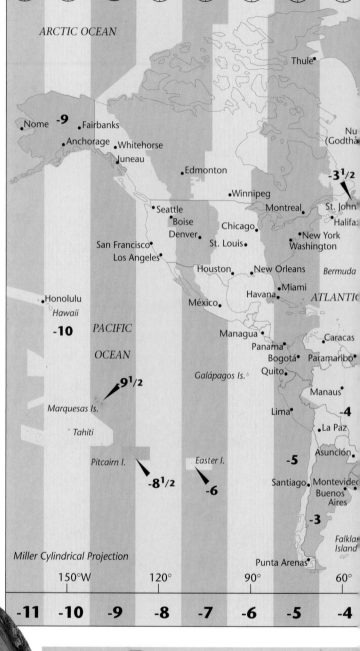

▶ **The prime meridian's** path is lit up by light bulbs strung across Greenwich Park just north of the Royal Observatory, in England. The photographer used a special lens called a fish-eye to make the park resemble a globe. Of course, on the real Earth, meridians and parallels (lines of longitude and latitude) are imaginary and cannot be seen.

▲ **A system of standard time** put trains on schedules, which helped reduce the chance of collisions and the loss of lives and property caused by them.

Web Link for information on time zones: http://tycho.usno.navy.mil/tzones.html

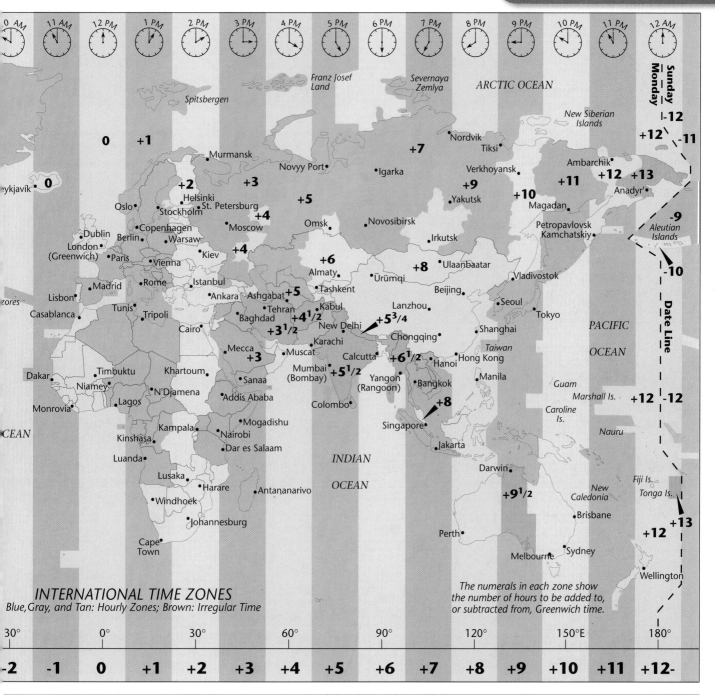

| 10 AM | 11 AM | 12 PM | 1 PM | 2 PM | 3 PM | 4 PM | 5 PM | 6 PM | 7 PM | 8 PM | 9 PM | 10 PM | 11 PM | 12 AM |

**ARCTIC OCEAN**

Franz Josef Land

Severnaya Zemlya

Spitsbergen

New Siberian Islands

Sunday / Monday

| -12 |

**0**    **+1**

•Murmansk

+12 / -11

Nordvik•  •Tiksi

Ambarchik•

+12 +13

Anadyr'•

•Reykjavík **0**

Novyy Port•  •Igarka

Verkhoyansk•

+11

**+2**   **+3**

**+7**

**+9**

**+10**

+12 +13

-9

Aleutian Islands

Oslo•  •Helsinki  •St. Petersburg

•Yakutsk

Magadan•

Stockholm•

**+5**

•Omsk  •Novosibirsk

Petropavlovsk Kamchatskiy•

-10

•Copenhagen **+4**  •Moscow

•Irkutsk

•Vladivostok

London (Greenwich)•  •Berlin  •Warsaw

**+4**

**+6**

**+8**  •Ulaanbaatar

•Seoul

Date Line

•Dublin  Paris•  •Vienna  •Kiev

Almaty•

•Ürümqi

•Beijing

•Tokyo

**PACIFIC**

•Madrid  •Rome  •Istanbul  •Ankara  Ashgabat•  **+5**  •Tashkent

Lanzhou•

•Shanghai

**OCEAN**

Lisbon•  Tunis•  Tehran•  **+4 1/2**  •Kabul

•Chongqing

Casablanca•  •Tripoli  Baghdad•  **+3 1/2**  New Delhi•  **+5 3/4**

Taiwan•

Cairo•  •Karachi

Calcutta•  **+6 1/2**  •Hong Kong

•Hanoi

Mecca•  •Muscat

Mumbai (Bombay)•  **+5 1/2**

Yangon (Rangoon)•  •Bangkok

•Manila

Guam•

Marshall Is.

+12 -12

Dakar•  •Timbuktu  Khartoum•  •Sanaa  Colombo•

**+8**

Caroline Is.

Niamey•  N'Djamena•  •Addis Ababa

•Singapore

Nauru

Monrovia•  •Lagos  •Mogadishu

•Jakarta

Kampala•  •Nairobi

Darwin•

OCEAN

Kinshasa•  •Dar es Salaam

**INDIAN**

Luanda•

**OCEAN**

Fiji Is.

Lusaka•  Antananarivo•

New Caledonia

Tonga Is.

+12 +13

Harare•

•Windhoek

**+9 1/2**

•Brisbane

•Johannesburg

Perth•

+12

Cape Town•

Melbourne•  •Sydney

•Wellington

## INTERNATIONAL TIME ZONES
Blue, Gray, and Tan: Hourly Zones; Brown: Irregular Time

The numerals in each zone show the number of hours to be added to, or subtracted from, Greenwich time.

| 30° | 0° | 30° | 60° | 90° | 120° | 150°E | 180° |

| -2 | -1 | 0 | +1 | +2 | +3 | +4 | +5 | +6 | +7 | +8 | +9 | +10 | +11 | +12- |

# Date Line

*The date line (180°) is directly opposite the prime meridian (0°). As Earth rotates, each new day officially begins as the 180° line passes 12 midnight. If you travel west across the date line, you advance one day; if you travel east across the date line, you fall back one day.*

*Notice on the map how the line zigs to the east as it passes through the South Pacific so that the islands of Fiji will not be split between two different days. Also notice that India is 5 1/2 hours ahead of Greenwich time, and China has only one time zone, even though the country spans more than 60 degrees of longitude. These differences are the result of decisions made at the country level.*

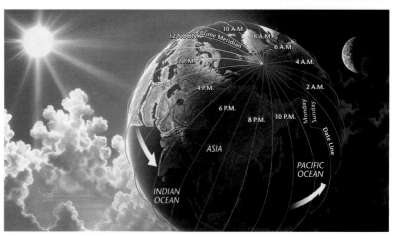

# Antarctica

**A**bout 180 million years ago Antarctica broke away from the ancient supercontinent Gondwana. Slowly the continent drifted to its present location at the southernmost point on Earth. Approximately 98 percent of the continent lies under permanent ice sheets that are nearly 3 miles (5 km) thick in places. It is estimated that if all of Antarctica's ice were to melt, the global ocean level would rise more than 200 feet (60 m).

## Facts & Figures

▶ **Land area:** 5,100,400 sq mi (13,209,000 sq km)

▶ **Population:** no permanent residents

▶ **Highest point:** Vinson Massif: 16,067 ft (4,897 m)

▶ **Lowest point:** Bentley Subglacial Trench: 8,366 ft (2,550 m) below sea level

▶ **Number of independent countries:** 0

▶ **Number of countries claiming land:** 7

▶ **Number of countries operating research stations:** 23

▶ **Number of research stations:** 44

▶ **Coldest temperature recorded:** minus 128.6°F (minus 89°C), July 21, 1983

▶ **Average precipitation on the polar plateau:** less than 2 in (5 cm) per year

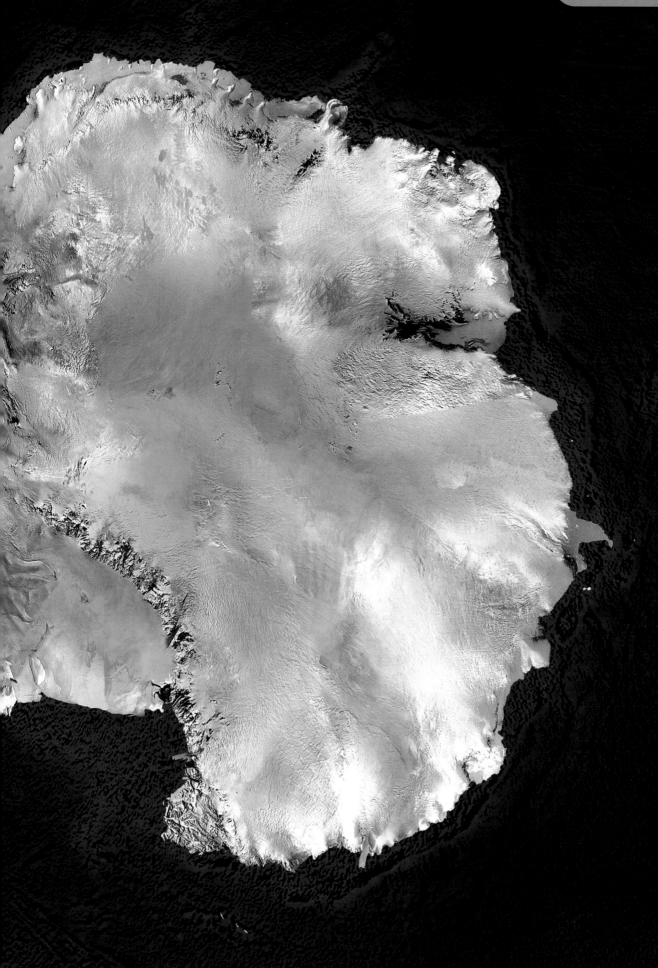

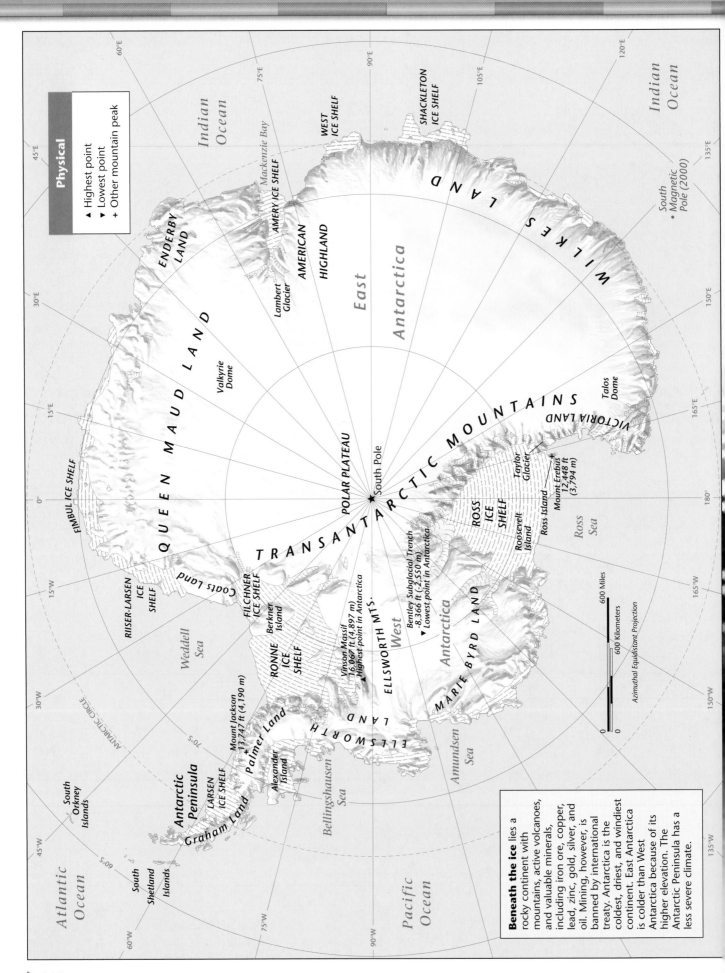

**Physical**

- ▲ Highest point
- ▼ Lowest point
- + Other mountain peak

*Atlantic Ocean*

*Indian Ocean*

*Indian Ocean*

*Pacific Ocean*

*Ross Sea*

*Weddell Sea*

*Bellingshausen Sea*

*Amundsen Sea*

ENDERBY LAND

QUEEN MAUD LAND

East Antarctica

West Antarctica

WILKES LAND

VICTORIA LAND

MARIE BYRD LAND

ELLSWORTH LAND

AMERICAN HIGHLAND

Coats Land

Graham Land

Palmer Land

ELLSWORTH MTS.

TRANSANTARCTIC MOUNTAINS

POLAR PLATEAU

South Pole

South Magnetic Pole (2000)

ANTARCTIC CIRCLE

Antarctic Peninsula

FIMBUL ICE SHELF

RIISER-LARSEN ICE SHELF

AMERY ICE SHELF

WEST ICE SHELF

SHACKLETON ICE SHELF

FILCHNER ICE SHELF

RONNE ICE SHELF

LARSEN ICE SHELF

ROSS ICE SHELF

Lambert Glacier

Mackenzie Bay

Valkyrie Dome

Talos Dome

Taylor Glacier

Berkner Island

Roosevelt Island

Ross Island

Alexander Island

South Orkney Islands

South Shetland Islands

Mount Erebus
12,448 ft
(3,794 m)

Vinson Massif
16,067 ft (4,897 m)
▲ Highest point in Antarctica

Bentley Subglacial Trench
-8,366 ft (-2,550 m)
▼ Lowest point in Antarctica

Mount Jackson
13,747 ft (4,190 m)

600 Miles

600 Kilometers

Azimuthal Equidistant Projection

**Beneath the ice** lies a rocky continent with mountains, active volcanoes, and valuable minerals, including iron ore, copper, lead, zinc, gold, silver, and oil. Mining, however, is banned by international treaty. Antarctica is the coldest, driest, and windiest continent. East Antarctica is colder than West Antarctica because of its higher elevation. The Antarctic Peninsula has a less severe climate.

# Antarctica

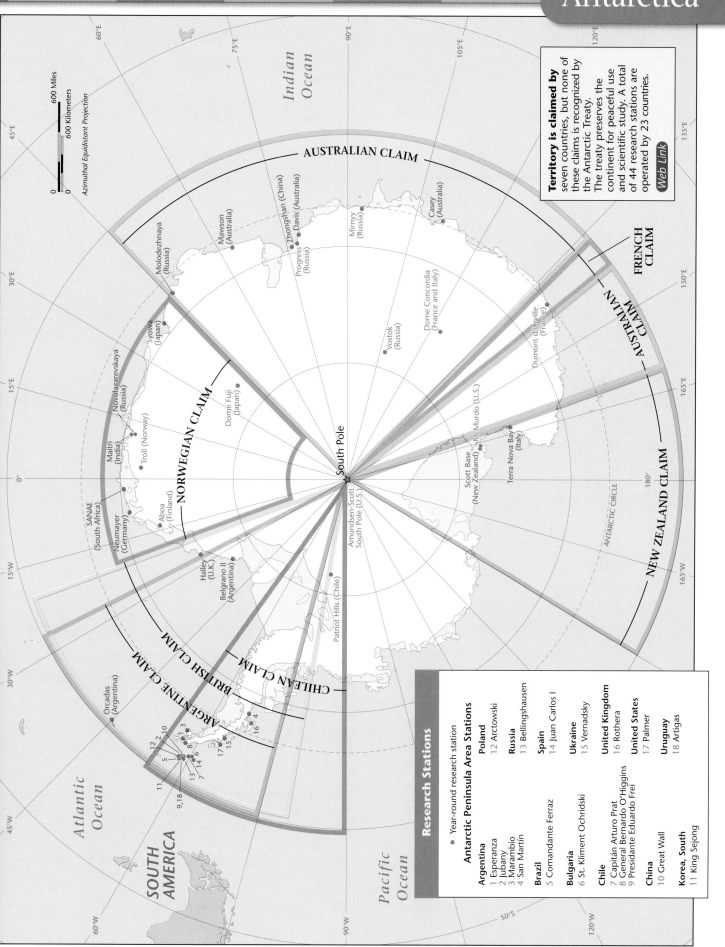

AUSTRALIAN CLAIM

FRENCH CLAIM

AUSTRALIAN CLAIM

NEW ZEALAND CLAIM

NORWEGIAN CLAIM

CHILEAN CLAIM

BRITISH CLAIM

ARGENTINE CLAIM

**Territory is claimed by** seven countries, but none of these claims is recognized by the Antarctic Treaty. The treaty preserves the continent for peaceful use and scientific study. A total of 44 research stations are operated by 23 countries.

Web Link

*Indian Ocean*

*Atlantic Ocean*

*Pacific Ocean*

SOUTH AMERICA

South Pole

ANTARCTIC CIRCLE

600 Miles
600 Kilometers
*Azimuthal Equidistant Projection*

Molodezhnaya (Russia)
Mawson (Australia)
Zhongshan (China)
Davis (Australia)
Progress (Russia)
Mirnyy (Russia)
Casey (Australia)
Syowa (Japan)
Novolazarevskaya (Russia)
Dome Concordia (France and Italy)
Vostok (Russia)
Dumont d'Urville (France)
Maitri (India)
Troll (Norway)
Dome Fuji (Japan)
Terra Nova Bay (Italy)
McMurdo (U.S.)
Scott Base (New Zealand)
SANAE (South Africa)
Neumayer (Germany)
Aboa (Finland)
Amundsen-Scott South Pole (U.S.)
Halley (U.K.)
Belgrano II (Argentina)
Patriot Hills (Chile)
Orcadas (Argentina)

## Research Stations

• Year-round research station

**Antarctic Peninsula Area Stations**

**Argentina**
1 Esperanza
2 Jubany
3 Marambio
4 San Martín

**Brazil**
5 Comandante Ferraz

**Bulgaria**
6 St. Kliment Ochridski

**Chile**
7 Capitán Arturo Prat
8 General Bernardo O'Higgins
9 Presidante Eduardo Frei

**China**
10 Great Wall

**Korea, South**
11 King Sejong

**Poland**
12 Arctowski

**Russia**
13 Bellingshausen

**Spain**
14 Juan Carlos I

**Ukraine**
15 Vernadsky

**United Kingdom**
16 Rothera

**United States**
17 Palmer

**Uruguay**
18 Artigas

The flags and fact boxes below represent the world's 191 independent countries—those with national governments that are the highest legal authority over the land and people within their boundaries. The flags shown are national flags recognized by the United Nations. Area figures are for land only. They do not include surface areas for inland bodies of water. Population figures are for the year 2000 as provided by the Population Reference Bureau of the United States. The languages listed are either the ones most commonly spoken within a country or official languages of a country.

# NORTH AMERICA

## Antigua and Barbuda
**Area:** 170 sq mi
(440 sq km)
**Population:** 68,000
**Capital:** St. John's
**Languages:** English, local dialects

## Bahamas
**Area:** 5,382 sq mi
(13,939 sq km)
**Population:** 310,000
**Capital:** Nassau
**Languages:** English, Creole

## Barbados
**Area:** 166 sq mi
(430 sq km)
**Population:** 259,000
**Capital:** Bridgetown
**Language:** English

## Belize
**Area:** 8,867 sq mi
(22,965 sq km)
**Population:** 254,000
**Capital:** Belmopan
**Languages:** English, Spanish, Mayan, Carib

## Canada
**Area:** 3,849,670 sq mi
(9,970,610 sq km)
**Population:** 30,764,000
**Capital:** Ottawa
**Languages:** English, French (both official)

## Costa Rica
**Area:** 19,730 sq mi
(51,100 sq km)
**Population:** 3,589,000
**Capital:** San José
**Languages:** Spanish, English

## Cuba
**Area:** 42,804 sq mi
(110,861 sq km)
**Population:** 11,139,000
**Capital:** Havana
**Language:** Spanish

## Dominica
**Area:** 290 sq mi
(751 sq km)
**Population:** 76,000
**Capital:** Roseau
**Languages:** English, French patois

## Dominican Republic
**Area:** 18,816 sq mi
(48,734 sq km)
**Population:** 8,443,000
**Capital:** Santo Domingo
**Language:** Spanish

## El Salvador
**Area:** 8,124 sq mi
(21,041 sq km)
**Population:** 6,280,000
**Capital:** San Salvador
**Languages:** Spanish, Nahuatl

## Grenada
**Area:** 133 sq mi
(344 sq km)
**Population:** 98,000
**Capital:** St. George's
**Languages:** English, French patois

## Guatemala
**Area:** 42,042 sq mi
(108,889 sq km)
**Population:** 12,670,000
**Capital:** Guatemala City
**Languages:** Spanish, Amerindian dialects

## Haiti
**Area:** 10,714 sq mi
(27,750 sq km)
**Population:** 6,423,000
**Capital:** Port-au-Prince
**Languages:** French, Creole

## Honduras
**Area:** 43,277 sq mi
(112,088 sq km)
**Population:** 6,130,000
**Capital:** Tegucigalpa
**Languages:** Spanish, Amerindian dialects

## Jamaica
**Area:** 4,244 sq mi
(10,991 sq km)
**Population:** 2,609,000
**Capital:** Kingston
**Languages:** English, Creole

## Mexico
**Area:** 756,066 sq mi
(1,958,201 sq km)
**Population:** 99,639,000
**Capital:** Mexico City
**Languages:** Spanish, regional indigenous languages

## Nicaragua
**Area:** 50,193 sq mi
(129,999 sq km)
**Population:** 5,074,000
**Capital:** Managua
**Languages:** Spanish, English, Amerindian dialects

## Panama
**Area:** 29,762 sq mi
(77,082 sq km)
**Population:** 2,857,000
**Capital:** Panama City
**Languages:** Spanish, English

## St. Kitts and Nevis
**Area:** 101 sq mi
(261 sq km)
**Population:** 43,000
**Capital:** Basseterre
**Language:** English

## St. Lucia
**Area:** 238 sq mi
(617 sq km)
**Population:** 157,000
**Capital:** Castries
**Languages:** English, French patois

## St. Vincent and the Grenadines
**Area:** 150 sq mi
(388 sq km)
**Population:** 112,000
**Capital:** Kingstown
**Languages:** English, French patois

## Trinidad and Tobago
**Area:** 1,981 sq mi
(5,131 sq km)
**Population:** 1,295,000
**Capital:** Port of Spain
**Languages:** English, Hindi, French, Spanish

## United States
**Area:** 3,717,796 sq mi
(9,629,091 sq km)
**Population:** 275,600,000
**Capital:** Washington, D.C.
**Languages:** English, Spanish

## SOUTH AMERICA

**Argentina**
**Area:** 1,068,302 sq mi
(2,766,889 sq km)
**Population:** 37,048,000
**Capital:** Buenos Aires
**Languages:** Spanish,
English, Italian, German

**Bolivia**
**Area:** 424,164 sq mi
(1,098,581 sq km)
**Population:** 8,281,000
**Capitals:** La Paz, Sucre
**Languages:** Spanish,
Quechua, Aymara (all official)

**Brazil**
**Area:** 3,286,488 sq mi
(8,511,965 sq km)
**Population:** 170,115,000
**Capital:** Brasília
**Languages:** Portuguese,
Spanish, English

**Chile**
**Area:** 292,135 sq mi
(756,626 sq km)
**Population:** 15,211,000
**Capital:** Santiago
**Language:** Spanish

**Colombia**
**Area:** 439,737 sq mi
(1,138,914 sq km)
**Population:** 40,037,000
**Capital:** Bogotá
**Language:** Spanish

**Ecuador**
**Area:** 109,484 sq mi
(283,561 sq km)
**Population:** 12,646,000
**Capital:** Quito
**Languages:** Spanish,
Quechua

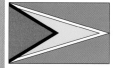

**Guyana**
**Area:** 83,000 sq mi
(214,969 sq km)
**Population:** 698,000
**Capital:** Georgetown
**Languages:** English,
Amerindian dialects

**Paraguay**
**Area:** 157,048 sq mi
(406,752 sq km)
**Population:** 5,505,000
**Capital:** Asunción
**Languages:** Spanish, Guaraní

**Peru**
**Area:** 496,225 sq mi
(1,285,217 sq km)
**Population:** 27,136,000
**Capital:** Lima
**Languages:** Spanish,
Quechua (both official),
Aymara

**Suriname**
**Area:** 63,037 sq mi
(163,265 sq km)
**Population:** 434,000
**Capital:** Paramaribo
**Languages:** Dutch, English,
Sranang Tongo (Taki-Taki),
Hindustani, Javanese

**Uruguay**
**Area:** 68,037 sq mi
(176,215 sq km)
**Population:** 3,313,000
**Capital:** Montevideo
**Languages:** Spanish,
Portunol, Brazilero

**Venezuela**
**Area:** 352,144 sq mi
(912,050 sq km)
**Population:** 24,170,000
**Capital:** Caracas
**Language:** Spanish

## EUROPE

**Albania**
**Area:** 11,100 sq mi
(28,748 sq km)
**Population:** 3,431,000
**Capital:** Tirana
**Languages:** Albanian, Greek

**Andorra**
**Area:** 175 sq mi
(453 sq km)
**Population:** 67,000
**Capital:** Andorra la Vella
**Languages:** Catalan,
French, Spanish

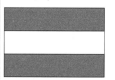

**Austria**
**Area:** 32,377 sq mi
(83,856 sq km)
**Population:** 8,094,000
**Capital:** Vienna
**Language:** German

**Belarus**
**Area:** 80,154 sq mi
(207,598 sq km)
**Population:** 10,004,000
**Capital:** Minsk
**Languages:** Belorussian,
Russian

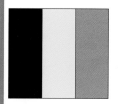

**Belgium**
**Area:** 11,783 sq mi
(30,518 sq km)
**Population:** 10,246,000
**Capital:** Brussels
**Languages:** Flemish,
French, German

**Bosnia and
Herzegovina**
**Area:** 19,741 sq mi
(51,129 sq km)
**Population:** 3,809,000
**Capital:** Sarajevo
**Language:** Serbo-Croat
(Bosnian)

**Bulgaria**
**Area:** 42,823 sq mi
(110,912 sq km)
**Population:** 8,152,000
**Capital:** Sofia
**Language:** Bulgarian

**Croatia**
**Area:** 21,829 sq mi
(56,538 sq km)
**Population:** 4,600,000
**Capital:** Zagreb
**Language:** Serbo-Croat

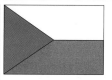

**Czech Republic**
**Area:** 30,450 sq mi
(78,864 sq km)
**Population:** 10,275,000
**Capital:** Prague
**Languages:** Czech, Slovak

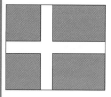

**Denmark**
**Area:** 16,638 sq mi
(43,092 sq km)
**Population:** 5,330,000
**Capital:** Copenhagen
**Languages:** Danish,
Faeroese, Greenlandic

**Estonia**
**Area:** 17,413 sq mi
(45,099 sq km)
**Population:** 1,433,000
**Capital:** Tallinn
**Languages:** Estonian,
Russian, Ukrainian

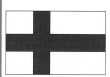

**Finland**
**Area:** 130,558 sq mi
(338,145 sq km)
**Population:** 5,177,000
**Capital:** Helsinki
**Languages:** Finnish,
Swedish (both official)

**France**
**Area:** 210,026 sq mi
(543,965 sq km)
**Population:** 59,353,000
**Capital:** Paris
**Language:** French

## Germany
**Area:** 137,857 sq mi
(357,046 sq km)
**Population:** 82,141,000
**Capital:** Berlin
**Language:** German

## Greece
**Area:** 50,962 sq mi
(131,990 sq km)
**Population:** 10,596,000
**Capital:** Athens
**Languages:** Greek, English,
French

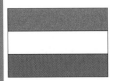

## Hungary
**Area:** 35,919 sq mi
(93,030 sq km)
**Population:** 10,020,000
**Capital:** Budapest
**Language:** Hungarian

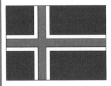

## Iceland
**Area:** 39,769 sq mi
(103,001 sq km)
**Population:** 281,000
**Capital:** Reykjavík
**Language:** Icelandic

## Ireland
**Area:** 27,137 sq mi
(70,284 sq km)
**Population:** 3,795,000
**Capital:** Dublin
**Languages:** English, Irish
(Gaelic)

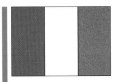

## Italy
**Area:** 116,324 sq mi
(301,277 sq km)
**Population:** 57,820,000
**Capital:** Rome
**Languages:** Italian,
German, French

## Latvia
**Area:** 24,942 sq mi
(64,599 sq km)
**Population:** 2,416,000
**Capital:** Riga
**Languages:** Latvian,
Lithuanian, Russian

## Liechtenstein
**Area:** 62 sq mi
(160 sq km)
**Population:** 33,000
**Capital:** Vaduz
**Languages:** German,
Alemannic dialect

## Lithuania
**Area:** 25,174 sq mi
(65,200 sq km)
**Population:** 3,697,000
**Capital:** Vilnius
**Languages:** Lithuanian,
Polish, Russian

## Luxembourg
**Area:** 998 sq mi
(2,586 sq km)
**Population:** 438,000
**Capital:** Luxembourg
**Languages:**
Luxembourgian, German,
French

## Macedonia
**Area:** 9,928 sq mi
(25,713 sq km)
**Population:** 2,033,000
**Capital:** Skopje
**Languages:** Macedonian,
Albanian

## Malta
**Area:** 122 sq mi
(316 sq km)
**Population:** 390,000
**Capital:** Valletta
**Languages:** Maltese,
English (both official)

## Moldova
**Area:** 13,217 sq mi
(33,999 sq km)
**Population:** 4,276,000
**Capital:** Chişinău
**Languages:** Moldavian,
Russian

## Monaco
**Area:** 0.6 sq mi
(1.9 sq km)
**Population:** 34,000
**Capital:** Monaco
**Languages:** French,
English, Italian

## Netherlands
**Area:** 16,023 sq mi
(41,499 sq km)
**Population:** 15,921,000
**Capital:** Amsterdam
**Language:** Dutch

## Norway
**Area:** 125,182 sq mi
(324,220 sq km)
**Population:** 4,487,000
**Capital:** Oslo
**Language:** Norwegian

## Poland
**Area:** 120,725 sq mi
(312,677 sq km)
**Population:** 38,648,000
**Capital:** Warsaw
**Language:** Polish

## Portugal
**Area:** 35,672 sq mi
(92,389 sq km)
**Population:** 10,013,000
**Capital:** Lisbon
**Language:** Portuguese

## Romania
**Area:** 91,699 sq mi
(237,499 sq km)
**Population:** 22,432,000
**Capital:** Bucharest
**Languages:** Romanian,
Hungarian, German

## Russia
**Area:** 6,592,692 sq mi
(17,074,993 sq km)
**Population:** 145,231,000
**Capital:** Moscow
**Language:** Russian

## San Marino
**Area:** 24 sq mi
(61 sq km)
**Population:** 27,000
**Capital:** San Marino
**Language:** Italian

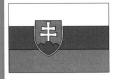

## Slovakia
**Area:** 18,921 sq mi
(49,006 km)
**Population:** 5,401,000
**Capital:** Bratislava
**Languages:** Slovak,
Hungarian

## Slovenia
**Area:** 7,819 sq mi
(20,251 sq km)
**Population:** 1,968,000
**Capital:** Ljubljana
**Languages:** Slovene,
Serbo-Croat

## Spain
**Area:** 194,897 sq mi
(504,782 sq km)
**Population:** 39,466,000
**Capital:** Madrid
**Languages:** Spanish,
Catalan, Galician, Basque

## Sweden
**Area:** 173,732 sq mi
(449,964 sq km)
**Population:** 8,866,000
**Capital:** Stockholm
**Language:** Swedish

## Switzerland
**Area:** 15,941 sq mi
(41,288 sq km)
**Population:** 7,142,000
**Capital:** Bern
**Languages:** German,
French, Italian, Romansch

## Ukraine
**Area:** 233,206 sq mi
(604,001 sq km)
**Population:** 49,509,000
**Capital:** Kiev
**Languages:** Ukrainian,
Russian, Romanian

## United Kingdom
**Area:** 94,248 sq mi
(24,101 sq km)
**Population:** 59,750,000
**Capital:** London
**Languages:** English, Welsh,
Gaelic

## Vatican City
**Area:** 0.2 sq mi
(0.4 sq km)
**Population:** 1,000
**Languages:** Italian, Latin

## Yugoslavia
**Area:** 39,450 sq mi
(102,173 sq km)
**Population:** 10,662,000
**Capital:** Belgrade
**Languages:** Serbo-Croat,
Albanian

# AFRICA

## Algeria
**Area:** 919,595 sq mi
(2,381,741 sq km)
**Population:** 31,471,000
**Capital:** Algiers
**Languages:** Arabic, French,
Berber dialects

## Angola
**Area:** 481,354 sq mi
(1,246,700 sq km)
**Population:** 12,878,000
**Capital:** Luanda
**Languages:** Portuguese,
Bantu

## Benin
**Area:** 43,484 sq mi
(112,622 sq km)
**Population:** 6,396,000
**Capitals:** Porto-Novo,
Cotonou
**Languages:** French, Fon,
Yoruba, indigenous languages

## Botswana
**Area:** 231,805 sq mi
(600,372 sq km)
**Population:** 1,576,000
**Capital:** Gaborone
**Languages:** English, Setswana

## Burkina Faso
**Area:** 105,869 sq mi
(274,200 sq km)
**Population:** 11,946,000
**Capital:** Ouagadougou
**Languages:** French,
indigenous languages

## Burundi
**Area:** 10,747 sq mi
(27,834 sq km)
**Population:** 6,054,000
**Capital:** Bujumbura
**Languages:** Kirundi,
French (both official)

## Cameroon
**Area:** 183,569 sq mi
(475,442 sq km)
**Population:** 15,422,000
**Capital:** Yaoundé
**Languages:** French, English
(both official), 24 major
African language groups

## Cape Verde
**Area:** 1,557 sq mi
(4,033 sq km)
**Population:** 401,000
**Capital:** Praia
**Languages:** Portuguese,
Crioulo

## Central African
## Republic
**Area:** 240,535 sq mi
(622,984 sq km)
**Population:** 3,513,000
**Capital:** Bangui
**Languages:** French,
Sango, Arabic, Hunsa

## Chad
**Area:** 495,755 sq mi
(1,284,000 sq km)
**Population:** 7,977,000
**Capital:** N'Djamena
**Languages:** French, Arabic
(both official), Sara, Sango,
more than 100 different
languages and dialects

## Comoros
**Area:** 719 sq mi
(1,862 sq km)
**Population:** 578,000
**Capital:** Moroni
**Languages:** Arabic, French
(both official), Comoran

## Congo
**Area:** 132,047 sq mi
(342,000 sq km)
**Population:** 2,831,000
**Capital:** Brazzaville
**Languages:** French,
Lingala, Monokutuba, many
local languages, dialects

## Congo, Democratic
## Republic of the
**Area:** 905,568 sq mi
(2,345,409 sq km)
**Population:** 51,965,000
**Capital:** Kinshasa
**Languages:** French,
Lingala, Kingwana

## Côte d'Ivoire
**Area:** 124,504 sq mi
(322,463 sq km)
**Population:** 15,980,000
**Capitals:** Yamoussoukro,
Abidjan
**Languages:** French,
Dioula, 60 native dialects

## Djibouti
**Area:** 8,958 sq mi
(23,200 sq km)
**Population:** 638,000
**Capital:** Djibouti
**Languages:** French, Arabic
(both official)

## Egypt
**Area:** 386,662 sq mi
(1,001,449 sq km)
**Population:** 68,344,000
**Capital:** Cairo
**Languages:** Arabic,
English, French

## Equatorial Guinea
**Area:** 10,831 sq mi
(28,051 sq km)
**Population:** 453,000
**Capital:** Malabo
**Languages:** Spanish,
French (both official), pid-
gin English, Fang, Bubi, Ibo

## Eritrea
**Area:** 46,842 sq mi
(121,320 sq km)
**Population:** 4,142,000
**Capital:** Asmara
**Languages:** Afar, Amharic,
Arabic, Tigre

## Ethiopia
**Area:** 424,934 sq mi
(1,100,574 sq km)
**Population:** 64,117,000
**Capital:** Addis Ababa
**Languages:** Amharic,
Tigrinya, Orominga,
Guaraginga, Somali, Arabic

## Gabon
**Area:** 103,347 sq mi
(267,667 sq km)
**Population:** 1,226,000
**Capital:** Libreville
**Languages:** French, Fang,
Myene, Bateke, Bapounou/
Eschira,Bandjabi

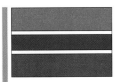

### Gambia
**Area:** 4,361 sq mi
(11,295 sq km)
**Population:** 1,305,000
**Capital:** Banjul
**Languages:** English,
Mandinka, Wolof, Fula

### Ghana
**Area:** 92,100 sq mi
(238,537 sq km)
**Population:** 19,534,000
**Capital:** Accra
**Languages:** English,
African languages (includ-
ing Akan, Moshi-Dagomba,
Ewe and Ga)

### Guinea
**Area:** 94,926 sq mi
(245,857 sq km)
**Population:** 7,466,000
**Capital:** Conakry
**Languages:** French,
indigenous languages

### Guinea-Bissau
**Area:** 13,948 sq mi
(36,125 sq km)
**Population:** 1,213,000
**Capital:** Bissau
**Languages:** Portuguese,
Crioulo, indigenous languages

### Kenya
**Area:** 228,861 sq mi
(592,747 sq km)
**Population:** 30,340,000
**Capital:** Nairobi
**Languages:** English,
Swahili (both official),
indigenous languages

### Lesotho
**Area:** 11,720 sq mi
(30,355 sq km)
**Population:** 2,143,000
**Capital:** Maseru
**Languages:** English,
Sesotho, Zulo, Xhosa

### Liberia
**Area:** 43,000 sq mi
(111,369 sq km)
**Population:** 3,164,000
**Capital:** Monrovia
**Languages:** English,
indigenous languages

### Libya
**Area:** 679,362 sq mi
(1,759,540 sq km)
**Population:** 5,114,000
**Capital:** Tripoli
**Languages:** Arabic, Italian,
English

### Madagascar
**Area:** 226,658 sq mi
(587,041 sq km)
**Population:** 14,858,000
**Capital:** Antananarivo
**Languages:** French,
Malagasy (both official)

### Malawi
**Area:** 45,747 sq mi
(118,484 sq km)
**Population:** 10,385,000
**Capital:** Lilongwe
**Languages:** Chewa,
English (both official)

### Mali
**Area:** 478,841 sq mi
(1,240,192 sq km)
**Population:** 11,234,000
**Capital:** Bamako
**Languages:** French,
Bambara, numerous
African languages

### Mauritania
**Area:** 397,955 sq mi
(1,030,700 sq km)
**Population:** 2,670,000
**Capital:** Nouakchott
**Languages:** Hasaniya
Arabic, Wolof (both offi-
cial), Pula, Soninke, French

### Mauritius
**Area:** 788 sq mi
(2,040 sq km)
**Population:** 1,189,000
**Capital:** Port Louis
**Languages:** English,
Creole, French, Hindi,
Urdu, Hakka, Bojpoori

### Morocco
**Area:** 275,117 sq mi
(712,550 sq km)
**Population:** 28,778,000
**Capital:** Rabat
**Languages:** Arabic, Berber
dialects, French

### Mozambique
**Area:** 308,642 sq mi
(799,380 sq km)
**Population:** 19,105,000
**Capital:** Maputo
**Languages:** Portuguese,
indigenous dialects

### Namibia
**Area:** 318,261 sq mi
(824,292 sq km)
**Population:** 1,771,000
**Capital:** Windhoek
**Languages:** English,
Afrikaans, German, indige-
nous languages

### Niger
**Area:** 489,191 sq mi
(1,267,000 sq km)
**Population:** 10,076,000
**Capital:** Niamey
**Languages:** French, Hausa,
Djerma

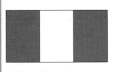

### Nigeria
**Area:** 356,669 sq mi
(923,768 sq km)
**Population:** 123,338,000
**Capital:** Abuja
**Languages:** English,
Hausa, Yoruba, Igbo

### Rwanda
**Area:** 10,169 sq mi
(26,338 sq km)
**Population:** 7,229,000
**Capital:** Kigali
**Languages:** Kinyarwanda,
French, English (all official),
Kiswahili (Swahili)

### Sao Tome and
### Principe
**Area:** 372 sq mi
(964 sq km)
**Population:** 160,000
**Capital:** São Tomé
**Language:** Portuguese

### Senegal
**Area:** 75,955 sq mi
(196,722 sq km)
**Population:** 9,481,000
**Capital:** Dakar
**Languages:** French, Wolof,
Pulaar, Diola

### Seychelles
**Area:** 175 sq mi
(453 sq km)
**Population:** 82,000
**Capital:** Victoria
**Languages:** English, French
(both official), Creole

### Sierra Leone
**Area:** 27,699 sq mi
(71,740 sq km)
**Population:** 5,233,000
**Capital:** Freetown
**Languages:** English,
Mende, Temne, Krio

### Somalia
**Area:** 246,201 sq mi
(637,657 sq km)
**Population:** 7,253,000
**Capital:** Mogadishu
**Languages:** Somali, Arabic,
Italian, English

### South Africa
**Area:** 471,445 sq mi
(1,221,037 sq km)
**Population:** 43,421,000
**Capitals:** Pretoria (adminis-
trative), Cape Town (legisla-
tive), Bloemfontein (judicial)
**Languages:** Afrikaans, English
Ndebele, Pedi, Sotho, Swazi,
Tsonga, Tswana, Venda,
Xhosa, Zulu (all official)

### Sudan
**Area:** 963,600 sq mi (2,495,712 sq km)
**Population:** 29,490,000
**Capital:** Khartoum
**Languages:** Arabic, Nuban, Ta Bedawie

### Swaziland
**Area:** 6,704 sq mi (17,364 sq km)
**Population:** 1,004,000
**Capital:** Mbabane
**Languages:** English, Swazi (both official)

### Tanzania
**Area:** 364,900 sq mi (945,087 sq km)
**Population:** 35,306,000
**Capital:** Dar es Salaam
**Languages:** Swahili, English (both official), Arabic, many local languages

### Togo
**Area:** 21,925 sq mi (56,785 sq km)
**Population:** 5,019,000
**Capital:** Lomé
**Languages:** French, Ewe, Mina, Kabye, Dagomba

### Tunisia
**Area:** 63,170 sq mi (163,610 sq km)
**Population:** 9,619,000
**Capital:** Tunis
**Languages:** Arabic, French

### Uganda
**Area:** 91,134 sq mi (236,036 sq km)
**Population:** 23,318,000
**Capital:** Kampala
**Languages:** English, Ganda or Luganda

### Zambia
**Area:** 290,586 sq mi (752,614 sq km)
**Population:** 9,582,000
**Capital:** Lusaka
**Languages:** English, indigenous languages

### Zimbabwe
**Area:** 150,804 sq mi (390,580 sq km)
**Population:** 11,343,000
**Capital:** Harare
**Languages:** English, Shona, Sindebele

# ASIA

### Afghanistan
**Area:** 251,773 sq mi (652,090 sq km)
**Population:** 26,668,000
**Capital:** Kabul
**Languages:** Pashto, Dari, Turkic languages

### Armenia
**Area:** 11,583 sq mi (30,000 sq km)
**Population:** 3,809,000
**Capital:** Yerevan
**Languages:** Armenian, Russian

### Azerbaijan
**Area:** 33,591 sq mi (87,000 sq km)
**Population:** 7,734,000
**Capital:** Baku
**Languages:** Azeri, Russian, Armenian

### Bahrain
**Area:** 267 sq mi (691 sq km)
**Population:** 691,000
**Capital:** Manama
**Languages:** Arabic, English, Persian, Urdu

### Bangladesh
**Area:** 55,598 sq mi (143,998 sq km)
**Population:** 128,133,000
**Capital:** Dhaka
**Languages:** Bengali, English

### Bhutan
**Area:** 18,147 sq mi (47,001 sq km)
**Population:** 877,000
**Capital:** Thimphu
**Languages:** Dzonkha, Tibetan, and Nepali dialects

### Brunei
**Area:** 2,226 sq mi (5,765 sq km)
**Population:** 331,000
**Capital:** Bandar Seri Begawan
**Languages:** Malay, English, Chinese

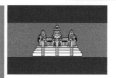

### Cambodia
**Area:** 69,898 sq mi (181,035 sq km)
**Population:** 12,127,000
**Capital:** Phnom Penh
**Languages:** Khmer, French

### China
**Area:** 3,705,820 sq mi (9,598,032 sq km)
**Population:** 1,264,536,000
**Capital:** Beijing
**Languages:** Chinese, Mandarin, dialects

### Cyprus
**Area:** 2,277 sq mi (5,897 sq km)
**Population:** 882,000
**Capital:** Nicosia
**Languages:** Greek, Turkish, English

### Georgia
**Area:** 27,027 sq mi (70,000 sq km)
**Population:** 5,454,000
**Capital:** T'bilisi
**Languages:** Georgian, Russian, Armenian

### India
**Area:** 1,269,346 sq mi (3,287,591 sq km)
**Population:** 1,002,142,000
**Capital:** New Delhi
**Languages:** Hindi, 14 other official languages, English

### Indonesia
**Area:** 741,101 sq mi (1,919,443 sq km)
**Population:** 212,207,000
**Capital:** Jakarta
**Languages:** Bahasa Indonesia, English, Dutch, Javanese and other local dialects

### Iran
**Area:** 636,296 sq mi (1,647,999 sq km)
**Population:** 67,411,000
**Capital:** Tehran
**Languages:** Persian, Turkic, Kurdish, Luri

### Iraq
**Area:** 169,235 sq mi (438,317 sq km)
**Population:** 23,115,000
**Capital:** Baghdad
**Languages:** Arabic, Kurdish (official in Kurdish regions), Assyrian, Armenian

### Israel
**Area:** 8,019 sq mi (20,770 sq km)
**Population:** 6,227,000
**Capital:** Jerusalem
**Languages:** Hebrew, Arabic, English

### Japan
**Area:** 145,875 sq mi (377,815 sq km)
**Population:** 126,876,000
**Capital:** Tokyo
**Language:** Japanese

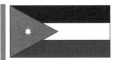

**Jordan**
**Area:** 35,467 sq mi
(91,860 sq km)
**Population:** 5,083,000
**Capital:** Amman
**Languages:** Arabic, English
understood

**Kazakhstan**
**Area:** 1,049,039 sq mi
(2,716,998 sq km)
**Population:** 14,865,000
**Capital:** Astana
**Languages:** Kazakh,
Russian

**Korea, North**
**Area:** 46,540 sq mi
(120,538 sq km)
**Population:** 21,688,000
**Capital:** Pyongyang
**Language:** Korean

**Korea, South**
**Area:** 38,230 sq mi
(99,016 sq km)
**Population:** 47,275,000
**Capital:** Seoul
**Languages:** Korean,
English widely taught

**Kuwait**
**Area:** 6,880 sq mi
(17,818 sq km)
**Population:** 2,190,000
**Capital:** Kuwait
**Languages:** Arabic, English

**Kyrgyzstan**
**Area:** 76,834 sq mi
(198,999 sq km)
**Population:** 4,929,000
**Capital:** Bishkek
**Languages:** Kirghiz,
Russian (both official)

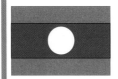

**Laos**
**Area:** 91,429 sq mi
(236,800 sq km)
**Population:** 5,218,000
**Capital:** Vientiane
**Languages:** Lao, French,
English, ethnic

**Lebanon**
**Area:** 4,015 sq mi
(10,399 sq km)
**Population:** 4,202,000
**Capital:** Beirut
**Languages:** Arabic, French,
English

**Malaysia**
**Area:** 127,317 sq mi
(329,749 sq km)
**Population:** 23,253,000
**Capital:** Kuala Lumpur
**Languages:** Malay, English,
Chinese

**Maldives**
**Area:** 115 sq mi
(298 sq km)
**Population:** 286,000
**Capital:** Male
**Languages:** Maldivian
Divehi, English

**Mongolia**
**Area:** 604,250 sq mi
(1,565,000 sq km)
**Population:** 2,472,000
**Capital:** Ulaanbaatar
**Languages:** Khalkha
Mongol, Turkic, Russian,
Chinese

**Myanmar**
**Area:** 261,218 sq mi
(676,552 sq km)
**Population:** 48,852,000
**Capital:** Yangon (Rangoon)
**Languages:** Burmese,
minority ethnic

**Nepal**
**Area:** 54,362 sq mi
(140,797 sq km)
**Population:** 23,930,000
**Capital:** Kathmandu
**Languages:** Nepali, 20
other languages

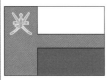

**Oman**
**Area:** 82,030 sq mi
(212,457 sq km)
**Population:** 2,353,000
**Capital:** Muscat
**Languages:** Arabic,
English, Baluchi, Urdu

**Pakistan**
**Area:** 307,374 sq mi
(796,095 sq km)
**Population:** 150,648,000
**Capital:** Islamabad
**Languages:** Urdu, English,
Punjabi, Sindhi

**Philippines**
**Area:** 115,831 sq mi
(300,001 sq km)
**Population:** 80,298,000
**Capital:** Manila
**Languages:** Tagalog,
English (both official)

**Qatar**
**Area:** 4,247 sq mi
(11,000 sq km)
**Population:** 591,000
**Capital:** Doha
**Languages:** Arabic, English

**Saudi Arabia**
**Area:** 830,000 sq mi
(2,149,690 sq km)
**Population:** 21,607,000
**Capital:** Riyadh
**Language:** Arabic

**Singapore**
**Area:** 239 sq mi
(618 sq km)
**Population:** 4,001,000
**Capital:** Singapore
**Languages:** Chinese,
Malay, Tamil, English

**Sri Lanka**
**Area:** 25,332 sq mi
(65,610 sq km)
**Population:** 19,169,000
**Capitals:** Colombo,
Sri Jayewardenepura Kotte
**Languages:** Sinhalese,
Tamil, English

**Syria**
**Area:** 71,044 sq mi
(184,004 sq km)
**Population:** 16,482,000
**Capital:** Damascus
**Languages:** Arabic,
Kurdish, Armenian

**Tajikistan**
**Area:** 55,213 sq mi
(143,001 sq km)
**Population:** 6,374,000
**Capital:** Dushanbe
**Languages:** Tajik, Russian

**Thailand**
**Area:** 198,457 sq mi
(514,001 sq km)
**Population:** 62,043,000
**Capital:** Bangkok
**Languages:** Thai, English,
regional dialects

**Turkey**
**Area:** 300,948 sq mi
(779,452 sq km)
**Population:** 65,311,000
**Capital:** Ankara
**Languages:** Turkish,
Kurdish, Arabic

**Turkmenistan**
**Area:** 188,418 sq mi
(488,000 sq km)
**Population:** 5,239,000
**Capital:** Ashgabat
**Languages:** Turkmenian,
Russian, Uzbek

## United Arab Emirates
**Area:** 32,278 sq mi (83,600 sq km)
**Population:** 2,835,000
**Capital:** Abu Dhabi
**Languages:** Arabic, Persian, English, Hindi, Urdu

## Uzbekistan
**Area:** 172,588 sq mi (447,001 sq km)
**Population:** 24,760,000
**Capital:** Tashkent
**Languages:** Uzbek, Russian, Tajik

## Vietnam
**Area:** 127,242 sq mi (329,556 sq km)
**Population:** 78,697,000
**Capital:** Hanoi
**Languages:** Vietnamese, Chinese, English, French, Khmer, indigenous languages

## Yemen
**Area:** 203,850 sq mi (527,968 sq km)
**Population:** 17,030,000
**Capital:** Sanaa
**Language:** Arabic

# AUSTRALIA & OCEANIA

## Australia
**Area:** 2,968,000 sq mi (7,687,000 sq km)
**Population:** 19,195,000
**Capital:** Canberra
**Languages:** English, indigenous languages

## Fiji Islands
**Area:** 7,056 sq mi (18,274 sq km)
**Population:** 811,000
**Capital:** Suva
**Languages:** English, Fijian, Hindi

## Kiribati
**Area:** 277 sq mi (717 sq km)
**Population:** 92,000
**Capital:** Tarawa
**Languages:** English, Gilbertese

## Marshall Islands
**Area:** 70 sq mi (181 sq km)
**Population:** 68,000
**Capital:** Majuro
**Languages:** English, local dialects, Japanese

## Micronesia
**Population:** 271 sq mi (702 sq km)
**Population:** 119,000
**Capital:** Palikir
**Languages:** English, Trukese, Pohnpeian

## Nauru
**Area:** 8 sq mi (21 sq km)
**Population:** 12,000
**Capital:** Yaren
**Languages:** Nauruan, English

## New Zealand
**Area:** 103,883 sq mi (269,057 sq km)
**Population:** 3,836,000
**Capital:** Wellington
**Languages:** English, Maori

## Palau
**Area:** 188 sq mi (487 sq km)
**Population:** 19,000
**Capital:** Koror
**Languages:** English, Palaun, 3 local official

## Papua New Guinea
**Area:** 178,260 sq mi (461,691 sq km)
**Population:** 4,810,000
**Capital:** Port Moresby
**Languages:** 715 indigenous languages

## Samoa
**Area:** 1,093 sq mi (2,831 sq km)
**Population:** 176,000
**Capital:** Apia
**Languages:** Samoan (Polynesian), English

## Solomon Islands
**Area:** 10,985 sq mi (28,450 sq km)
**Population:** 434,000
**Capital:** Honiara
**Languages:** Melanesian pidgin, 120 indigenous languages, English

## Tonga
**Area:** 270 sq mi (699 sq km)
**Population:** 108,000
**Capital:** Nuku'alofa
**Languages:** Tongan, English

## Tuvalu
**Area:** 10 sq mi (26 sq km)
**Population:** 10,000
**Capital:** Funafuti
**Languages:** Tuvalu, English

## Vanuatu
**Area:** 5,700 sq mi (14,760 sq km)
**Population:** 195,000
**Capital:** Port-Vila
**Languages:** English, French, pidgin (Bislama)

# Glossary

*Note: Terms defined within the main body of the atlas text are not listed below.*

**Alkaline** term describing soil or natural body of water that has a high salt content; most often found in dry areas where soluble salts have not been washed away or where evaporation rates are high (p. 84)

**Arid climate** type of dry climate in which annual precipitation is often less than 10 inches (25 cm); experiences great daily variations in day-night temperatures (pp. 18–19)

**Boundary** line established by people to separate one political or mapped area from another; physical features, such as mountains and rivers, or latitude and longitude lines sometimes act as boundaries (p. 10)

**Breadbasket** geographic region that is a principal source of grain (p. 34)

**Brine** solution containing a much higher concentration of salt than seawater (p. 84)

**Canadian Shield** region containing the oldest rock in North America; areas are exposed in much of eastern Canada and some bordering U.S. regions (p. 42)

**Coastal plain** any comparatively level land of low elevation that borders the ocean (p. 50)

**Continental climate** mid-latitude climate zone occurring on large land-masses in the Northern Hemisphere and characterized by great variations of temperature, both seasonally and between day and night; **continental cool summer climates**

are influenced by nearby colder subarctic climates; **continental warm summer climates** are influenced by nearby mild or dry climates (pp. 18–19)

**Culture hearth** center from which major cultural traditions spread and are adopted by people in a wide geographic area (p. 86)

**Desert and dry shrub** vegetation region with either hot or cold temperatures that annually receives 10 inches (25 cm) or less of precipitation (pp. 22–23)

**Ecosystem** term for classifying Earth's natural communities according to how all the things in an environment, such as a forest or a coral reef, interact with each other (p. 10)

**Fault** break in Earth's crust along which movement up, down, or sideways occurs (pp. 14–15)

**Flooded grassland** wetland dominated by grasses and covered by water (pp. 22–23)

**Fossil fuel** group of nonrenewable mineral resources—coal, oil, natural gas—formed over millions of years from plant and animal remains (pp. 38–39)

**Geothermal energy** heat energy generated within Earth (p. 39)

**Glacier** large, slow-moving mass of ice that forms over time from snow (p. 42)

**Gondwana** name given to the southern part of the supercontinent Pangaea; made up of what we now call Africa, South America, Australia, Antarctica, and India (pp. 14, 84)

**Hemisphere** one-half of the globe; the Equator divides Earth into Northern and Southern Hemispheres; the prime meridian and the 180 degree meridian divide it into Eastern and Western Hemispheres (p. 5)

**Highland/upland climate** region associated with mountains or plateaus that varies depending on elevation, latitude, continental location, and exposure to sun and wind; in general, temperature decreases and precipitation increases with elevation (pp. 18–19)

**Humid subtropical climate** region characterized by hot summers, mild to cool winters, and year-round precipitation that is heaviest in summer; generally located on the southeastern margins of continents (pp. 18–19)

**Ice cap climate** one of two kinds of polar climate; summer temperatures rarely rise above freezing, and what little precipitation occurs is mostly in the form of snow (pp. 18–19)

**Indigenous** native to or occurring naturally in a specific area or environment (p. 102)

**Infiltration** process that occurs in the water, or hydrologic, cycle when gravity causes surface water to seep down through the soil (p. 36)

**Isthmus** narrow strip of land that connects two larger landmasses and has water on two sides (p. 56–57)

**Landform** physical feature shaped by uplifting, weathering, and erosion; mountains, plateaus, hills, and plains are the four major types (p. 20)

**Language family** group of languages that come from a common ancestry (pp. 30–31)

**Latin America** cultural region generally considered to include Mexico, Central America, South America, and the West Indies; Portuguese and Spanish are the principal languages (pp. 28–29)

**Llanos** extensive, mostly treeless grasslands in the Orinoco River basin of northern South America (p. 58)

**Lowlands** fairly level land at a lower elevation than surrounding areas (p. 12)

**Mangrove vegetation** tropical trees and shrubs with dense root systems that grow in tidal mud flats and extend coast-lines by trapping soil (pp. 22–23)

**Marine west coast** type of mild climate common on the west coasts of continents in midlatitude regions; characterized by small variations in annual temperature range and wet, foggy winters (pp. 18–19)

**Median age** midpoint of a population's age; half the population is older than this age; half is younger (p. 27)

**Mediterranean climate** type of mild climate common on the west coasts of continents, named for the dominant climate along the Mediterranean coast; characterized by mild rainy winters and hot dry summers (pp. 18–19)

**Mediterranean shrub** low-growing, mostly small-leaved evergreen vegetation, such as chaparral, that thrives in Mediterranean climate regions (p. 22–23)

**Melanesia** one of three major island groups that make up Oceania; includes the Fiji Islands, New Guinea, Vanuatu, the Solomon Islands, and New Caledonia (pp. 102–103)

**Melanesian** indigenous to Melanesia (p. 102)

**Mestizo** person of mixed Native American and European ancestry; most commonly used in Latin America (p. 53)

**Microclimate** climate of a very limited area that varies from the overall climate of the surrounding region (p. 20)

**Micronesia** one of three major island groups that make up Oceania; made up of some 2,000 mostly coral islands, including Guam, Kiribati, the Mariana Islands, Palau, and the Federated States of Micronesia (pp. 102–103)

**Micronesian** indigenous to Micronesia (p. 102)

**Monsoon** seasonal change in the direction of the prevailing winds, which causes wet and dry seasons in some tropical areas (p. 90)

**Mountain grassland** vegetation region characterized by clumps of long grass that grow beyond the limit of forests at high elevations (pp. 22–23)

**Nonrenewable resource** elements of the natural environment, such as metals, minerals, and fossil fuels, that form within Earth by geological processes over millions of years and thus cannot be readily replaced (pp. 38–39)

**Northern coniferous forest** vegetation region composed primarily of cone-bearing, needle-leafed or scale-leafed evergreen trees that grow in regions with long winters and moderate to high annual precipitation; also called boreal forest or taiga (pp. 22–23)

**Oceania** name for the widely scattered islands of Polynesia, Micronesia, and Melanesia; often includes Australia and New Zealand (pp. 96–107)

*Pampas* temperate grassland primarily in Argentina between the Andes and the Atlantic Ocean; one of the richest agricultural regions in the world (pp. 56, 58)

*Patagonia* cool, windy, arid plateau region primarily in southern Argentina between the Andes and the Atlantic Ocean (p. 58)

*Plain* large area of relatively flat land; one of the four major kinds of landforms (p. 16)

*Plate tectonics* study of the interaction of slabs of Earth's crust as molten rock within Earth causes them to slowly move across the surface (pp. 14–15)

*Plateau* large, relatively flat area that rises above the surrounding landscape; one of the four major kinds of landforms (pp. 16–17)

*Polar climates* climates that occur at very high latitudes; generally too cold to support tree growth; include tundra and ice cap (pp. 22–23)

*Polynesia* one of three major regions in Oceania made up mostly of volcanic and coral islands, including the Hawaiian Islands, the Society Islands, Samoa, and French Polynesia (pp. 102–103)

*Polynesian* indigenous to Polynesia (p. 102)

*Predominant economy* main type of work that most people do to meet their wants and needs in a particular country (pp. 32–33, 47, 63, 73, 83, 93, 103)

*Province* land governed as a political or administrative unit of a country or empire; Canadian provinces, like U.S. states, have substantial powers of self-government (p. 49)

*River basin* area drained by a single river and its tributaries (p. 58)

*Sahel* in Africa the semiarid region of short tropical grassland that lies between the dry Sahara and the humid savanna and that is prone to frequent droughts (p. 78)

*Savanna* tropical tall grassland with scattered low trees (p. 23)

*Selva* Portuguese word referring to tropical rain forests, especially in the Amazon Basin (p. 64)

*Semiarid* dry climate region that experiences great daily variation in day-night temperatures; receives enough rainfall to support grasslands (pp. 18–19)

*Silt* mineral particles that are larger than grains of clay but smaller than grains of sand (p. 65)

*Sisal* tropical plant with leaves made up of strong fibers that are used to make rope (p. 84)

*Steppe* Slavic word referring to relatively flat, mostly treeless temperate grasslands that stretch across much of central Europe and central Asia (p. 88)

*Subarctic climate* region characterized by short, cool, sometimes freezing summers and long, bitter cold winters; most precipitation falls in summer (pp.18–19)

*Subcontinent* large landmass such as India that, although part of a continent, is considered a separate feature either geographically or politically (p. 84)

*Subtropical climate* region between tropical and continental climates characterized by distinct seasons but with milder temperatures than continental climates (pp. 18–19)

*Temperate broadleaf forest* vegetation region with distinct seasons and dependable rainfall; predominant species include oak, maple, and beech, all of which lose their leaves in the cold season (pp. 22–23)

*Temperate coniferous forest* vegetation region that has mild winters with heavy precipitation; made up of mostly evergreen, needleleaf trees that bear seeds in cones (pp. 22–23)

*Temperate grassland* vegetation region where grasses are dominant and the climate is characterized by hot summers, cold winters, and moderate rainfall (pp. 22–23)

*Territory* land under the jurisdiction of a country but that is not a state or a province (p. 43)

*Tropical coniferous forest* vegetation region that occurs in a cooler climate than tropical rain forests; has distinct wet and dry seasons; made up of mostly evergreen trees with seed-bearing cones (pp. 22–23)

*Tropical dry climate* region characterized by year-round high temperatures and sufficient precipitation to support savannas (pp. 18–19)

*Tropical dry forest* vegetation region that has distinct wet and dry seasons and a cooler climate than tropical moist forests; has shorter trees than rain forests and many shed their leaves in the dry season (pp. 22–23)

*Tropical grassland and savanna* vegetation region characterized by scattered individual trees; occurs in warm or hot climates with annual rainfall of 20 to 50 inches (50–130 cm) (pp. 22–23)

*Tropical moist broadleaf forest* vegetation region occurring mostly in a belt between the Tropic of Cancer and the Tropic of Capricorn in areas that have at least 80 inches (200 cm) of rain annually and an average annual temperature of 80°F (20°C) (pp. 22–23)

*Tropical wet climate* region characterized by year-round warm temperatures and rainfall ranging from 60 to150 inches (150–400 cm) annually (pp. 18–19)

*Troposphere* region of Earth's atmosphere that is closest to the surface; where weather occurs (p. 5)

*Tundra* vegetation region at high latitudes and high elevations characterized by cold temperatures, low vegetation, and a short growing season (pp. 22–23)

*Tundra climate* region with one or more months of temperatures slightly above freezing when the ground is free of snow (pp. 18–19)

*Upland climate* see *Highland/upland climate*

# Web Sites (Web Link)

*Antarctica:* http://www.nsf.gov/od/opp/antarct/start.htm

*Earth's Climates:* http://www.worldclimate.com

*Earth's Geologic History:*

 *Earthquakes:* http://earthquake.usgs.gov/

 *Volcanoes:* http://www.geo.mtu.edu/volcanoes/

*Earth's Vegetation*: http://www.earthobservatory.nasa.gov/Library/LandCover/

*Map Projections:* http://www.colorado.edu/geography/gcraft/notes/mapproj/mapproj.html

*Political World:* http://www.cia.gov/cia/publications/factbook/index.html

*Predominant World Economies:* http://www.wto.org/english/res_e/statis_e/overvwf_e.htm

*Types of Maps:* http://magma.nationalgeographic.com/education/

*World Cities:* http://www.un.org/esa/population/urbanization.htm

*World Cultures:* http://highschoolhub.org/hub/language.htm

*World Energy:* http://www.bp.com/worldenergy/

*World Food:* http://www.cgiar.org/areas.htm

*World Population:* http://www.census.gov/ipc/www/idbnew.html

*World Water:* http://water.usgs.gov/

# Thematic Index

## U
United Kingdom 74
  Greenwich Park **106**
United Nations
  Educational,
  Scientific, and
  Cultural
  Organization
  (UNESCO) 94
United States
  natural hazards
    54, map 55
  population
    pyramid 27
  roads **39**
Urban areas 28
  maps 28–29

## V
Vegetation **22, 23**
  map 22–23
Volcanoes **54, 84**

## W
Washington (state),
  U.S.
  logging **32**
  volcanoes **54**
Water
  map 36–37
  sources 37
Wheat 34, **34**
  map 34–35
Wildfires **54**, map 55
Winds 21, 39
World
  cities map 28–29
  cultures map 30–31
  energy and minerals
    map 38–39
  food map 34–35
  land and water
    features 16–17
  physical map 12–13
  political map 24–25
  population map
    26–27
  predominant
    economies map
    32–33
World Heritage Sites
  **94**, 94–95, **95**
  map 95

# Place-name Index

Due to limited space,
only countries, their
capitals, cities with
populations of one
million or more, and
selected physical
features are listed here.

## A
Abidjan, Côte d'Ivoire
  79
Abu Dhabi, United
  Arab Emirates 89
Abuja, Nigeria 79
Accra, Ghana 79, 82
Aconcagua, Cerro
  (mountain),
  Argentina 58
Addis Ababa, Ethiopia
  79, 82
Adelaide, Australia 99,
  102, 103, 104
Afghanistan 89, 90,
  91, 92, 93
Ahaggar Mountains,
  Algeria 78
Alaska (state), U.S. 43,
  44, 45, 46, 47, 51
Albania 69, 70, 71,
  72, 73
Aleutian Islands,
  Alaska 42, 50
Alexandria, Egypt
  79, 82
Algeria 79, 80, 81,
  82, 83
Algiers, Algeria 79,
  82, 83
Almaty, Kazakhstan
  89, 92
Alps (mountains),
  Europe 68
Altay Mountains, Asia
  88
Amazon (river), Brazil
  58, 64–65
Amazon Basin, Brazil
  58, 61, 63
American Highland,
  Antarctica 110
American Samoa 99,
  100, 101, 102, 103
Amery Ice Shelf,
  Antarctica 110
Amman, Jordan 89
Amsterdam,
  Netherlands 69, 72

Andes (mountains),
  South America 58,
  62, 63
Andorra 69, 70, 71,
  72, 73
Angel Falls, Venezuela
  58
Angola 79, 80, 81, 82, 83
Ankara, Turkey 89, 92
Antananarivo,
  Madagascar 79, 82
Antarctica 108–111
Antigua & Barbuda
  43, 46
Apennines (moun-
  tains), Italy 68
Apia, Samoa 99
Appalachian
  Mountains, U.S.
  42, 50
Arabian Peninsula,
  Asia 88
Aral Sea, Kazakhstan-
  Uzbekistan 88
Argentina 59, 60, 61,
  62, 63
Arkansas (river), U.S.
  42, 50
Armenia 89, 90, 91,
  92, 93
Ashgabat,
  Turkmenistan 89
Asmara, Eritrea 79
Assal, Lake, Djibouti
  78
Astana, Kazakhstan 89
Asunción, Paraguay
  59, 62
Atacama Desert, Chile
  58, 61
Athens, Greece 69,
  72, 73
Atlanta, Georgia 43,
  46, 47, 51
Atlas Mountains,
  Africa 78
Auckland, New
  Zealand 99, 102,
  103, 105
Australia 96–104
Austria 69, 70, 71,
  72, 73
Azerbaijan 69, 70, 71,
  72, 73, 89, 90, 91,
  92, 93

## B
Baffin Island, Nunavut
  42, 48, 49
Baghdad, Iraq 89,
  92, 93
Bahamas 42, 43, 46
Bahrain 89, 90, 91,
  92, 93
Baikal, Lake, Russia 88

Baja California (penin-
  sula), Mexico 42, 52
Baku, Azerbaijan 69,
  89, 92
Balkan Peninsula,
  Europe 68
Baltimore, Maryland
  46, 51
Bamako, Mali 79, 82
Bandar Seri Begawan,
  Brunei 89
Bangalore, India 89, 92
Bangkok, Thailand 89,
  92, 93
Bangladesh 89, 90, 91,
  92, 93
Bangui, Central
  African Republic 79
Banjul, Gambia 79
Barbados 43, 46
Barranquilla,
  Colombia 59, 62
Basseterre, St. Kitts and
  Nevis 43
Beijing, China 89,
  92, 93
Beirut, Lebanon 89, 92
Belarus 69, 70, 71,
  72, 73
Belém, Brazil 59,
  62, 63
Belgium 69, 70, 71,
  72, 73
Belgrade, Yugoslavia
  69, 72
Belize 43, 44, 45,
  46, 47
Belmopan, Belize 43
Belo Horizonte, Brazil
  59, 62
Benin 79, 80, 81,
  82, 83
Bentley Subglacial
  Trench, Antarctica
  108, 110
Berlin, Germany 69,
  72, 73
Bermuda Islands,
  North Atlantic
  Ocean 42
Bern, Switzerland 69

Bhutan 89, 90, 91,
  92, 93
Birmingham, England
  69, 72
Bishkek, Kyrgyzstan 89
Bissau, Guinea-Bissau
  79
Black Sea 68, 69, 70,
  71, 72, 88
Bloemfontein, South
  Africa 79
Blue Nile, Ethiopia-
  Sudan 78
Bogotá, Colombia 59,
  62, 63
Bolivia 59, 60, 61,
  62, 63
Borneo (island),
  Indonesia 88
Bosnia and
  Herzegovina 69, 70,
  71, 72, 73
Bosporus, Turkey 68
Boston, Massachusetts
  43, 46, 47, 51
Botswana 79, 80, 81,
  82, 83
Brasília, Brazil 59, 62
Bratislava, Slovakia 69
Brazil 59, 60, 61,
  62, 63
Brazilian Highlands,
  Brazil 58
Brazzaville, Congo
  79, 82
Bridgetown, Barbados
  43
Brisbane, Australia 99,
  102, 103, 104
Brooks Range, Alaska
  42, 50
Brunei 89, 90, 91, 92,
  93
Brussels, Belgium
  69, 72
Bucharest, Romania
  69, 72
Budapest, Hungary
  69, 72
Buenos Aires,
  Argentina 59, 62,
  63
Buffalo, New York
  46, 51
Bujumbura, Burundi
  79
Bulgaria 69, 70, 71,
  72, 73
Burkina Faso 79, 80,
  81, 82, 83
Burundi 79, 80, 81,
  82, 83

## National Geographic Society

John M. Fahey, Jr.
*President and Chief Executive Officer*

Gilbert M. Grosvenor
*Chairman of the Board*

Nina D. Hoffman
*President, Books and School Publishing Group*

William R. Gray
*Vice President and Director of the Book Division*

Ericka Markman
*Vice President and Director, School Publishing*

## Staff for this book

### Children's Books

Nancy Laties Feresten
*Publishing Director, Children's Books*

Suzanne Patrick Fonda
*Project Editor*

Carl Mehler
*Director of Maps*

Marianne R. Koszorus
*Design Director*

Dorrit Green
*Art Director and Designer*

Martha B. Sharma
*Writer and Chief Consultant*

Marilyn Mofford Gibbons
*Illustrations Editor*

Jerome N. Cookson
*Map Production Manager*

Matt Chwastyk
Thomas L. Gray
Nicholas P. Rosenbach
Gregory Ugiansky
Martin S. Walz
National Geographic Maps
XNR Productions
*Map Research and Production*

Marcia Pires-Harwood
*Text Research*

Marilyn "Minh" Le
Jessica Ann Peterson
Anjali M. Shenai
*Research Assistance*

Stuart Armstrong
*Graphs*

Sharon K. Berry
*Illustrations Assistant*

Connie B. Binder
*Indexer*

Ellen Teguis
*Director*
*Trade Sales and Marketing*

Lawrence M. Porges
*Marketing Specialist*

R. Gary Colbert
*Production Director*

Lewis R. Bassford
*Production Manager*

Vincent R. Ryan
*Manufacturing Manager*

### School Publishing Division

Steve Mico
*Editorial Director*

Richard Easby
*Editorial Manager*

Carolyn Hatt
Lydia Lewis
*Editors*

Jean Stringer
Anika Trahan
*Associate Editors*

### Education Foundation

Lanny Proffer
*Executive Director*

Joe Ferguson
*Director of Programs*
*Geography Education Outreach*

Christopher Shearer
*Program Officer*

### Consultants

Deborah Batchelor
*Specialist*
*Baltimore City Public School System*
*Baltimore, Maryland*

Sari J. Bennett
*Department of Geography*
*& Environmental Systems*
*University of Maryland*
*Baltimore County*

*Acknowledgments:* We are grateful for the assistance of Richard W. Bullington, Jan D. Morris, Karla H. Tucker, and Alfred L. Zebarth of NG Maps; the National Geographic Image Collection; and Jo H. Tunstall, Robert W. Witt, and Lyle Rosbotham, NG Book Division

*Illustrations Credits:* Abbreviations for terms appearing below: (t) top; (b) bottom; (l) left; (r) right; (c) center; NGS: National Geographic Staff

Locator globes on pages 2–3 and in chapter openers created by Theophilus Britt Griswold

Graphs created by Stuart Armstrong

Continent chapter openers: NASA/JPL/California Institute of Technology/Advanced Very High Resolution Radiometer Project/Cartographic Applications Group

Cover: NOAA satellite mosaic prepared for National Geographic Television by NASA/ JPL, color enhanced by Alfred L. Zebarth; background art digitally created by Slim Films

Back cover: photograph, Steve Raymer; satellite image map, NOAA/NESDIS/NGDC

**About The Earth**
4 (art) © NGS; 4–5 (t) Shusei Nagaska; (b) Earth Satellite Corporation; 5 (bl) Robert Hynes; 6–7 (art) Shusei Nagaska; 10 (l) Vlad Kharitonov NGS; 11 (t–b) NASA/GISS, NOAA/NESDIS/NGDC, NASA/GSFC, University of Miami; 14–15 (t) NASA/JPL/CalTech/CAG, (b) Christopher R. Scotese/PALEOMAP Project, U. of TX, Arlington; 16–17 (t) NOAA/ NESDIS/NGDC; 22–3 (l–r) Jen & Des Bartlett; Raymond Gehman; Cosmo Condina/stone; Walter M. Edwards; Tom Bean/stone; Steve Jackson; Timothy G. Lamar; Medford Taylor; 26 Stuart Franklin; 32 (graph) Theopholis Britt Griswold, revised by Stuart Armstrong; 32–3 (l–r) Martin Rogers; James P. Blair; Phil Schermeister; James L. Stanfield; Mark Thiessen NGS; © NGS; 34 (l) Steve Raymer; (c) Sisse Brimberg; (r) Stephen G. St. John; 36–7 (l–r) Steve Winter; Annie Griffiths Belt; Loren McIntyre; Jim Brandenburg; 39 (tl) James A. Sugar/Black Star; (tr) Marc Moritsch; (bl) Bob Krist; (r) stone

**North America**
54 (tl) Roger Werth/Woodfin Camp Inc; (tr) Ravi Miro Fry; (b) Chris Stewart/Black Star

**South America**
65 (bl, br) Michael Nichols NGS; (tr) Bill Curtsinger; (c) Mattias Klum

**Europe**
74 Bert Blokhuis/stone; 75 (br) Index Stock

**Africa**
84 (l) Paul Zahl; (tr, br) Chris Johns NGS

**Asia**
94 (t) James L. Stanfield; (b) Steve McCurry; 95 (l) James P. Blair; (r) Lynn Funkhouser

**Australia**
106 (l) Bob Sacha; (r) The Granger Collection; 107 Shusei Nagaska

Library of Congress Cataloging-in-Publication Data

National Geographic Society (U.S.)
National Geographic student atlas of the world.
p. cm.
Includes index and glossary.
ISBN 0-7922-7221-8 (pbk.)
ISBN 0-7922-7235-8 (hc.)
 1. Children's atlases. 2. Earth—remote-sensing images. 3. Physical geography—Maps for children.
[1.Atlases.] I. Title: Student atlas of the world. II. Title.
G1021 .N42 2001
912-dc21                                    00-030006

Published by the National Geographic Society
1145 17th St. N.W.
Washington, D.C. 20036-4688
Copyright © 2001 National Geographic Society